CHICKEN SOUP FOR THE TEENAGE SOUL IV

Chicken Soup for the Teenage Soul IV
Stories of Life, Love and Learning
Jack Canfield, Mark Victor Hansen, Kimberly Kirberger, Mitch Claspy

Published by Backlist, LLC,
a unit of Chicken Soup for the Soul Publishing, LLC. www.chickensoup.com

Front cover art by Jesse Kirberger
Originally published in 2004 by Health Communications, Inc.

Back cover and spine redesign by Pneuma Books, LLC

Distributed to the booktrade by Simon & Schuster. SAN: 200-2442

Publisher's Cataloging-in-Publication Data
(Prepared by The Donohue Group)

Chicken soup for the teenage soul IV : stories of life, love, and learning / [compiled by] Jack Canfield ... [et al.].

   p. : ill. ; cm.

  Originally published: Deerfield Beach, FL : Health Communications, c2004.
  ISBN: 978-1-62361-023-4

  1. Teenagers--Conduct of life--Anecdotes. 2. Anecdotes. I. Canfield, Jack, 1944-

BJ1661 .C174 2012
158.1/28/0835   2012944188

PRINTED IN THE UNITED STATES OF AMERICA
on acid free paper
21 20 19 18 17 16 15 14 13 12   01 02 03 04 05 06 07 08 09 10

CHICKEN SOUP
FOR THE
TEENAGE SOUL
IV

Stories of Life, Love
and Learning

Jack Canfield
Mark Victor Hansen
Kimberly Kirberger
Mitch Claspy

Backlist, LLC, a unit of
Chicken Soup for the Soul Publishing, LLC
Cos Cob, CT
www.chickensoup.com

Contents

6. TOUGH STUFF

7. OVERCOMING OBSTACLES

8. GROWING UP

Introduction

Dear Teens,

Our lives are full of stories. Some of our stories are happy, some are sad and most of them fall somewhere in between. What's important is that we understand that they are for our learning. We usually look at our actions as good or bad, right or wrong, or experiences that place us above or below others. If we can adjust our thinking and look at our stories as tools for our growth, then we can be grateful for all the things that we have to go through. If we can remember to love ourselves and have compassion for our "mistakes," then we can live with more gratitude and joy.

The people who have written stories for this book have shared them with you in hopes that their experiences can help you. Many of the authors have said that even though their stories are about something painful they went through or something they felt guilty about, if someone else can learn from it, then their story is worth sharing.

All the books that we have compiled have been with these thoughts in mind. We want you to know that we all have to deal with heartbreak, family issues, fights with friends and the most difficult of all, the death of someone we love. It is our hope that with these stories you can find answers to questions, guidance in difficult moments and the understanding that you are not alone in anything you are going through.

We love you guys and hope that you find support and comfort within this book.

All our love,

Kimberly, Jack, Mark and Mitch

$\overline{1}$

FRIENDSHIP

Friendship is the inexpressible comfort of feeling safe with a person, having neither to weigh thoughts nor measure words.

George Eliot

The Friend That You've Outgrown

Here's to the friend that you've outgrown,
The one whose name is left unknown.
The one who wiped away your tears,
And sought to hold your hand,
When others turned the other way,
No beginning, just an end.

She's the one you turned to,
The one that you called friend.
She laughed with you, she cried with you,
And felt it was her duty,
To remind you of your worth,
And all your inner beauty.

When others' eyes could only dwell,
Upon your exposed outer shell.
They saw a fat girl steeped in braces,
Not seeing you they turned their faces.
But she was there to whisper,
When others didn't care.

She held your secrets in her heart,
That friends like you could share.
You never had to be alone,
But now she is, 'cause you've outgrown
Her for those others whose laughs you share,
As you run carefree through the air.

Time has eased your form and face,
But she's the one who knew your grace
When those who you now call your friend
Saw no beginning . . . only end.

C. S. Dweck

My Friend, Forever

When we were merely little girls, still full of innocence and wonder, I tied your shoes and made sure your lip wasn't bleeding. "Best friends since third grade," we've always said. We've been to hell and back, with our bleeding hearts and tampered souls.

We've watched each other slip helplessly into the realms of addiction, holding mercilessly onto one another's palms, simply praying that it was just some horrid nightmare.

You held me with your soothing tones over the phone when my heart first broke in pain. You told me it would be okay and that I was much too strong to let some stupid boy topple me over the edge.

When I felt as though no one could possibly understand the torment going on within my soul, you were always there to reassure me that one day it would pass, and that I could always turn to you. The pain I held back with others, I could share with you—and you with me.

I suppose all I want is for you to know that I know you've been through far too much for seventeen years, and that you are the most beautiful person I have ever known. The distance that separates us now doesn't change my love for you, my sweetest friend. I can feel your thoughts from miles away and when I close my eyes I can see you there in all of your beauty.

We will rise above this. We will travel the world, write poetry and dazzle the hearts of everyone we meet.

I will never let go of your palms, my friend, and I will always be there to lift you up and tie your shoes. Best friends since third grade—to hell and back.

Love always,
Mell

Melissa Malloy

There Is No End in Friend

Lauren and I met during summer camp after fifth grade. We were stargazing. She was looking for Orion and I was lying on my back searching the night sky for the Little Dipper when she tripped over me and fell backwards.

"Oh sorry! I was trying to find the stars in Orion's belt and . . ."

I took her hand and pointed with it to the sky. "Just over there."

She smiled and introduced me to the Little Dipper. That was right where it all began, a chance encounter with a fellow camper as curious as I was about the stars.

Lauren and I were instant friends, spending the remainder of the summer together jumping rope, swimming in the lake, crushing over the cute camp counselor and gushing over our diaries by candlelight. We were attached at the hip—partners in crime, secret handshakes and lazy-day promises over fresh-squeezed lemonade to remain friends forever. She beat me at checkers and I was the chess champion. We both had June birthdays, annoying younger brothers and last names that started with W. We both loved books, funny movies and laughing until we cried.

Lauren and I lived two hours apart, so during the school year we went months without seeing each other. We maintained our long-distance friendship by telephone and e-mail. When boys broke my heart, she was there to console me at 2:00 A.M. on a school night and when Lauren's parents divorced when we were in ninth grade, Lauren came to visit for a long weekend and cried on my shoulder into pockets-full of Kleenex.

No matter what happened in our lives, we knew we would get through it because we had each other. We were convinced that a good friend was the best medicine, especially a friend that could make you laugh.

"There's no end in friend," Lauren said.

"You're right . . ."

"You are the sugar in my tea."

"Today I feel like coffee."

"Okay then. I'm the cream in your coffee."

"Half-and-half."

Through thick and thin, love lost and found, family tragedy and fair-weather friends, we always knew that the other was only a couple of hours drive up the coast, an instant message, an e-mail or a phone call away.

When Lauren met her high-school sweetheart, she sent me photographs and made sure he called me on the phone so I could approve of him. His name was Isaac and he seemed really nice. She promised to dig up one of his friends so we could double-date the next time I went to visit her.

"Awesome. I love you to death," I said, laughing.

"Oh yeah! Well, I love you to life!" Lauren exclaimed, voice creaking through the phone.

And she was right. She always knew how to rewrite the rules so that things made perfect sense. She modernized clichés and came up with secret passwords and sayings that suited us like twin, red dresses and matching pigtails.

The distance between our homes couldn't separate the bond we had. Lauren and I would be best friends forever. She was my soul mate, finishing my sentences and blowing me kisses from her backyard to mine.

Lauren and Isaac broke up about a year later, and I had just broken up with my boyfriend, Jake, a few weeks previously. Sweet sixteen was right around the corner for both of us and school was almost out for the summer. For some time, Lauren and I had been talking about going back to camp and now that we were old enough to attend as counselors with a summer salary to boot, we decided to return.

We spent our summer the same way we had six years earlier—stargazing, river rafting and crushing on the cute counselors over juice and pretzels. It was the first time since junior high we were able to spend the entire month together. We had grown up. Once upon a time we were little girls, whispering after lights-out and misspelling words in our diaries. Now we had driver's licenses, SAT prep courses and unrequited love stories. We had mastered the art of kissing boys, acing English papers and coming up with good excuses for getting home after curfew. We swapped stories, gave advice, listened and talked through the night. Virtually exhausted every afternoon, we napped in a heap on the counselors' couch.

On the last night of camp, we hiked to the top of Silver Mountain with our flashlights, and sprawled out in the dirt and grass, young women giggling and reminiscing about the first night we met.

"It was right over there," I said, pointing.

"I tripped over you just like this!" Lauren laughed, pushing me into the dirt.

Lying on our backs, eyes to the sky Lauren raised her hand. "You see that up there? That's Gemini."

I looked over her shoulder. "Where?" I asked.

"See the two heads? And the legs coming down—like that."

I squinted and sure enough there they were. Twins joined at the hip, best friends forever hanging out in the sky.

Rebecca Woolf

Sketches

Friendship is a horizon—which expands whenever we approach it.

E. R. Hazlip

During fifth-grade recess, my girlfriends and I wouldn't play kickball with the other kids. Instead, we stayed behind at the benches and made pencil sketches on blue-lined binder paper.

We sketched puppies, flowers, kittens, and my personal favorite—the future prom dress, with every detail, down to the long staircase (for the big entrance) and a crystal chandelier.

I was ten then; prom was seven years away. I was Chinese, so I didn't have a quinceanera, debutante ball or Bat Mitzvah. Prom was the one shot I had to live my Cinderella story. My only other opportunity to live the princess fantasy would be my wedding day—and I wasn't going to wait that long!

I needed prom. It was what high school was all about. Where even the most gawky of girls (me) could become a swan. It was puberty's heyday.

The dresses I sketched were fit for a night of being swept away by a prince. But I could never get a sketch quite right. All the other girls drew their dresses so evenly, earnestly and beautifully. I couldn't do it. All the while, I had a very picture-perfect vision of my prom even though it never translated well onto paper.

Years into my teenage life I still sketched these future moments. Not with paper, but in my mind—sometimes down to the last syllable of imagined dialogue. Sometimes down to the most minute detail of weather or scenery. I sketched first kisses, weddings, relationships and big, important events that transform a life into "a life."

Sometimes I think I've spent more time sketching than living.

Two days before the prom my boyfriend left me for someone else. He had a new girlfriend and a new date for the prom. I ended up going with my best friend, Danielle.

I wore a black slip dress. As Danielle and I danced, I tried not to look at my ex while he danced with and kissed his date. I tried not to cry about how wrong this whole scene was.

There was no romancing. No grand entrance. And it was expensive, the pictures especially, considering my eyes were closed and puffy. But I had Danielle, my best friend, to keep me from breaking down and crying through the night. I came home before midnight—not how I imagined my prom would turn out.

Danielle called me the other week while I was at work.

She said, "Remember the prom we went to? Can you believe it? That was a pretty funny night. And we are probably the only couple from that night who still talk to each other now!"

"Yeah, I guess that's true. I'm sure nobody is still as close to their prom date as we still are. Do you think it's too late to get a refund on those prom pictures? My eyes are closed in them!" Danielle started laughing, then I started laughing, and before we knew it, we were laughing hysterically on both ends of the phone as we relayed details back and forth from that night.

When we hung up, I realized it's the "little stuff" in life that's important, like a phone call from a friend and a good laugh.

Kristina Wong

Love Poem

The light breeze from the open window sent chills running up and down my spine. It's not that the air was all that cold—for a September afternoon, it was rather warm, in fact. It's just that my nerves were so fragile, so on-edge, that any unexpected movement could have set off fireworks in my heart.

"You ready?" he asked, clearing his voice as he lifted the tattered notebook from where it lay open on his desk.

I gulped and giggled nervously, not quite sure if I knew how to answer that question truthfully. Bryan laughed, too, and I could tell by the uneasiness of his smile that he was just as nervous.

Bryan's poetry was his greatest source of pride and accomplishment. Sometimes, we'd spend all day together and ideas would strike him like lightning, prompting him to pull out that notebook and jot down a note or two. Each night, he'd seek solace in his father's empty study, where only the stillness and the silence mingled with the moonlight, where he'd pour his heart into a poetic masterpiece.

Until that autumn day in my senior year, nearly two years after I'd first fallen in love with his mischievous smile, Bryan had never shared his poetry with another soul, a policy I'd always respected, despite the depth of our conversations otherwise. But this poem, he'd told me, was special. He'd been perfecting it for weeks, and finally, with me standing just inches before him in the privacy of the study, he was ready to share the most heartfelt piece he'd ever written.

"Go ahead," I encouraged him, unable to stand seeing such worry hang over his gorgeous features.

Bryan gripped the notebook with both hands and moved his sparkling green eyes from my face down to the ink-covered page. "It seems like I'll never truly get over you," he began, his voice sounding stiff, but his words ringing sincere all the same. "I'll never hear the word 'love' without feeling your heart beat in my soul/Never will I kiss a pair of lips without wishing they were yours."

Bryan became more emotional with every word he read, still afraid to meet my admiring gaze, but comfortable enough to bare his soul to the only person who, regardless of difficult times and a shaky relationship, loved him and his inspired heart beyond all measure, whether he felt confident about it or not.

Bryan continued reciting the poem, even occasionally making quick eye contact with me as he professed his feelings in a way I'd never heard before. With every line Bryan read, every word he spoke, I was twice as tempted to run over and melt into his arms, to rest my head on his shoulder and numb his senses with the scent of my shampoo. I wanted to tell him right then and there that it was the most beautiful poem I'd ever heard, that his words touched my heart like no others ever had.

Still captivated by the sound of Bryan's voice as he read the final few lines of the poem, I forced myself to remain still. The overwhelming urge to hold him close faded as I began to drown in the reality of Bryan's feelings. "I hesitate to kiss you sometimes, because I know I'll never want to stop/And while the clock ticks away the moments until we part forever/I can't let a second escape without telling you 'I love you.'"

Bryan swallowed hard and stared at the poem for a moment before looking into my adoring eyes. He stood there like a young boy who knew I was his biggest admirer. "Oh, Bryan," I said breathlessly, clutching my heart as he sheepishly smiled at the positive reaction his sentiments had evoked.

"You really liked it?" he asked quietly, placing his hands over mine and pressing his soft pink lips to my forehead. "I hoped you would."

I nodded, resisting the urge to laugh at my overly emotional reaction to Bryan's words. Stepping back, I looked into his green eyes that were so full of hope. He stood confidently before me, finally ready to shout his honest declarations of love to the world, but reciting it to one more important girl in his life.

"Don't worry," I told him, squeezing his trembling hands. "Tiffany will love this. She'll love you for writing this for her."

My heart began to crumble as he beamed at me, dreaming only of someone else's sweet kisses and loving embrace. After years as Bryan's number two girl, I could only hope that Tiffany saw in him everything that I did— a beautiful spirit, a caring soul and a heart that deserved more love than one person was capable of giving. As I sat back and watched their relationship grow, I hoped she knew how lucky she truly was.

As Bryan's gaze toward me conveyed an appreciative sense of friendship, I basked in his affection, however unromantic. It occurred to me that I was lucky to at least have the confidence of a friend whom I truly admired, and someday, Bryan might be privileged enough to hear my outpourings of love for another person—someone whom I hoped would admire me in the very same way.

Cortney Martin

Unfaithful

Some friends play at friendship but a true friend sticks closer than one's nearest kin.

Proverbs, 18:24

When Jason and Rebecca broke up in April of our senior year, I felt like I was the one being dumped. Rebecca and I had been best friends since before kindergarten. Jason had been her boyfriend for the last two years, and during that time I'd gone from being resentful of his claims on my friend's time to really liking the guy. He was easy to like: funny, nice, an all-around good guy. Plus, as captain of the football team he always had lots of cute football player friends I got to hang out with.

Rebecca didn't just break up with him, she cheated on him with Robert Mitchell, a shrimpy, dorky troublemaker no one liked. During spring break Jason visited his grandma upstate, I skied with my family, and, as I found out from rumors swirling around school after we all got back, Rebecca and Robert were at home making out. I knew Robert had been writing her love letters for the past

few months, even though she kept asking him to stop.
And I knew things were kind of awkward between
Rebecca and Jason since he got into his first-choice college
and she'd been rejected, but I never expected anything as
low as this from her.

Everyone was disgusted at Rebecca's unfaithfulness.
Even Rebecca's dad, who considered Jason part of the
family, sided against his daughter.

Rebecca and I never discussed what happened. Other
friends would talk about what a terrible thing she'd done,
and I never felt like she deserved to be stood up for.
Sometimes I even contributed to the criticism.

At first we tried to pretend things were the same; we
went to dance class after school and to the beach with our
group of girlfriends on the weekend. One weekend
Rebecca brought Robert to our Saturday beach outing. We
all ignored him as much as we could without being obvious. We had no interest in making friends with someone
who'd pursued another guy's girlfriend. The next weekend we "forgot" to invite her along.

Rebecca didn't want to go to parties where she knew
Jason and his friends would be, so I'd go without her, even
if we'd made plans to hang out that night. She tried to set
me up with a friend of Robert's for prom, so we could go
to dinner before and share a limo like we'd always
planned, but I made excuses and found another date.

As graduation approached we spent less and less time
together. I missed the goofy fun we used to have, but I
thought it wasn't my fault things had changed. She was
the one who had done something terrible.

One Saturday morning during dance rehearsal, I was
talking with some girlfriends about a party that night that
Rebecca hadn't been invited to.

"I'm not deaf," I heard behind me. I turned to see
Rebecca with tears welling in her eyes. "I thought we were

best friends." She stormed off and drove home.

Later, her sister called me.

"Rebecca's been in her room crying all day," she said. "I think you should come talk to her."

"Why?" I almost asked. But I knew why: because for the last twelve years she had come over to my house every time I had cried and needed her.

I brought her a plate of homemade snickerdoodle cookies, our favorite treat to cook and eat.

"I know what I did to Jason was wrong," she said. "Everyone at school, even my family, looks down on me. I didn't expect you to approve. But I didn't expect you to abandon me. I've heard what you say behind my back."

I'd never said anything that wasn't true. Just that Rebecca had been wrong to let Robert keep writing her those letters, that she'd always been too much of a flirt— then I realized, this wasn't how you were supposed to talk about your best friend. I had been unfaithful. A friend's job was not to pass judgment, but to be there, no matter what.

I apologized and for the next few hours we hugged, talked and ate snickerdoodles. She told me how upset and lonely she'd felt when she'd found out she didn't get into the school Jason and I would be going to. I told her how bummed I was that we wouldn't be roommates next year, but I was glad we wouldn't be that far away. And most importantly, I'd be there for her, not as a critic, but as a friend.

Chiara Tomaselli

Bacon and Eggs

True friendship is like sound health; the value of it is seldom known until it is lost.

Charles Caleb Colton

I was standing beneath the doors that led to my high school's gymnasium, music blaring, the stands packed with family and friends. I was waiting anxiously to make my entrance and had mixed feelings. This was it. The moment I had long awaited.

"Are you nervous?" someone asked behind me.

I turned around and saw the brown corkscrew curls of my old friend from elementary school, Beth Ann.

"Yeah, kinda. It just feels so weird," I said.

"Yeah, I know. It seems like yesterday we were playing line soccer and bacon-and-eggs at recess," she said with a reminiscent smile.

Bacon-and-eggs, as we called it back then, was a game we played every day at recess. It involved two people on different swings locking their arms and legs together as tight as they could and other people pushing them from all directions to try to break them apart. No matter how rough the ride seemed, Beth Ann and I never let go. We were inseparable.

Someone's hand reached out and nudged me along. It was my turn to walk. As I rounded the corner all I could see were thousands of people, and all I could hear was "Pomp and Circumstance." I had heard the song a dozen times before, but this time it had meaning. It seemed to take over my whole body, and my heart seemed to beat along with the notes. Tears filled my eyes as I realized this was the last time I would ever walk with my friends. I marched underneath the flowered arches and turned down the aisle to my seat. When I sat down, I took a deep breath and took in everything around me—the people yelling and waving, my heart still beating with the song, all of my old elementary-school friends in their caps and gowns, the class banner. The banner read: "The end of a decade, a century, a millennium, the beginning of a dream." At that moment I realized that it was finally time to live the dream I had been planning for years. This was it. This was the moment I was to grow up and become the person I wanted to be. On the other hand, it also meant leaving everything behind.

The ceremony was long and hot—very hot. My gown was drenched with sweat and tears, and it made me itch. I went hoarse from yelling for my friends when their names were called, and my mouth ached from laughing at the teachers who, after four years, still mispronounced our names. I grinned from ear to ear as I received my diploma and saw Mom and Dad looking down at me with eyes of pride. And, of course, I cried at every reference made toward this day as being our last. But I made it through to the end.

As I marched out of the gymnasium I looked to the people who had impacted my life through the years—to the people who made my life worth living, the people I would always carry with me. I looked to my parents, my family, my teachers and, finally, to my best friend from elementary school.

Through the years the group of us had grown apart, and we had all gone our separate ways. But Beth Ann was right. It seemed like yesterday we were playing in the schoolyard and dreaming of high school, which seemed, at the time, to be forever away.

I remembered the time Beth Ann and I were sitting outside on the stoop that led to our elementary school's doors. We had just finished a game of hopscotch, and we were throwing rocks across the parking lot.

"I can't wait till we're in high school," I said, wiping the sweat off my forehead.

The sun was hot and beating down on my toes. I was wearing new, hot pink jelly shoes that I had begged my mother for weeks to buy.

"I can't either. And when we get our licenses we can drive to each other's houses and go to the movies or swimming anytime we want," Beth Ann rambled on.

"I know. I can't wait. We'll go everywhere together . . . we'll always be together," I promised.

"Best friends, forever!" Beth Ann said.

"Yeah . . . best friends, forever," I nodded.

We sat on that stoop planning out our future together—the places we'd go, the things we'd do and the people we'd marry. We planned on getting married at the same time to best friends just like us. We planned on teaching our kids to play bacon-and-eggs and teaching them how to never let go.

As I walked out of the gymnasium, I thought about all the plans we had made in elementary school and how none of them had come true. I realized that there was still a place in my heart that wanted us to always be together, even after all the years apart.

I followed the long line into the cafeteria to meet my family and friends. I received thousands of hugs and took hundreds of pictures. I was pulled in a million directions, but I couldn't shake my thoughts of Beth Ann. We had made so many plans and so may promises. But now it was time to let go—to say good-bye.

I searched for her through the crowd. I looked for ten minutes, and when I was about to give up, I turned the corner and there she was, surrounded by a bunch of people. I walked over to her and pulled her to the side.

"Beth . . ."

We called her "Beth" now because she felt that she had outgrown "Beth Ann."

" . . . I don't know what to say. I guess I just felt like I had to come over and say good-bye."

At that last word, "good-bye," she pulled me into her arms and gave me a big hug. We held onto each other for what felt like hours, but was probably only a few moments. When we pulled away we both had tears in our eyes.

She whispered to me, "I just want to thank you for the memories. I love you. I'm gonna miss you. . . ." She was staring into my watery eyes and gripping my fingers so tightly they were turning purple. "I'll never forget you."

"I'll never forget you. . . ." I repeated, as I slowly let my fingers slip away. I was finally able to let go. I turned and walked away.

I walked out of my high school's doors that night by myself, with my thoughts dashing around in a hundred places. I realized as I walked out that I was beginning a new life—a life without my elementary-school best friends, a life of new friends and new connections, and hopefully a life of bacon-and-eggs with friends who can hold on as tightly as Beth Ann.

Beth Dieselberg

Andy

A friend may well be reckoned the masterpiece of nature.

Ralph Waldo Emerson

If you watch television or movies, you've heard a gunshot before. That loud fiery blast that rings from the screen and bounces around in your ears. It's unmistakable. War films, mob movies, cop dramas—they're all wrought with them. Gunshots. You think you know what one sounds like.

I didn't, no matter how many of the fake kind I heard in my childhood.

When I was still in fifth grade my best friend, Andy, was shot. Right through the head. It was a freak accident. I saw it, but more importantly, I heard it. There was no bang. No fiery blast. The shot came from an air rifle; it was just a soft crack and a hiss—and Andy fell down. Sounds and images that I will never, ever forget.

The doctors didn't expect him to live. The pellet had gone through his temple and lodged in his brain. Fluid built up around it, and he went into a coma. His family and friends were in shock. People hoped, they prayed, they cried, anything they felt they could do to bring Andy back, but the outlook was grim. There was no one to blame, but still we searched for answers that weren't there. I, for one, tormented myself with the thought of, *Why not me?* I was torn between feelings of guilt that it wasn't me in his place . . . and undeniable relief . . . that it wasn't me in his place. There were too many feelings and I tried to figure out what feeling was "correct."

Then came the day when Andy woke up. He opened his eyes, and later he sat up in his bed. I went to the clinic and played catch with him with a foam ball. It was all he could do, really. He couldn't even speak. He had to essentially relearn everything, and they said he would never walk again. But then they had said he wouldn't pull through either. It didn't take long before Andy was in therapy, tirelessly working his way from the bed, to crutches, to his own two legs and feet.

Throughout high school, Andy and I were, as always, the best of friends. He was still handicapped from the accident and couldn't use his left arm, but he worked it seamlessly into his daily life. He could shoot a basketball as well as ever. He taught himself how to play even the most complicated video games with one hand on the control. But even more impressive and inspiring to those of us who love Andy was that he just went back to being a kid. He went to school every day, did his homework, played sports, was active with his church and had a girlfriend he was crazy about. He was always aware of his injury and accepted it as part of who he was, but it didn't consume him. And so it was for the rest of us.

Andy taught me what it means to be a friend. To be genuinely happy when they achieve, to feel real pain when they hurt, to smile when they smile. To find hope and strength in the gravest situations. Whether you believe in miracles or not, Andy's recovery was something truly special. Andy used to thank me on occasion, telling me things like, "I couldn't have gotten through it without you." The ironic thing is that *I* couldn't have gotten through it without *him*.

Scott T. Barsotti

For Claire

We giggled like the children we were as we balanced on the ledge of the girls' bathroom and dangled our fingers out of the open window, trying to catch the snowflakes. We were supposed to be in class, but the teacher had left the room, and we'd run away for a moment to get a better view of the whitening world outside. Minutes later, we ran out of the bathroom and right into the principal. He'd seen our arms flailing around from his office in the building across the playground.

Wiping the snow from our freezing hands onto our navy blue V-neck sweaters, we were marched back into our classroom and reprimanded loudly in front of everybody. I twiddled my pigtails around my trembling fingers. You glanced at me nervously with beet-red cheeks. That's the day we became friends.

I'll always remember how we crashed that go-cart into your horrible neighbor's fence. How we stood there as the paint chipped off and the white post fell broken and twisted into the garden. How each of us waited for the other to laugh first as we ran away, each of us shocked at the discovery of a conscience, at the realization that what we'd done wasn't funny, it was just wrong. We hid in your bedroom behind blankets that hung from the top bunk, waiting for the inevitable ring of the doorbell—as long as we were invisible, we were untouchable. Your neighbor was angry. We wished we were cooler kids who didn't care.

That same summer we stole a basket from a farmer's field. We didn't even need it for the miniscule amount of blackberries that grew along the roadside—we only wanted it because it wasn't ours. The farmer caught us and shouted and screamed as we snickered shamelessly behind our hands. By then, we were far *too* cool to care.

We found a ripped-up page from an adult magazine scattered in a hedge and put the pieces back together with sticky tape. It was a male sailor in a compromising position, probably thrown out of the window of a passing truck. We'd never seen anything like it, but we both said we had. We took *The Joy of Sex* from the bookshelf and hid it behind a book of cartoons so that when your brothers came in the room where we sat, we wouldn't look as naughty as we felt.

We had an argument once about some yogurt. You had two left in your fridge. One was banana and one was blackberry, and you asked me which I'd prefer. Of course, I wanted the blackberry—who likes banana? But you wanted it, too. I said you should have it. You told me not to be stupid. I said, don't call me stupid, I don't even *like* blackberry. You called me a liar. We didn't speak for two days.

I had my first kiss before you did, and when I told you, you burnt the rice pudding you were cooking on purpose. We were supposed to have our first kisses on the same night at the school dance, with boys who were best friends, too, so we could be couples that double-dated. You had a real boyfriend before me. I always wished we still lived in the same town, so we could double-date. And I could burn your dessert like I said I would.

You rescued me from my first job at a fish shop for which I was getting paid so little. You asked your parents if I could be a waitress at their hotel. I learned to serve potatoes with fancy silverware and lock people in the refrigerator for kicks.

We used to have gymnastic lessons in the sports center every Saturday before we went swimming. We thought it was cool to wear bikinis to the local pool, even though it was full of granddads and mothers with babies. At the pool you showed me how to do a backward flip into the deep end and wouldn't give up on me until I did it. I felt so proud of myself. Once I showed some people I had never met my new talent. The force of the water pulled my bikini bottoms down to my feet, and I still go red when I think about it.

You taught me how to ride a horse. I was always scared of them, but because you were my best friend, I followed you to the riding school every weekend and watched from the fence. You always looked so calm and controlled. Eventually you got your own pony. He was really tiny and always smelled like poop. You taught me how to trot. I was really bad and always afraid, but I grew to love that smelly pony almost as much as you did.

A few months ago I wrote you a letter with some of these memories and all my gossip on four long pages. I sent a photo of me smiling and wrote a big "Hello" on the bottom in black Sharpie. I realized that too much time had passed between us. I really hope you read it. We went our separate ways in our quests to conquer the world. Life got in the way. But everything we did, in ways both big and small, led to this very moment. It's so easy to forget why we do what we do, or why we are where we are. I never want to forget.

You never wrote back.

Today I heard you'd died, and I went shopping. I don't know why I had to go shopping. I left what I was doing and went straight into Herald Square, lost myself in the clothes racks, emptied my brain of meaningful thoughts and filled it with passing snippets of other people's mindless conversation. "How's your dog?" "Do you want chicken for dinner?" "No, Tommy, you can't have an ice cream!" It all seemed so trivial. Everything they said seemed invalid. Didn't they know the world was different now?

Back in school we had a friend who died. She was fourteen. We took flowers to the scene of her car crash and remembered her smile. We never understood how God could have taken her away, but maybe now she can tell you. And you can tell me one day why you had to go, too.

Claire, I hope you're as happy now as you are in my memories, laughing and smiling and chasing your dreams. I'll remember you whenever I jump into a swimming pool at the deep end, whenever I see a kid ride a go-cart, and whenever I stick my hands out of a window to touch the falling snow.

Rebecca Wicks

Jonathon

Friends are as companions on a journey, who ought to aid each other to persevere in the road to a happier life.

Pythagoras

If we hadn't thought our girlfriends were cheating on us with Jonathon, I don't think Ben and I would ever have become friends. Since our coach was making us run about three miles a day, and we ran at the same pace, we had plenty of time to talk about this weird thing we had in common.

Grace and I had been together for over a year, but we'd spent a lot of that time fighting. Jonathon had been my best friend since fifth grade; since he and Grace had become close friends, he frequently had to play referee.

Being our referee wasn't an easy job, because Grace and I fought about everything. We were a dramatic couple, as our whole school knew, and we probably spent as much time broken up as we spent together, maybe even more.

But Jonathon was having problems of his own. He and

his mom hadn't been getting along, so he had been living with my family for several months. He slept upstairs, in the old bedroom I'd abandoned for the room my brother had vacated for college.

My new room downstairs was like a little bachelor pad, with a TV, its own bathroom and doors to the kitchen and outside. I could go anywhere and no one would know. Except for one thing: without my own car, "anywhere" meant "within walking distance."

Jonathon, on the other hand, had inherited a tiny white jalopy from a distant cousin that was years past its prime, but it was still a car. He could come and go as he pleased. My parents left him alone. It was torture: with all the independence my new room conferred, I still needed my parents' permission to go anywhere.

Having Jonathon's car around changed things dramatically: instead of my mom and I sharing her car, with one of us dropping the other off at school or work, Jonathon was now my ride. I was completely dependent on him to get from home to school, from school to practice and everywhere else. But even though we were on the same team and spent a lot of time together, Jonathon had his own life. He skipped practices or went out late, and when he wasn't available, I had to beg other people for rides or call my mom. I felt like the only child in a family with three parents.

To make things worse, Grace and Jonathon were spending a lot of time together. Frequently, they would hang out at my house while I was at practice, though Jonathon and I played for the same team, our coach let him skip practices without consequence.

Jonathon and Grace had their inside jokes, like one where they would rub their feet together: they called it "foot sex." I was the monkey in the middle, supposed to play along. It seemed like I was always the butt of their jokes that I didn't understand. Jonathon was taking everything that was mine—my girlfriend, my house, my independence—leaving me running around in circles.

My running partner, Ben, was in the same boat. His girlfriend, Melisa, was also spending time with Jonathon while we were at practices that Jonathon was able to avoid. There were the same inside jokes, traded smirks and rolled eyes; he was growing uncomfortable, too.

Ben and I talked about it constantly for weeks, trying to figure out what the three of them were doing. I was much angrier, thanks to Jonathon's omnipresence in my life, but we were both confused and growing more irritated. Then, one day as we finished up a run, Ben turned to me and said, "Listen, I can't tell you why, but you don't have to worry about Jonathon and Grace."

I asked what he knew, and how.

"Just trust me. I guarantee she's not cheating on you. Not with him, at least."

"What about Melisa?" I asked.

"It's fine," he said. "I promise."

Unfortunately, I didn't believe him. His advice only made things worse. Now I was left out of another group—first my family, then my relationship with Grace and now the people who "knew" that nothing was going on.

Meanwhile, my relationship with Jonathon grew worse. I would barely speak to him when he came home, which made him come home later and later to avoid the discomfort. Finally, it all came to a head.

"Can we talk?" he asked. It'd been a while since we'd really spoken: he had as much reason to expect a "no" as a "yes."

My fists balled up as I said, "Yes."

He suggested we go for a walk, so I followed him out the door toward the wetlands behind my house. There were acres of dried-out swamp with train tracks cutting through the middle. We had played on the tracks as kids, placing coins on the rails to see them deform into blank strips of copper.

Barely concealing my rage, I stood in front of him with my fists still balled up behind me, ready to do anything at all to take back my girlfriend, my house and my sanity.

He looked at me and said quietly, "So you know how Grace and I have been spending a lot of time together, lately?"

Prepared as I was, I couldn't believe he was about to say it. As my heart skipped, I glared back, too angry to respond.

"Well, she's been helping me figure something out. And we didn't tell you, but I know that Ben knows, and since you're my best friend, it's only fair that I tell you. . . ."

As he trailed off, I pictured us wrestling on the tracks, a train approaching.

". . . Dan, I'm gay."

"You're *what*?" I asked.

"I'm gay," he said. It was clearly not an easy thing for him to say.

This wasn't what I had expected. He was still stealing my girlfriend, though, right? Slowly I began to piece together that if he were gay, he might not want a girlfriend.

I was still suspicious: "So, you're not sleeping with Grace?"

He laughed. "Um, I'm gay, Dan."

"Are you sure that that's it?" I asked. I still wasn't convinced.

"Uh, yeah, that's about it," he replied.

"Oh. Okay. I thought you were going to tell me something bad that could have ended our relationship."

That was the end of an ugly chapter in our lives. Jonathon returned home, and to refereeing other things Grace and I found to fight about. But I always found it funny that the one thing he seemed ashamed of was the only thing I wanted to hear.

Dan Levine

Going Away

Plant a seed of friendship; reap a bouquet of happiness.

Lois L. Kaufman

I couldn't believe Loni was leaving. Since she'd become friends with my sister Sara when I was in eighth grade, she'd been a part of my family. Her friendliness, laughter and jokes had quickly made her a favorite visitor, and soon she didn't have to knock, anymore. The familiar honking of the Ford we teased her about always signaled her arrival. The dog would bark, and Laura, my youngest sister, would run to the door to wait for her, eager to grab her hand and lead her off to show her something new: a rare Pokemon card, a new Beanie Baby, a new species of plant growing only in our backyard, which would lead to an inevitable nature walk—Laura the tour guide, Loni the eager student.

Over the years, she'd become a friend of mine as well as Sara's. And now, after countless bike rides, phone calls and nights spent talking she was leaving. I wasn't sure how I felt about it.

I pulled into the familiar driveway with gravel crunching under my tires, a sound that meant home to me. I eased the car around the bend and parked up close to the garage, watching carefully for the kittens I knew were there somewhere. Sliding out of the car, I scanned the yard.

The large shed that held the farm equipment was farther back, its doors a dazzling new shade of white, a product of hours of work in the summer sun. Loni, the artist, still stood on a ladder, holding a paintbrush in her hand and squinting up at the doors, searching for spots she may have missed. She hadn't noticed me yet.

"Hey," I called, moving closer to the shed.

"Hey," she called back, grinning at me from up high. She wiped her hands on her jean shorts, already flecked with paint. Climbing down from the ladder, she looked almost apologetic as she said, "I'm almost done."

"It's all right; I have until ten or so." School was starting the next day and my curfew had been reinstated, a sure sign that summer was ending. In the bright sun of that day, it was hard to believe summer was really gone and school was about to start.

She finished up on the ladder, and I followed her into the garage, helping her put lids on cans of thick white paint, pounding them shut with the handles of screwdrivers. She spoke of things she needed to do, things she needed to buy and places she needed to go before she left for the University of Michigan on Wednesday.

"So after I get all that stuff at Meijer, I think I'll be okay . . . do you think I need a wastebasket? Maybe I should call my roommate . . . I got the carpet, though. That's okay, right? I mean, everyone likes blue. . . ."

We headed into the house, where it was air-conditioned and cool. The kitchen floor was smooth and clean under my bare feet, and I sat down at the table as Loni poured glasses of red cherry Kool-Aid. As she poured, her eyes widened, and she smacked herself on the forehead, a gesture of forgetfulness.

"I bought all this Kool-Aid for my room . . . but I forgot sugar! Don't let me forget to write it down."

We headed upstairs with the glasses, the too-bright red of the juice staining our lips as we drank, making us look like kids who'd been playing in our mothers' makeup. I fidgeted as usual, tracing the rim of my glass with a finger. Her room had the mess of someone trying to decide what to take and what to leave. Piles of clothing, towels, books and CDs towered shakily, threatening to topple at any moment. There were crates and boxes and suitcases, some half-packed and some empty, some already taped shut. We stood in the middle of it all, looking around, unsure.

"I don't know where to start," she sighed, plopping down. "I mean, what to pack, where to put it all. . . ."

"Start with clothes," I suggested, and she started pulling clothes from the closet, rolling them into bulky tubes and stacking them in a suitcase.

"I saw this on *Oprah* . . . they're not supposed to wrinkle."

"Really?"

"I wonder how many pairs of jeans I'll need . . . it'll be cold soon . . . do I need sweaters?"

We talked like that for a while, about things that didn't really matter, until I looked up. She was standing, framed by the closet door, holding a pair of rolled-up jeans. I glanced at the suitcase and realized that we'd packed nearly every article of clothing she owned. One suitcase alone was packed almost entirely with just pants. She shrugged.

"I'm not going to have to do laundry for a while, right?"

I laughed. I think I was almost as surprised as she was when my laughter dissolved into tears. She came forward to hug me, and I choked out a muffled, "I can't believe you're leaving."

"I know." There were tears in her eyes, too, and we cried for a while, talking about things we'd done: about basketball games we'd played in the dark, the times we'd gone to the mall and walked around talking in the loudest, most obnoxious voices we could, the movies where we'd thrown popcorn at the screen.

Eventually our tears dried, and we gave up on packing for the night, reasoning that she did "have two more days left." We went downstairs and got ourselves popcorn and more cherry Kool-Aid, and watched *The Simpsons*, laughing at Homer and Bart until I had to leave.

As I drove home that night, I listened to a tape she'd made me for my sixteenth birthday, still a little sad about the prospect of losing one of my best friends. But the more I thought about it, the more I realized I wasn't really losing her. The person who had taught me so much about life and laughter, the person who had helped me grow to be myself, was just going away for a while, to do some growing and learning of her own.

Bethany Trombley

SPF 1,000

Cameron and I met in the ninth grade, at a time when we were both covered in acne and our mouths were full of metal. Until I met Cam, I had a few good friends with whom I shared many of the same interests, but never in my life had I experienced a friendship quite like the one I shared with her.

"I'm Cameron. Friends call me Cam," she said, introducing herself to me.

"Cool, I'm Lauren. Friends call me Lauren or Lauren."

Cam and I shared everything. At times it even seemed like we shared a brain. Cam and I both had a thing for snapping photos of our shadows in the moonlight. Some nights we would ditch everyone else, and walk around school, the park, even train tracks with our cameras—searching for the perfect shot of a our shadows, imprinted on the sidewalk beside us.

A few months before I met Cameron, I was diagnosed with a rare nervous system disease that progresses if left untreated. I was misdiagnosed for months. Consequently, a lot of time was wasted on the wrong treatments and I was getting worse and worse. Cam was the first friend I ever told about my situation.

"Eventually I might not be able to walk, be in the sun, digest food, eat like a normal person. Or worse," I said as we sat on a bench one day after school. She was quiet for a moment.

"Well, if you can't walk, I'll push you and if you can't eat, I'll have a food fight with you anyway, and if you become allergic to light we'll still be able to go shadow-hunting. I'll be your emotional sunscreen—SPF 1,000."

"My SPF 1,000, huh?"

"Yup," she laughed.

I hugged her. "Thank you."

Days turned into weeks, weeks turned into months and my health deteriorated. It was getting increasingly difficult for me to get around. Soon I lost the ability to walk entirely. Cam was there with me, every "step" of the way. Finally, things got bad enough that I was forced to leave school. Over the next four years, I was in and out of the hospital. It became my home away from home and I was often there for months at a time. I was very sick and unable to stay in contact with friends, even Cam.

I remained bedridden for those four years but eventually gained a lot of my strength back. I had a nurse who gave me my medicine and made sure I was okay. I was never "alone" but that didn't change the fact that I felt lonely. I needed someone to talk to, a friend.

"Cam, it's me."

"Lauren, oh my gosh. How are you? I have missed you so much. How are you feeling?"

Hearing Cam's voice filled me with an inner peace I hadn't felt in a long time.

"I'm fine, now," I said, relieved. Everything was going to be okay.

Things slowly began to improve. I received a power wheelchair for my eighteenth birthday, which for me meant FREEDOM! Finally, I could get around again! I could go outside at night, smell the grass, feel the wind against my face. I could take photographs with a flash. I could live. I called Cam and told her the news.

"I'm on my way!" she said.

That night, I took my first walk in four years. Cam brought her camera, and I brought mine. We walked and talked and laughed like we were kids again. We made shadow puppets in the dark with our hands, against the pavement.

Having her back was a relief. There were so many things I wanted to tell her, so many questions I had about myself.

"Sometimes I wonder about my purpose, Cam. Why am I here? What's going to happen to me? I mean, I'm lucky to be alive. I'm appreciative of every moment and every day. The thing is, though, I don't just want to "exist." I want more than that. I want to break free. I'm tired of being the patient patient. I want to change the world. I want to be great, I want to help people and I don't want to be alone. It's just that, I'm terrified of being alone again . . . ," I trailed off.

"You will never be alone, Lauren," she said shaking her head, smiling. "You will be great. You will do whatever you want to do and you will never, ever be alone." She paused to snap a picture of a tree and then continued. "Think of me as your shadow. No matter how far you walk, no matter how dark the night becomes, I'll always be behind you."

We stopped and took pictures of our shadows. She looked at the screen on her digital camera. "Hot!" she exclaimed. "I think we finally got the perfect shot!"—two forms, dancing across the sidewalk, side by side, best friends back together again.

I looked over at Cameron and laughed. "What would I do without my SPF 1,000?"

She kissed me on my cheek and we kept on down the road.

Lauren Henderson

More than Just Sisters

Is solace anywhere more comforting than that in the arms of a sister.

Alice Walker

My sister and I have always had a special kind of bond. Being the only kids in the family, we were stuck with each other. Not that it was bad or anything, but we had our share of arguments and fights.

Although I would never admit it, I always looked up to her. Somewhere along the way, she became known as Sissy, and my nickname became JulieBug. I would try to hang out with her and her friends, only to be kicked out of her room, eventually eavesdropping at her door on their juicy conversations. Whenever she had a date, you could always catch my friend Ruth and me peaking out the window or hiding in the bushes, giggling. My sister and I even went through a "prank phase." I don't remember who started it, but we went through weeks of Saran-wrapped toilet seats, Vaseline-covered phones, short-sheeted beds and frozen underwear—yes, *frozen underwear.* Eventually our parents had to break it up, for some of the tricks were getting out of hand, and although they were intended for each other, sometimes the effects ricocheted off our parents. Of course, being sisters, we also experienced our share of fighting over clothes and stealing, I mean borrowing, each other's things. Even though we occasionally, okay daily, got in fights, we could never remain angry at each other for long.

When I was in middle school and she was in high school, she started letting me hang out with her friends. Once in a while she asked if I would like to go out with them, and I would eagerly reply yes. Sometimes she even let me tag along with her and her boyfriend to the movies or out to eat. Whenever I needed help with my homework she always made herself available to tutor me. When she turned sixteen and got her first car, she usually found time to take me to the Dairy Queen for a treat and on occasion brought me lunch at school.

The day we took her to college for her freshman year was the hardest day for me. Though my dad tried to comfort me on the long four-and-a-half-hour ride home, I cried from the time my sister and I said good-bye to when my parents and I reached our hometown. I missed her more than anything. I became the "only child" at home and, although I thought it was going to be great to receive all the extra attention, I hated it. I had more fights with Mom, more supervision and, worst of all, *more chores.* Adjusting to her absence at home wasn't easy, and occasionally I would catch myself walking out the door in the morning yelling, "Bye Mom, bye Dad, bye Ann Marie!"

Late one Saturday night, she called me, frustrated with school, friends, boys and life. We had always been able to call each other and talk about stuff, but this conversation was different. She told me her troubles and, although I can't remember our conversation as well as she can, I tried my best to comfort her and give her good advice. That night I went from being her little sister to being a trusted source of listening and support. I told her that night, before we hung up, that she was my best friend. Later that week, I received a letter from her and this poem:

Sister

I met my best friend last night.
She's been under my nose for a while.
How could I have been so blind?
She's been with me all my life.
Younger,
and more intelligent than me,
because she was the first one to see it:
The tremendous friendship we possess,
that binds us together as sisters,
and as friends.

That night we both came to the realization that we are more than just sisters, we are the best of friends.

Julie Hoover

$\overline{\underline{2}}$

MAKING A DIFFERENCE

It's the curiosity that drives me. It's making a difference in the world that prevents me from ever giving up.

Deborah Meier

Just Being There

It was my junior year of high school, and I needed to knock out twenty hours of community service—and fast. My ethics teacher had given us months to get it done, but with everything else I had going on, I'd managed to procrastinate right down to the last two weeks of the semester.

Lucky for me, there was a convalescent home a few blocks down the street from my school. To be honest, I wasn't looking forward to it. I'd always had an aversion to hospitals and convalescent homes. Still, I needed the hours—and how bad could it be? I could walk over after class let out, spend a few hours there, and voila, obligation fulfilled in no time.

On my first afternoon there, one of the nurses introduced me to a group of wheelchair-bound ladies playing penny-ante poker out in the central courtyard, under the shade of a gazebo. They always met to play poker at that same time each afternoon, so I became a member of their bunch. They couldn't walk, but their minds were sharp. We'd joke and share stories between each hand.

My last day of volunteering at the convalescent home was a Friday. I was in high spirits as I arrived that afternoon. As much as I enjoyed the sassy grandmothers and their stories, I was still a teenager. I had other things I wanted to do and people my own age with whom to hang out.

But the gazebo was empty. A nurse explained that the physical therapy sessions earlier that day had put everybody's normal schedule out of whack. There'd be no poker under the gazebo that afternoon.

I asked the nurse what I should do. Not having anything specific for me, she led me to the lounge reserved for the residents with Alzheimer's. It was a gloomy, cavernous room. Those within sat quietly on couches or trembled from place to place with no specific destination. It was age, sickness, loss of mental faculties and impending death. It was, in short, everything that frightened me about the idea of growing old.

There was a small, old-fashioned organ sitting in the corner. There was no rhyme or reason to its being there. The nurse noticed me looking at it.

"Why don't you play for them?" she said.

"But I can't play the organ," I protested. "I can't even play piano!"

"They won't know the difference," she said, leaning in confidentially. Before I could reply, she'd turned and walked out.

So there I was—seventeen years old, surrounded by Alzheimer's patients and not a clue as to what I should do. I looked around the room again, hunting for that one face, that one pair of eyes that wasn't adrift in a sea of memories. I didn't find it.

Suddenly, that organ was looking pretty good.

I sat down at it and fiddled with the different keys, buttons and levers. After that, I tried to plunk out simple songs, one key at a time. "La Cucaracha" and "Daisy" had never sounded so bad. If that organ could think, it would have crawled away in shame.

Halfway through my off-season rendition of "Joy to the World," I noticed movement out of the corner of my eye. I looked over and saw an old man in a bright red sweater shuffling toward me. He walked slowly, but with purpose.

"Hey, young fella," he said, wiping at his wet mouth with a shaking handkerchief. "You play pretty good."

"No . . . I mean, thanks, but . . . I'm just messing around. . . ."

"It's a good job, playing piano. That, and plumbing."

"Yeah . . . I guess."

"Plumbers and piano players, fella. They can find work anywhere. No matter where they go in the whole wide world, they'll find work."

"I hadn't thought of that."

He patted me on the shoulder with a hand that was gnarled and dry with age.

"You keep up with that piano playing, young fella. It'll take you places. Piano players and plumbers. They work anywhere—you remember that."

With that, he turned and shuffled away, as randomly as he'd appeared in the first place.

As soon as he was gone, the nurse hurried over to me. I didn't realize she'd been watching. Not knowing what I'd done wrong, I panicked.

"Was he talking to you?" she asked.

"Yeah," I said.

She stared at me.

"I'm sorry," I blurted. "I didn't mean to cause . . ."

"Sorry? You didn't do anything wrong." She looked over at the old man. He was sitting on one of the couches at the other end of the room, a faint smile on his lips. "He and his wife got sick around the same time. They've both lived here for years. She died a month ago. He hasn't spoken a word to anybody since then. Until now. What did you say to him? How'd you get him to open up?"

"I didn't say anything. I didn't do anything. I was just here."

Sometimes that's all it takes.

Patrick Seitz

I Hope You Dance

This past year, Valentine's Day took on a whole new meaning for me. I met Bill two years ago, as a freshman in high school when we were in the same drama class. Bill was very popular—it seemed like everyone knew him. He had a way of finding joy in every detail of life.

This is all the more remarkable because Bill is in a wheelchair. The thing is, he doesn't seem to notice it—and before long, you don't either. He doesn't let a tragedy like being paralyzed stop him from making the most of every opportunity. Whereas most teens in his place take special classes separate from the rest of the school, Bill instead has chosen to immerse himself in the normal high-school environment, in an effort to be just like every other ordinary teenager. But I knew from the moment I met him that Bill was anything but ordinary. Indeed, he was extraordinary.

Bill was a hit in drama class. Everyone wanted to act in a scene with him, because he was so fun to be around. He never failed to captivate the audience with his expressive face, bright toothpaste-ad smile and effortless charisma. Bill also took part in our school's annual student art parade, ingeniously building a "race car" around his wheelchair. No greater applause was heard than the cheers that erupted from the student body when Bill was wheeled past, honking the horn and dramatically turning the steering wheel of his "car."

I am a member of the Interact club at my school, which is geared toward bringing students together in positive ways and breaking down barriers. Every year, we sponsor a Valentine's Day dance at lunch that is held especially for students like Bill who have special needs. As freshmen and sophomores, my friends and I went to the dance together, but last Valentine's Day things changed. Many of my friends now had boyfriends and wanted to use the extended lunch period to go out for a romantic lunch. So I, alone in my "single status," attended the dance solo.

I'm ashamed to admit that I was feeling a bit left out and sorry for myself. Here it was, another Valentine's Day, and it seemed like everyone else had found that special someone to spend it with. Except for me. I was alone—without a boyfriend, and now without my close friends, as well. I considered skipping the dance altogether, but then I remembered how much work had gone into it and how my fellow Interact Club members were counting on me. So, feeling like I was doing a good deed, I went.

At the dance, I saw Bill immediately—in his wheelchair, in the middle of the dance floor, surrounded by a group of people. He saw me and smiled, so I headed over to join the cluster of students around him, all of them laughing and dancing and having a good time. Many of us are a bit self-conscious when it comes to dancing, but not Bill. A quadriplegic, he was only able to move his arms a little bit, but when he did, everyone around him began to excitedly chant, "Go Bill! Go Bill!" and he displayed the kind of smile five-year-olds flash on Christmas morning. Indeed, he seemed to be having the time of his life.

Bill's enthusiasm was contagious. Before I knew it, I was dancing and laughing, too. As I gazed around the gym at the joy and excitement on everyone's faces, I realized that my Valentine's Day was, in fact, special and filled with love. I had thought that by coming to the dance I was doing a favor for others, but I was really giving a priceless gift to myself. Simply by being himself, Bill showed me how to forget my fears and just *dance*.

Dallas Nicole Woodburn

The Greatest Audience

They may forget what you said, but they will never forget how you made them feel.

Carl W. Buechner

I was sixteen years old, and like many other teenage boys, I was in a band. We played a mix of hard rock and heavy metal, covering our favorite bands. We weren't great, but we were good enough to come in third place at our school's talent show, so we decided to see if we could get some local gigs. When we found out we'd gotten booked for a charitable event at a large rehabilitation hospital, we were ecstatic. It wouldn't pay much, but it was our first real job. For two weeks we practiced hard, getting together every day after school to hone our skills and learn enough songs to fill a one-hour show.

The day of the concert, we showed up early in order to check out the stage. It was nerve-racking to stand there and look out at the hundred or so chairs lined up below us. To my eyes it seemed like those chairs went on forever. We set up and did a quick sound check, then went backstage to have a soda and rest, anything to calm our nerves. While we were back there the hospital's entertainment director came over to talk to us.

"Okay, boys, I just want to fill you in on a couple of important details," she told us. "A lot of the people in the audience are suffering from severe physical and/or mental disabilities. Also, many of them are older, in their sixties and seventies. Don't let that alarm you. These patients have very few chances to see live entertainment of any kind, so they enjoy any kind of musical talent that we can bring in. Just play your regular show, and you'll do fine." With that, she left, going into the auditorium to help the volunteers and staff that were assisting the patients to their seats.

Soon enough it was show time. We made our way through the thick, dusty curtain that separated the backstage area and stepped out onto the creaking wood floor of the stage. As we picked up our instruments and plugged them in, we got our first real look at the audience. I think to one degree or another we all felt a kind of nervousness that had nothing to do with how we would perform. The auditorium was packed, and there were at least two or three rows of wheelchairs in both the front and the back of the big room. The majority of the people watching us had either been seriously injured in accidents or born with major congenital birth defects. Many of them were missing limbs. Some were talking quietly among themselves, but most were just sitting there, intently watching the stage. The quiet was unnerving, especially to a group of young men used to rowdy, energetic audiences.

Tommy, the lead singer, signaled us to start the first song, and we broke into the opening chords. Everything was perfect, and we played probably the best show of our lives. We hardly missed a note on any of our songs, even the ones that we'd only recently learned. My guitar solos seemed to flow effortlessly out of my fingers, and I felt surrounded by a wall of music. I knew I was getting a taste, just the merest glimpse, of what real musicians must feel when they're on stage. Unfortunately, we couldn't enjoy our performance.

As each song finished, there was a short pause, maybe three or four seconds, before we launched into our next number. This was the time when the audience would normally applaud. Now, we were realistic enough to know that even at our best, we weren't professional musicians by any means. We didn't expect thundering applause or standing ovations. No illusions of greatness here. But polite applause is usually a given, even if the audience doesn't like you. We were getting nothing. Zero. If there was anything there, it was Zen applause—the sound of one hand clapping. To say it was disheartening would be an understatement. The deafening silence only made us more determined to win the audience over. We played each successive piece stronger, more furiously than the last, striving for perfection. Loud songs, mellow songs, it made no difference. Each time we concluded a number the audience just continued their imitations of statues. After forty-five minutes we decided to end our set early. Why bother finishing when no one was appreciating us anyway?

We unplugged our instruments and went backstage. A moment later, the entertainment director ran back and confronted us. "What are you doing?" she asked. "I thought we agreed that you'd play for an hour!"

"Well, that was before we realized that the audience was going to hate us," Tommy replied, disgust and embarrassment evident in his tone.

"What are you talking about?" asked the director. "They love you. Get back out there and finish your show. You can even play some extra songs if you want."

"Love us?" exclaimed Pete, our bass player. "That's the worst audience I've ever seen!"

"You don't understand," the director continued. "Most of these people don't know they're supposed to clap. In fact, many of them can't. I've been out there talking to them, and they can't believe how good you are. They'll be so hurt if you don't finish."

The four of us looked at each other. None of us really believed her, but we decided that we should honor our word and finish the show. Returning to the stage, we played our final three songs—and added two more for good measure.

Finally, the show was over and we gratefully began packing up our instruments. We had still received no applause, not even when we said good night. Backstage the director told us, "When you're done packing up, please come back inside the auditorium. Some of the patients want to thank you for coming."

We didn't want to do it, but hey, we felt obligated. I mean, after all, it was a charity event. Of all the things I expected, what happened next shocked me more than anything. At least fifty people, ranging in age from ten to seventy, had gathered by the stage. All of them wanted to thank us; some shook our hands, and one small girl even asked me for my autograph. Several told us that we were the best band that had played for them in years. We couldn't believe it. The director had been right all along; they loved us! We ended up staying there for more than half an hour, saying hello to people, telling them about ourselves and talking about music.

While I knew I was never going to end up having a career in music, I did play a few more small shows with different bands. But no matter how much the audience cheered, I never felt as good as I did that one special night.

Greg Faherty

Understanding Jenny

If someone listens, or stretches out a hand, or whispers a kind word of encouragement, or attempts to understand a lonely person, extraordinary things will begin to happen.

Loretta Girzartis

I jumped into my mother's car, threw my cross-country team bag into the backseat, slammed the car door and fought with my seat belt.

"I'm so sick of it!" I said and pulled my hair back into its frizzy ponytail.

"I can see that," my mom answered, then turned on the blinker, looked over her shoulder and pulled out into the traffic. "I'm guessing this isn't about your hair."

"It's Jenny, playing her mind games again. Training is less tiring than dealing with her and her feelings."

"Which one is Jenny?" my mom asked.

"She's been here about a month. She lives at the Timmers."

"Oh, yes, Gloria told me they had a new foster kid. Said

she's been moved around, but she's getting decent grades and joining school activities."

"I just wish she hadn't joined my activity."

"Why's that?" My mom was pretty good about listening to me vent.

"I mean, we've been training for weeks: stretching, running, pacing, lifting weights and making ourselves into a team. Then in strolls Jenny, the goddess of cross-country or something. A coach's dream. She paces around the course with us, and suddenly she's so far ahead that she makes the loop and is running back towards us like we're standing in place. A smile on her face, her perfect hair swinging behind her."

"So are you upset because your team has someone who can earn you some real points, or because she has a talent that she enjoys or because her hair stays so perfect?" My mom leaned over and pushed my damp-curled bangs out of my face.

"Mom, I'm not that shallow."

"I know, honey. Sorry. Just trying to see the problem here."

"Jenny's the problem. She helps all of us run faster by upping the pace. She cheers us on. She trains harder, and so do we. We were voted cocaptains. Then, this week, she cops an attitude. I spent most of my time running after her."

"No pun intended!"

"Mom! Please! This is serious," I sighed and took a drink from my water bottle. "Our first meet is tomorrow. Jenny keeps saying she won't run with the team. She has all sorts of reasons from leg cramps to a headache. I have to beg her. I have to tell her over and over that she can't do that to the rest of the team. It goes on all day, between classes, at lunch, on the way to practice. She wears me out. What's her deal?"

"She ends up running though, right?"

"Yeah, but we're all tired of it. She's so needy."

Mom pulled into our driveway. Instead of rushing into the house to start dinner, she turned and looked at me.

"Cindy, you gave yourself the answer."

Great, I'm pouring it all out, and Mom's going to give me a pop quiz. "Make this easy, would you, Mom?"

"Well, Gloria told me a little about Jenny. She and her little brother have been together all this time in foster care. They're really close. Her caseworker said that Jenny took good care of her little brother. Every time they would move, Jenny would say that as long as they were together, they had a family."

My heart sank. "Please, don't tell me something happened to her little brother."

"No, he's fine. His father, Jenny's stepfather, earned custody of him. He came for him this week. He had gifts and hugs and big plans for their future."

"Really? That's good."

"Yes, but he had nothing for Jenny. She wasn't even a little part of his big plans."

My chest felt tight. "Why?"

"Well, Jenny's mom and stepfather weren't together that long. Jenny and her brother have been in foster care for a while now. I guess he didn't consider Jenny his."

"What about her mom?"

"Her mom wants her drugs and alcohol more than she wants Jenny."

"Poor Jenny, not to have a family." I was close to tears. "Not to feel wanted or needed."

My mother patted my knee. "That's it, honey. You got it." And I did.

I didn't see Jenny during school the next day. I started to think I had understood too late, that Jenny wasn't going to show at all.

I was the last one to get on the team bus and was glad

there were still a few empty rows. I could take up two seats, put on my headsets and get some down time before the meet.

Then I spotted Jenny. She was sitting in the back, alone.

I started down the narrow aisle, causing quite a disruption trying to maneuver myself and my oversized bag to the back. By the time I got to my seat, most of the team was watching my progress.

"Can I sit by you?" I asked Jenny. She shrugged her shoulders. I took it as a yes. "I didn't see you today. I was afraid you weren't going to make it."

"I didn't think anyone would notice if I made it or not."

The girls around us groaned. Here she goes again.

I looked at Jenny. I saw past her attitude because I understood what she was really saying.

"We would've noticed if you weren't here, Jenny. We want you running with us. The team needs you."

Jenny seemed to fill up, to expand.

"Isn't that right, team?" I called. "Let's hear it for Jenny!"

There was silence. *Please,* I thought, *for Jenny's sake, give her what she needs.*

Slowly and then with building momentum, they cheered for their teammate. As they did, the atmosphere changed. They began to care more about Jenny.

Jenny felt it. The defiance drained out of her shoulders. Her face relaxed. She smiled and blushed with pleasure.

We didn't erase all the pain in Jenny's life, but neither had we added to it.

She ran with us that day. She won the individual blue ribbon and lifted our team to third place. She never threatened not to run again, and she led us to our best season record.

Through our simple offering of friendship and her willingness to accept it, we gave Jenny something more important to her than blue ribbons. We gave her what she desired the most: to know she was wanted and needed.

Cynthia M. Hamond

Sometimes We Dream

Sometimes I dream of Lesley
Sitting painfully
Corruption concealed behind eyes of happiness and silk.
Her plastic smile hides the affliction of the heart.
Deep inside there is a vengeance that
Seeps into her veins.
She cries out, but no one hears.
Someone will interrupt a nightmare.
Someone will help Lesley stand against vanity.

Sometimes I dream of Marcia
Her vibrant eyes hidden beneath a
Dark, dark hood.
Her soul is in cigarette butts, and old needles,
Thrown away.
Sometimes she literally sells herself short.
When her fingers reach, she grasps only at broken edges.
She cries out, but no one hears.
Someone will interrupt a nightmare.
Someone will help Marcia fight addiction.

Sometimes I dream of Jonathan
His eyes run without destination.
Away from his culture, away from himself.
A glass shell forms around his heart, filling it with shame.
As scissors snip his long, dark hair,
Shards of soul fall at his feet.
Colorless pieces.
He cries out, but no one hears.
Someone will interrupt a nightmare.
Someone will help Jonathan kill prejudice.

Sometimes I dream of Caitlyn
Her eyes are fatigued from the fight.
"It's hard to be liked," she says, "when you have those
   things others want."
Her riches have the power to
Destruct, deceive, demolish.
The power to make others covet
Rather than celebrate.
She cries out, but no one hears.
Someone will interrupt a nightmare.
Someone will help Caitlyn combat envy.

Sometimes I dream of Juan
With eyes black, beaten, and bruised.
No one notices when that single, solitary tear trickles
   down his cheek.
He sits in the deepest shadow of the darkest corner,
Dreading the afternoon bell.
He blames himself, though
It's hardly his fault.
He cries out, but no one hears.
Someone will interrupt a nightmare.
Someone will help Juan brave domestic violence.

Sometimes I dream of Kimberly
Her eyes downcast.
She tries to make friends, but to hope anymore is to be let
    down.
She walks through the halls, trying to pass by unnoticed.
She cannot help her clothes, her weight, her
    trembling chin.
She runs from the comments that shatter her dreams and
Build a wall around her heart.
She cries out, but no one hears.
Someone will interrupt a nightmare.
Someone will help Kimberly battle bullying.

As social issues start to shout,
Have no fear of standing out.
There is a difference to be made,
In harmony, nightmares will surely fade.

I can interrupt a nightmare.
I can help society conquer all . . .
Maybe the someone is me.

Olivia Heaney

My Amazing Brother

Those who trust us educate us.

T. S. Eliot

Mark was the most popular boy in his class. He had top grades, was a star athlete and was everyone's friend. His face belonged on the cover of magazines, and he was nicer than ice-cold lemonade on a scorching hot day. He was the classic "all-American boy." Girls chased after him with starry eyes and drooling mouths. Who could blame them? He was absolutely perfect. He also happened to be my little brother.

My brother and I had always been close, yet I had long felt slightly inferior to him. He just seemed to have everything. I, on the other hand, was a shy writer with relatively few close friends. I'm sure 95 percent of the class had no idea I even existed.

High school started, and Mark and I were at the same school; he was a freshman, and I was a senior. We got closer than ever that year. I don't know whether it was the rides to school when we gleefully sang along to the songs on the radio, the fact that we were both on the swim team and spent three months breathing chlorine fumes together or that we shared the same school gossip with each other. Whatever the reason, our bond grew by the day. We told each other everything. We were each other's confidant.

I helped him with his algebra problems, and he read my papers and assured me they were A^+ quality. We listened to CDs every night and danced around the den, laughing. We joked about our parents and their unjust curfew policy. We even hung out with each other at school functions, at the mall and at the movies. He introduced me to everyone he knew—basically the whole school—and I quickly gained more and more friends. People actually started knowing I existed. I was a "somebody."

One night, my brother and I were discussing the upcoming semiformal dance. Mark, of course, already had a date. I didn't have a date and hadn't even planned on going. I never had a date for anything, and I accepted that nothing was likely to change that. When Mark asked who I wanted to go with, I was shocked.

"It doesn't really matter, because I'm not going," was my curt reply.

"What do you mean you're not going? You have to go. It's your senior year!" Mark sincerely didn't understand why I wasn't going.

"Well, you kinda have to have a date to go, and there's not one person who would want to go with me," I told him, using the reasoning I'd repeated to myself over and over.

"You've got to be kidding, Care. There isn't one guy in the whole school who would turn you down. Do you realize how many guys like you?"

"How do *you* know?" I asked, wondering where my brother was getting such ridiculous ideas.

"Because you're the coolest girl in the world, that's how I know. Everybody thinks so. You're smart, funny, pretty, talented. . . . " Mark counted off on his fingers, as I sat on the edge of my bed in utter amazement. "Any guy who would turn you down has serious problems. I know. . . ."

I didn't hear what else my brother said. My mind was stuck on seven words that had rolled off his tongue: "You're the coolest girl in the world." I ran it through my mind nearly a hundred times before it sunk in. My brother believed any guy would go to the dance with me. My brother, the most popular boy in school, thought I was "the coolest girl in the world."

The rest of the year went by in an exuberant blur. By graduation, I knew nearly everyone at school and had been on many dates. I made new friends and tried new things like coffee, guitar, conversation and karaoke. I was happier than I'd ever been.

Later that summer Mark and I were having our normal nightly chat.

"Mark?" I asked.

"What, Care?" His question was as sweet as his heart.

I thought a minute before saying, "Thanks."

Mark looked puzzled. "Thanks for what?"

Thinking even longer, I replied, "For bringing the 'me' out of me."

Mark smiled and hugged me. "It's always been there, Care. You've always been wonderful you."

I smiled into the darkness as I thought to myself, *Yeah, it just took my amazing brother to make me realize it.*

Carrie O'Maley

Super Roy

The greatest truth must be recognition that in every man, in every child is the potential for greatness.

Robert Kennedy

"You're a halfback."

I looked over my shoulder at the empty field behind me. "Me?" I asked, pointing to my chest.

"Yes," the coach said again. "You're a halfback. Yep, no doubt about it."

The coach's name was Super Roy. Someone told me his real name once, but it never stuck. In my mind he'll always be Super Roy—football coach, mentor, philosopher and role model. He was the man who made a halfback out of a scrawny, scared little fellow on his first day of pony league practice. He was the man who shaped my life.

When I got to practice that day I was a small kid with little athletic experience or skill. I wondered if I belonged there at all. When I left I was the team's halfback, and I wondered what Super Roy had seen in me that I didn't see in myself.

"Are you sure I'm a halfback?" I asked him the next day.

"Let me see," he said, standing back to have a good glance at me. "Yep. You're a halfback. Might as well get used to it."

"Okay," I said, puzzled but beginning to accept the idea, strange as it seemed.

Later that day we started running plays. Time after time the quarterback put the ball right in my hands. Me, the nerdy fellow who had to be reminded how many points a touchdown was worth. I expected to go all season without touching the ball. I expected to be a bench warmer, and now the ball was in my hands—literally.

Super Roy had a routine he did every day. As practice wound down he would pick one of the players to step forward. The player had to recite a quote Super Roy had given him the day before. It was a very important moment in practice. No one wanted to forget his quote in front of the whole team.

After practice was over one day, Super Roy summoned me. "Your turn tomorrow," he said. "Ready for your quote?"

"Okay," I said, straining in deep concentration. "I'm ready."

"Well, here it is: 'It's not the size of the man you play, it's how you play the man.' Got it?"

"Yes, Coach."

Super Roy winked at me and gave me a pat on the shoulder.

The next day my mind played like a broken record. "It's not the size of the man you play, it's how you play the man." I repeated it to myself in the morning while I waited for the bus. I wrote it down time and time again during breaks in school, and all during practice I mumbled the quote to myself after each hit, just to be sure it hadn't been knocked out of my head.

When the time came I stepped forward proudly. "It's not the size of the man you play," I told my teammates, "it's how you play the man."

Super Roy gave me another smile and a wink.

I remembered my quote—I always will.

Years later I came to understand the genius of Super Roy's methods. He was the kind of coach who brought out the greatness in his players. He was a coach who understood what sports can do to shape character.

That year a scrawny little kid learned to believe in himself, to learn there is no problem so big he can't handle. It was a lesson that shaped my life.

Long after my pony league days were over I became a teacher at a school for troubled boys. Super Roy's lessons were never far from my mind, and I borrowed from him freely. Every day there was a new quote for a young man to remember, a quote made just for him. And I always looked for the good in my students that they never saw in themselves.

There was a young man in my class who had a gifted mind and a superb voice for public speaking. One day he gave a great answer to a question I'd posed to the class. "Good point, Mr. President," I told him.

After class he stopped me in the hallway. "Mr. Heisler, why did you call me Mr. President?"

"Because you are a president. It's just a matter of time. Might as well get used to it."

I gave him a wink and a pat on the shoulder. Super Roy would have been proud.

Jeff Heisler

Safe at Home

Great opportunities to help others seldom come, but small ones surround us daily.

Sally Koch

Coaching is one of the toughest jobs a man can do. He must please a platoon of people: parents who want the team to win; parents who want their sons to play; parents who are certain they could coach better than the one who is. There is no pleasing everyone.

It is not a job for the thin-skinned. It is best left for graying men.

But my most poignant memory of a coach didn't involve a man with silver in his sideburns and years of experience on his resume.

It involved a first-year coach who was just sixteen.

It was during the annual Babe Ruth Tournament one summer several years ago—the elimination round in the double-elimination format. The situation is this: The local team and their opponent are tied. It's the bottom of the last inning. The locals have two outs with a runner on first and the bottom of the order up to bat. The coach—a kid himself actually, because he's only sixteen—looks across his bench and sees a face that hasn't gotten to play that day.

He signals the boy to go in and pinch run. The boy looks surprised. He's been content to cheer on his teammates today. He knows the importance of this game. But he stands up and pulls his cap down low over his forehead, then limps out to first base.

He limps because he has cerebral palsy, you see.

The crowd exchanges glances, and the skeptics are already muttering about the inexperience (and inadequacies) of this sixteen-year-old coach.

Then the coach gives the steal sign and the crowd holds its breath. The boy tears toward second base, catching the pitcher unaware. As the pitcher wheels to try to pick him off, his throw is high and the ball rolls into center field. The boy picks himself out of the agrilime and runs toward third. He has to slide again. Because he doesn't have quite the grace that more agile players possess, he falls across the base. His hands and elbows are scraped raw from the ragged gravel, and the left knee is torn in his pants. Blood seeps through the white material.

But he is safe.

Then the pitch comes across the plate. It's a little high, but catches the outside corner. The twelve-year-old batter takes a mighty swing and drills the ball to right field. The fielder runs up and snags it on the first bounce.

And the coach sends the boy on third home.

The throw is there; the right fielder—for a twelve-year-old—has quite an arm.

But the boy who has been on the bench all day needs to prove to his coach that his was a wise choice.

His slide creates a cloud of dust. Both runner and catcher are lying, legs tangled, in the dirt. When the dust clears away the umpire looks at the position of the players at the plate, then asks the catcher to show him his glove.

"You're safe!" he decrees.

As his teammates hoisted their dusty, bloodied hero to their shoulders, I caught the eye of this oh-so-wise young coach.

The emotion of the moment had rendered many of us speechless. I could find no words to thank him. I hope he understood.

Mary Berglund

Sight and Insight

A moment's insight is sometimes worth a life's experience.

Oliver Wendell Holmes

On the back of a flatbed truck, probably meant for lumber, we hold on for dear life and sing "La Bamba" with our Nicaraguan compatriots. This is the fifth time we are singing it, so the foreign lyrics have finally seemed to stick—*"Yo no soy marinero, yo no soy marinero, soy capitan soy capitan soy capitan"* (I am not a sailor, I am a captain)—and we feel like just that: the captains of this day as we steer toward hours full of song, beach, friends and ocean. It has been a long week of clinics, and today is our day to relax. I feel comfortable, proud and lucky to be here.

I had come to Nicaragua with my father, a professor of optometry, and my older sister, Rachel. We were part of a group, an intrepid bunch of middle-class New Englanders, who had taken on the task of setting up an optometry clinic in the town's small elementary school.

My father had wanted to give Rachel and me a chance,

as volunteers, to use our Spanish and to see a new place. This was a completely new experience for us, and for the first few days, I think we must each have swallowed dozens of bugs with our jaws constantly dropped in wonder at everything we encountered. It was exciting. We had done a bit of traveling in our lives; my parents would take Rachel and me on long cross-country trips when we were little, exposing us to the rest of the country, the many landscapes, the people and the different ways in which they lived. Along with our little sister, Kate, we had been to Europe. This trip to Nicaragua, however, wasn't a standard vacation.

Almost immediately upon arrival here, I noticed how our new experiences differed from person to person. There was Kurt and Shelly, the seasoned professionals, who moved through the days with the graceful familiarity of skilled veterans. They have the history of many other clinics under their belts. There was Cynthia and her husband George, a nervous couple who refused to eat any of the food and brought suitcases of nonperishable snacks, so they wouldn't have to touch the local food. They even brought gallons of their own water.

During the week, working with local nurses and teachers, we saw nearly three thousand people. We had personally met all of them, given eye exams, dispensed advice on keeping their vision protected, and fitted them for prescription glasses. I met hundreds of other kids my age. The other sixteen-year-olds there had lives fairly different from my own. Many of them had jobs and were helping to take care of their families in ways I never had to. Some were farmers, working in the fields all day; others were fishermen, working on the trawlers day in and day out. There were some taking classes to become doctors and some headed off to the university in Managua for other types of education. Some had never even been to school before, and some had already started families of their own. Their lives were quite different from my own, but that did not make their lives abnormal.

A large part of what we had to do was help our patients understand what we were doing and why we were doing it. Many of them opened up and shared with us their lives, their experiences and their beautiful country. It was an amazing education.

I was always taught to respect people in whatever situations they are in, especially if I don't understand them. Some of those in our group seemed not to subscribe to that belief. People like Cynthia and George, who treated the people like exotic creatures, got only what they were looking for, an anecdote to take home to their friends. They felt fine—they had helped these people. They had missed the point. Those of us who approached the trip as a learning experience and a cultural exchange, and came to treat our Nicaraguan counterparts as equals, got just that.

On the beach, we eat lunch with our new friends, the local nurses and teachers. We smile and tell stories of the clinic, about how the old ladies were in shock when they could finally see their hands in detail, allowing them to sew as precisely as they had when they were teenagers. And of the babies who with their strong new glasses correcting a lazy eye, turning it forward, making them giggle.

Off in the distance throngs of gulls are swarming the fishing trawlers. We sit in the shade underneath the palms, tossing our leftovers to the vultures, large and sluggish with the heat of the midday sun. Hermit crabs leave tiny highways in the fine sand, crisscrossed patterns reminiscent of the major arteries and overpasses we temporarily left behind in Boston. I finally allow myself to close my eyes. I think about how Cynthia and George refused to go on this excursion. They didn't want to get dirty on the back of the flatbed truck. They had their anecdotes already and were ready to go home. I was okay with that. It is only what we are open to that we receive. Our initial motives might have been simple altruism, but I will admit, when we come back again it will also be for reasons a bit selfish. We give glasses and eye exams, yes, but what we get in return is so much greater; while we may give the gift of sight, we receive the gift of insight in return.

Eric J. Moore

$\overline{\underline{3}}$

RELATIONSHIPS

There is no mistaking love. You feel it in your heart. It is the common fiber of life, the flame that heats our soul, energizes our spirit and supplies passion to our lives.

Elizabeth Kubler-Ross

Reality Check

Best friends are the siblings God forgot to give us.

Anonymous

He was perfect. The exact mix of bad boy and intellectual that I was looking for, and good looking, as well. He was six feet, three inches, with a medium build, dark brown hair and deep brown eyes I just wanted to gaze at for days. And probably did, when I got the chance. As much as I like to pretend that I'm above all those cheesy crush feelings, I'm not.

The best part of this particular crush was that, unlike so many of my others, he actually knew my name. He had my number stored in his cell phone and even used it! I swear I used to hear wedding bells when I saw his name on my caller ID.

My friends were not his biggest advocates, to say the least, and you can bet they let me know it. I heard everything from "You can do so much better," to "He sucks, plain and simple." My logic remained unchanged. If I could do better, why wasn't I?

I couldn't understand why my girlfriends didn't like him. Okay, so maybe he used to show me his photo albums and point out all the girls he had dated. Yeah, he'd complain about the lack of an available hot girl in his life. But they didn't know him like I did. Isn't that always the case?

A few days before Valentine's Day, he sent me an instant message saying, "Red, pink, peach, white or yellow?" I immediately knew that he was asking me my preference in rose colors. I selected red, the most romantic kind. After the color, we debated between a dozen or a half-dozen. After that—to include a card or send them anonymously. He had mentioned during the conversation that he simply wanted to "make some girl's day." I was convinced that I was "some girl." Three hours after we began chatting, we had chosen a half-dozen red roses, to be sent anonymously. We had also, unfortunately, discussed all the possibilities among the girls he could surprise. When I playfully suggested that I be the recipient of the Valentine's Day bouquet, I was swiftly shut down. "Don't be greedy," was his reply.

After the incident, I immediately ran down the dorm hallway to relay the entire conversation to my friends. I was only partially upset about the outcome. I was more excited that he had just spent three hours asking *me* for advice. They rolled their eyes, knowing all they could do was wait it out, and eventually, I'd come to my senses.

Valentine's Day arrived, and since I had no date, I went about my business as I would any other day. When I returned to my dorm room after classes, I was shocked to find a vase of red roses on my dresser. I counted them— exactly six. I searched for a card and found none. *Could it be? I knew it!* He had gone through the pains of making me so sure I wasn't going to get those flowers just so I would be extra shocked when I found them. A few moments later, four of my closest friends bounded through the door. They handed me a small envelope. "It goes with the flowers," they said. I opened it, and it read:

> Roses are red
> Violets are blue
> He doesn't love you
> But we sure do

Yeah, I was disappointed, but only for a minute, because I realized at that moment how foolish I had been. I hugged my friends, and the unworthy boy was forgotten. My friendship with him has since faded, and frankly, I don't miss it. As for those four girls? They're keepers.

Arielle Jacobs

Only a Matter of Time

Love is everything it's cracked up to be. It really is worth fighting for, being brave for, risking everything for. And the trouble is, if you don't risk anything, you risk even more.

Erica Jong

The smoke billowed out of the second-floor windows. I covered my face with my backpack and used my chemistry book as a battering ram to bust through the windowpane. Smashing through the apartment door with one hand, I grabbed the child with the other and ran to safety, coughing but alive. And there was Bethany, who happened to be passing by. "You're a hero!" she said as she flung her arms around me.

I had a rich fantasy life. It all revolved around the object of my obsession, Bethany Howe. Everyone called her B.H. Except for me. I loved to say the name "Bethany"—to myself, of course, because I rarely got within ten feet of B.H.

I first saw Bethany during our freshman year. I noticed her because she wasn't trying to be cool. I stood in silent solidarity with her on that front. I had given up trying to be cool in junior high. I learned my lesson after an unfortunate skateboarding incident. I won't go into too much detail, but it involved board shorts my mom constructed out of a pair of my dad's old Levi's cotton Dockers—an attempt to make a fashion statement that failed miserably.

Not trying to be cool can be very liberating. It takes away a lot of pressure and stress. I didn't think Bethany had a skateboarding incident in her past. She was too cute for that. Her lack of coolness was just cool.

Two years went by and not much happened between B.H. and me. I would see her at lunch. Sometimes we had class together. The more I learned about her, the more I liked her. She had a part-time job at a day-care center after school. She liked to go to the beach. She had the most amazing smile.

I decided I would have to get her to notice me. I joined the track team for Bethany. I spent two hours hitting tennis balls off the backboard every day so I could make the tennis team—for Bethany. I read the newspaper every morning so I'd have something interesting to say in case Bethany decided to talk to me. Bethany was a good influence on me, even though we never spoke. I made new friends, became more talkative and outgoing, and got into pretty good shape. Now if I could only meet her.

One day, I was asked by one of my teachers, Mr. Houston, to go to the office to get some paper and videos. As I walked down the hall, I was lost in thought, having another Bethany fantasy. I loaded up on the paper for Mr. Houston and went to the AV room to get the videos. I was arranging the paper, thinking about Bethany. And then I heard a voice. "This tape is checked out."

"Huh?"

"Excuse me, but the tape you want is checked out."

I looked up. It was Bethany. She worked in the AV center.

"Hey, I know you," she said. "You're in my history class."

I stammered something, inaudibly.

Then she stammered something, inaudibly.

Then we both tried to speak at once.

I was flustered. I wasn't prepared. Our first meeting wasn't supposed to happen like this—it wasn't even a good hair day, for me. I started to leave, then turned back and muttered, "See ya, Bethany."

"What did you call me?"

"Bethany. Isn't that your name?"

"Yeah, but everyone calls me B.H."

"But Bethany is such a pretty name."

"Really?" She laughed nervously.

"Yeah."

I couldn't believe it. We were actually having a conversation.

"Aren't you on the tennis team? I go to the matches sometimes."

"Tennis?" I couldn't remember what that was. Something about a racket and a court was all I could remember as she spoke to me. Then I remembered I had a match that afternoon and before I could talk myself out of it, I invited her.

The bell rang before she could answer and I realized Mr. Houston was waiting for his supplies. After school, I suited up for my match. I scanned the stands for Bethany but didn't see her. I can't remember the score but I won. I hoped she saw when I made an especially good volley or an ace.

After the match, I still didn't see her. I started walking toward the locker room when I heard my name being called. I didn't even know she knew it. I'd always hated my name but it sounded like an angelic ballad when she said it.

That afternoon at the entrance to the guy's locker room

I asked Bethany out. She told me she'd had her eye on me since freshman year too, but our paths never seemed to cross. I'm kind of glad it took so long for us to get together. The day Bethany and I met, even though my hair was messed up and I wasn't wearing my favorite shirt, I was ready to meet her. And I didn't even have to brave a burning building.

Tal Vigderson

Drowning in Somebody I'm Not

I know for me the subject of how to be in a relationship is precious and complicated and challenging. It wouldn't be right to make it look too easy.

Helen Hunt

There is nothing like being young and in love. Your body trembles all over, and you long for that special person. I was sixteen when it first happened. Her name was Mary; she was one grade ahead and the most beautiful girl in the entire school. I was smaller than the rest of the guys my age but had many friends. I would walk by her locker, act cool and do just about anything to gain her attention.

Nothing worked.

I often pondered to myself, *How would such a beautiful and amazing girl ever fall for a guy like me?* I constantly thought that if I were a "hip guy," she would eventually have to notice. Once, I "accidentally" dropped my letter jacket by her feet, just so she would note my varsity pins—and me.

She only laughed.

Then, at a weekend gathering one evening, she was there with all of her frightening friends. I decided that this had to be it; I couldn't live with myself one second more without at least trying to talk to her. I checked my ego at the door—and decided to be myself. She was alone outside for one moment, and all I can remember is that she was so incredibly beautiful it made me dizzy. I walked up to her and said, "Hi, I'm Mark. You seem really nice; can we talk?" My belly rolled with butterflies while my head rushed with anxiety.

Time stood still for a moment.

She replied, "I know who you are; you're different when your friends aren't around." And then she smiled and said, "I'm walking up the street to meet a friend. Would you like to go?" I could hardly breathe: How could this beautiful girl ever talk to a guy like me? Needless to say, we walked and talked, and she was everything I thought she would ever be. We giggled about the world and how stupid our friends were.

Then, to my amazement, she gave me her phone number. That night, Mary revealed that dropping my letter jacket in front of her was a stupid thing to do. She didn't care about what sports guys lettered in, she only cherished wonderful people with substance. After I began being myself, we quickly fell for one another and became "high school loves."

We later went on to separate colleges and grew apart, but one thing that I learned from the experience has stuck with me my entire life. If you try to act like somebody you're not, any love or approval you gain won't mean anything.

It's best to just be yourself.

Mark Whistler

Eternity

I lie in bed at night and pray,
that you will think of me.
I cry until my eyelids close,
and dream—eternity.

I wake to sunlight on my face,
for a moment I forget.
Then a cloud passes by,
and I realize, this is it.

I carry on throughout the day,
feigning joy, and feeling pain.
I long to gaze upon your face,
and share a smile, an embrace.

The day is drawing to an end,
and still I think of you.
I try to relax, yet in my mind,
I wonder what to do.

So now I lay me down to sleep,
I pray the Lord, my soul will keep.
And should you chance to think of me,
know that I love you—eternally.

Deiah Haddock

Tom(my) Boy

When I was seven years old, I broke my wrist. I had gotten in a fight with Tommy Maducci over whether GI Joe was stronger than He-Man. Tommy had insisted that, because I was a girl, I didn't know what I was talking about. To prove him wrong, I punched him in the nose. He came at me and pushed me off the jungle gym. My arm was in a cast and he had two black eyes and a broken nose, all in the name of GI Joe. I was one of the few girls in my neighborhood, and as a result, I was introduced to bands named after comic-book characters and anarchists. I grew up in a world of boxer shorts and baseball bats— where Tony Hawk was Hero, and Barbie was Bar-b-cued.

I wouldn't call myself a tomboy. Tomboys wore overalls and had their own tree-house club. I was somewhere in the middle. I never cared to sell lemonade on sidewalk corners or finger paint in smock and skirt. My weekends were spent catching crawdads in hair nets. On Sunday afternoons I sneaked out of church to go play baseball with Danny and Tommy, who had forgiven me for the playground incident.

When Danny moved to the city, Tommy and I became

best friends. We built skateboard mini-ramps, mowed lawns together in the summers and shared slurpees and candy bars bought with our earnings.

Through elementary school everything was cool. Tommy could care less if girls had cooties and I didn't see boys as anything but playmates. But one day we woke up and we were teenagers. Tommy stopped calling me after school and I traded my skateboarding shoes for flip-flops and bought myself a skirt. Nothing too feminine, denim cutoff. We said "hello" on the bus to and from Woodberry Middle School and partnered up in science class, but that was the extent of our relationship.

Tommy flirted with girls in class and I rolled my eyes and passed notes. It was annoying to me the way Tommy smiled at pretty girls. It made me mad because he didn't smile at me like that, not even as a friend. In the afternoons after school, while circling the cul-du-sac on my skateboard, I thought about Tommy a lot. One day I went down to the park, where we used to skateboard together, hoping that he would be there. The ramp was gone and Tommy was nowhere to be found.

The next day at school he was holding hands with Kelly Nicholson. I hated them both. The spectacle annoyed me. *What made her "hang-out" worthy? What about me?*

One day Tommy came up to my table during lunch with some of his new guy friends.

"Hey, Zoe, how's it going?"

"It's going," I said, unwrapping my turkey sandwich from the clear plastic Saran wrap.

 "Jason is bringing the ramp over to Mike's house and we're all gonna skate on it after school if you want to come." Tommy nudged Mike and Mike winked at me.

Gross, I thought. Mike was not my type at all, but skating sounded like fun and it was cool of Tommy to invite me along, so I agreed.

"Sure, I'll come along."

My friend Alice pinched me. "Mike's cute," she said.

"He's not my type," I chewed.

"No one's your type, Zoe. Good grief."

I changed the subject and finished my lunch.

When I arrived at Mike's house the boys were already there: Tommy, Mike, Jason and Tommy's brother, Scotty, who I used to push around when Tommy and I were friends. Alice came with me and Kelly Nicholson came with Tommy. They were an "item," but I knew it would never last. She wasn't Tommy's type, at least I didn't think so.

"Hey Zoe, I bet you can't do a crooked grind off that ledge."

"Yes I can," I huffed.

Mike shrugged. "Let's see it." And in the background I could see Jason shaking his head, flirting with Alice and muttering something stupid, making her laugh a little bit.

"All right boys. This is how it's done."

I wiped the sweat from my forehead and pushed off. I made my way up onto the ledge with a 180, but lost my balance and fell backwards, my skateboard launching into the air, feet twisted up and arms outstretched.

Instead of breaking my fall I broke my wrist. I closed my eyes, trying to hold back my tears, more embarrassed than anything else.

When I opened my eyes Tommy was next to me. His eyes were wide and he looked scared. He yelled for Mike to get his mom and the four of us drove to the hospital: Mike's mom, Mike, Tommy and me.

"It hurts, it hurts."

Tommy put his arm around me. "Be brave, Zoe. We're almost there."

I looked over at Tommy's sweaty face, hair matted to his forehead, acne around his nose and nodded my head.

It turned out that I broke my wrist in the same place as when I hit Tommy in second grade. The doctors put me in a cast, scolded me for skateboarding without wrist guards and sent me home. Tommy stayed with me the whole time and was the first to sign my cast.

I couldn't sleep that night and it wasn't because I was in pain. It was something else completely. Every time I tried to close my eyes, all I could see was Tommy's face and his crystal blue eyes pleading with me not to cry.

The next morning, Mom opened my bedroom door.

"You have a visitor," she said.

Tommy peered his head in the door, nodded at me and came over to give me a high five.

"Very funny," I coughed.

Tommy sat down next to me on my bed. "Because of me, now you've broken your wrist twice."

"It isn't your fault or anything. I can usually make that move without falling. Sometimes things just happen."

"Well, you know what I think?" Tommy pulled an old Barbie off my shelf, head shaved on the sides.

"That's Mohawk Barbie," I laughed.

"Oh yeah? Well I bet Mohawk Barbie is stronger than GI Joe and He-Man put together." Tommy dropped the doll on the floor and looked over at me.

"Oh you do, do you . . .?"

And with that, Tommy Maducci kissed me, right there with Mohawk Barbie as a witness and me in my big ugly arm cast, hair unwashed, stinky sneakers on the floor. The room started spinning, my knees got weak and, boy, was I glad I broke my wrist.

"What about your girlfriend?" I asked, pulling away.

"She's not my girlfriend anymore," he said, shyly.

"Yeah, she wasn't your type anyway," I laughed.

"Nope." Tommy kissed my cheek.

That afternoon we took a walk down to the old 7-11 at

the edge of the neighborhood. Tommy held my casted hand the whole way, and bought me a slurpee and a candy bar. Just like the old days, except everything was different now.

Zoe Graye

First Love, First Loss

"What happened, where did we go wrong?" The words began to flow freely, as did the tears that were beginning to form and slowly slide down my already tear-stained cheeks. His soft-spoken "I don't know" did nothing to ease the ache I was feeling, and had been feeling, for several weeks. Standing at the foot of his bed, looking around his room, a room I had spent as much time in as my own, the memories surrounded me. Here I was, fifteen, in love and losing the person who had meant so much to me for two years. Raising my head, I looked into those familiar blue eyes and saw that they were also filling with tears. We did-n't have to speak; we both knew without talking that this was it.

He scooted down and pulled me into his arms, up against his chest. Standing, he stood a head taller than me; sitting, we were eye to eye. With my face buried in the place where his shoulder and neck meet, I cried. I cried for everything we had shared, both good and bad. I cried for the past and for my future without him.

Tyler had started off as a friend, but his charismatic attitude soon made him my best friend. I could tell him anything, and I did. He always had something to say to make me laugh; only he had the ability to bring out the sun on my grayest days. We soon evolved into more; I had never experienced anything like it before. We had our share of bad times—some more serious than others—and more ridiculous arguments than I could count. However, neither of us could stay mad at the other for long, and one of us would always give in.

But this time was different. We were over. This wasn't a fight that would end with an "I'm sorry." It was another sign that what we once had was over. We were together now because neither one of us could handle the idea of breaking up, but hanging on was becoming more painful than ending it.

We took a long walk that afternoon; the earlier rain had left the air damp but cool. The sun had come out, and I could hear the birds in the woods behind us. Walking hand in hand, we talked for about an hour, pausing every now and then for a quiet "I'll miss you" and "I'll miss you, too." We promised to remain friends and swore that we would still talk. Maybe one day, we said, after things got a little bit easier, we would go do something together. Neither one of us wanted to think of our lives without the other one in it.

As we neared my house and the walk ended, I asked for one more hug. His strong, tanned arms enclosed me, and then he lowered his lips for one last kiss. The hardest thing that afternoon was forcing myself to let go, pull away and walk home.

Moving on was hard; at times it seemed unbearable. Time has now healed the pain, and when I think of him I smile instead of cry. He will always have a special place in my heart.

Melody Mallory

Once Upon a Time I Lost Myself

This above all; to thine own self be true.

William Shakespeare

Sometimes we lose it. We fall into love like a pillowed net and lie there for months in LaLaLand. I've been there, in that net. I've been there countless times. It wasn't the first time or the last, but once upon a time I lost myself. He was the guy who I had watched from afar for months. His eyes drew me in from across the campus, the party, even the football game, and saturated my thoughts. He made me weak at the knees; he made me feel different.

When he finally asked me out, I was overjoyed. It felt as though everything I once questioned was suddenly clear. It was a wonderful moment, the first of its kind that actually lasted. We spent every afternoon together, every evening on the phone, every morning laughing at the bus stop.

On our three-month anniversary, he threw me a party. When we both showed up at the restaurant, our table for ten was empty. He had called my closest girlfriends, and not one of them showed up. We sat there under the darkness at a table much too big for two and had our anniversary alone. It didn't faze me that my friends hadn't shown up. It didn't matter that Billy and I were alone again. We were always alone, and it felt good that way. I didn't even question the fact that my girlfriends had fallen off the face of the planet. I couldn't see past my own two feet, and there was no room for anyone else but Billy. We were a couple. We were in love; our names sewn from the same string.

Dreams fall apart sometimes. We wake up and everything is different.

One day I woke up, and the fantasy that Billy and I had created was torn, revealing the reality on the other side of the wall we had formed. It was easy to be idealistic about love; I had never felt this way about anybody. We had built a cocoon around each other, wanting nothing more but to become butterflies together, and here we were, flying away.

As I emerged from the darkness that morning, I realized that isolation wasn't the answer. I had pushed my friends and my family out of my life. I had thrown down the truth, hidden my identity and dismissed the me that once was. I had lost myself in his eyes and in his arms, and now who was I?

I called Billy that afternoon. He wasn't there, though. He was gone. I knew he was. I had broken our paper chain, so delicate and so easily torn. When I finally reached him we agreed to meet at the bus stop where we had met every morning for the past few months.

I sat there in front of those blue eyes, the eyes that held me in and made me forget my own. The eyes that now looked different. I told him it was unfair for us to deprive ourselves of our lives. I told him I missed my friends, and I missed being called Becca instead of the "Becca and Billy" that had become our joint title. I wanted to be together, but not all the time. I wanted to be in love, but not in exchange for my identity. I wanted to look into his eyes and see him, not the glow of my own reflection. I didn't want to lose myself, and I feared I already had.

The lamppost shivered, and tears blurred us from each other. The wind shifted, and the light above us streamed down. Billy looked at me and smiled. He smiled, and then he kissed my eyelids. He knew I was right. He told me so later, and although we only stayed together another three weeks, that night was the first time we truly understood what it meant to be in love. That was the first night we walked without stepping on each other's shadow. That was the first night I was Becca and he was Billy. Two names. Two souls. Two selves.

Regardless of what may happen in the future, I learned a serious lesson through Billy. I learned that love doesn't mean losing oneself.

Rebecca Woolf

My First Date

The chemist who can extract from his heart's elements, compassion, respect, longing, patience, regret, surprise, and forgiveness and compound them into one can create that atom which is called love.

Kahlil Gibran

Like most every girl, I wanted to be noticed by the opposite sex. I was more than ready to start dating. However, I was practically ignored, and this began to make me feel unwanted and inferior to all the other gorgeous, popular girls at my high school. Eventually, my self-confidence started to wither, and I even started to think there was something wrong with me. I had always wanted to date a religious guy, although most of the guys at my school weren't, so that cut back my options.

Then, one Sunday, everything changed. I arrived at church, ready to teach a Sunday school class of perky five-year-olds, when I was greeted by Jeremy, a teenage helper like myself. Immediately, I could tell he had something on his mind. His eyes seemed to probe my face looking for any sign of emotion. Finally he inquired, "Did Brian ask you something?"

"Ask me what?" I replied.

"Oh . . . you'll see!" Jeremy said, with a slight twinkle in his eyes. As soon as he said it, I knew what he meant. Brian Jones, a shy, introverted senior, had liked me unceasingly for almost two years. Although aware of his crush, I hadn't been interested. I wanted to date someone with a more outgoing personality.

The rest of Sunday proceeded as usual. In the back of my mind, I was waiting for Brian to ask me out; however, it came time to leave and nothing had happened. Puzzled and somewhat relieved, I hopped in my dad's van for the ride home. A few minutes after I got home, my mom walked through the door holding a delicate, pink rose accompanied by a note. When she left church, the flower had been sitting on the hood of her car, waiting for me. I had taken the wrong vehicle! Looking at the beautiful flower, I absolutely melted. If Brian asked me out, I would say yes! I figured a guy nice enough to give a girl a flower was someone special.

At that instant, the phone rang, and I became almost numb with excitement. My dad answered and knowingly handed it to me. My hands trembled with nerves, but I realize now that Brian must have been even more nervous talking with me. I thanked him for the flower, telling him that I adored roses and that pink was my favorite color. He said he had known this about me. Evidently, he went out of his way to find out and get my favorite flower. I was so touched by his thoughtfulness. Obviously nervous, Brian asked me everything from, "How was your day?" to "What did you do yesterday?" After posing almost every question in the book except the one he had called to ask, we said good-bye.

I understood the anxiety he was experiencing trying to ask me on a date, so I waited patiently for him to call me back. Within a few minutes, Brian called again and asked me out for coffee. Without hesitation I said yes, and we agreed that he would be pick me up at one thirty. I began tearing apart my wardrobe, searching for the perfect outfit to wear on my very first date. I wanted something attractive, but not flamboyant, and I decided on my pink blouse and tan shorts. I did my hair up in twists and, just as I finished, Brian arrived!

The ride there was mostly a blur; I was so nervous I could hardly focus. At one point, Brian awkwardly asked me if I was nervous and, in the most confident voice I could muster, I answered, "No . . . well, maybe a little." I realize now that hiding my feelings probably made him feel even more anxious.

We arrived at the coffeehouse and ordered our drinks. I had my own money, but Brian insisted on paying for me. We sat across from each other at a small corner table. At first, our conversation was awkward and seemed to struggle along. However, as we learned more about each other, we realized that we shared similar likes and dislikes, and our staggered conversation transformed into a lively discussion. With every new, intriguing piece of information I learned about Brian, the more attractive he became. We talked for two hours about any topic that arose, and I discovered that he was incredibly smart, pleasant and down-to-earth. My previous notion that I would only enjoy dating someone outgoing was totally incorrect.

After we were finished, he drove me back to my house, told me he had a wonderful time and said he'd like to do it again. I agreed and we said good-bye, each of us glowing with excitement. The next day he called and invited me to the beach with him later that week. I happily agreed. Our relationship was off to a wonderful beginning.

Brian and I have now been together for seven months and one week. Every day we grow closer, and because we bonded so quickly and solidly, we can even see marriage as a possibility in our future. What started as my first date has flourished into a beautiful relationship.

Sarah Van Tine

Junior High Crush

Junior high. Just the thought of it plagued me for an entire summer. And it was finally given meaning the first day I walked into homeroom. I was late. Not too late, but late enough to gain unwanted attention from my classmates. I nervously glanced around the room for a friendly smile as my new sneakers squeaked on the shiny, waxed floor. Nicole, my best friend since first grade, motioned to me. I figured she wanted me to take the seat next to her, so I made a pirouette and walked in her direction.

"Miss Moore?" bellowed a male voice from behind.

"Yeah?" I spun on my heels and faced a kindly looking man.

"You can take the seat over there in the corner," he said, gently.

I smiled. He reciprocated, and I walked to my seat. I figured he would be my homeroom teacher for the rest of seventh grade. Maybe junior high wouldn't be as scary as I thought.

We were about a week into the fall semester when my English teacher, Ms. McKinney, inaugurated a new activity: "The Name Game." She split our class into two groups and had half of us stand up at the chalkboard and recite our names while the other half stayed in our seats, committing all the new names to memory. My group was called up, and I stood in line next to a tall, lanky guy wearing a dorky Hard Rock Cafe T-shirt from Jerusalem. We exchanged glances and a smile, and shifted our eyes to the boy at the front of the line.

"Cecilia Rivera." "David Sands." "Jeff Powers." One by one, my classmates delivered their monikers. The boy next to me in the Hard Rock Cafe T-shirt cleared his throat to speak. "Max Phillips."

His voice had cracked. Since I had never before been exposed to pubescent boys (I attended an all-girls elementary school), I turned red and barely choked out my own name.

"R-r-r-achel Moore," I managed to spit out between giggles. I glanced up at Max while covering my crimson cheeks with my sweaty palms. He blushed, but I could tell he was used to it. I tried to console him with a smile, but he was still red.

I ended up sitting next to him and finding out that he had caught the eyes of many girls, including Nicole. On our bus ride home she gushed about his "adorable" Hard Rock Cafe T-shirt and how they "totally flirted in English today." I talked about my computer teacher and asked if I could borrow her science notes. Needless to say, Nicole was getting popular, and I was getting left in the dust.

Maybe it was because I felt I needed to fit in, or maybe because there was no one else to like, but I began to start thinking about Max in another kind of way. He wasn't just that nerdy, tall guy who sat next to me in English. He was a god. Suddenly his repugnant skater shoes became "fabulously stylish," and I worshipped every sheet of loose-leaf notebook paper he crumpled up and casually tossed aside. I began to wear my Hard Rock Cafe T-shirt from Tijuana, the one Mom got from her Mexican vacation with her boyfriend. The one I swore I'd never wear outside the vicinity of our house. Then, after two months of silent adoration, he spoke to me.

"Did you like Tijuana?" Max asked me one day, while our class was paraphrasing a sonnet from *Julius Caesar*.

"Huh?" I replied. Was he talking to me? Me? Rachel Louise Moore? The girl who spied on him from across the quad at lunch while he played Hackey Sack with his friends?

"Tijuana. Is it nice?" he repeated.

"Uh . . . yeah! It's great!" I lied. Who was I kidding? I had never even been out of the United States. Well, I obviously fooled him.

"Neat," he replied coolly. *Whoa, he just talked to me.* Which, in junior-high girl language, automatically meant, "He likes me!"

I strutted through the hallways that day. Nicole begged me to tell her why I was so happy.

"Ahhh . . . no reason. Must be the fall breeze!" I responded, with a smirk.

"Okaaaaay . . . whatever, Rachel. You're freakin' me out!" Nicole countered. But nothing could get me off this wonderful feeling.

The next day was a Thursday, but I had a cold, so I stayed home. That evening I called my new friend Jackie for our English homework.

"Soooo Jackie . . . anything interesting happen in English today?" I asked, coyly.

"Actually, yeah. Max asked Nicole to the homecoming dance," Jackie said, matter-of-factly.

My jaw dropped. I was completely dumbfounded. I had built my entire pathetic seventh-grade existence around Max, making witty comments about how boring Shakespeare was every time he asked what page we were on, intentionally dropping my pen so he might take time out of his busy-boy schedule to pick it up for me.

"He what?" I asked with a lump in my throat.

"He asked her out. Today. In third-period English. She was wearing that cute Hard Rock Cafe T-shirt from San Francisco. He told her he went there over the summer, and they spent nearly the entire period talking about it. Ms. McKinney practically had to separate their desks to keep them from talking."

Ugh. I had heard enough. I got the homework assignment and hung up. I couldn't believe this! He was supposed to like me! All the signs pointed to me! Why was this happening? I read the assigned pages of *Julius Caesar* but wasn't concentrating at all. All I could think about was how they would walk down the halls hand in hand for the rest of the year while I stood idly by, more pathetic than ever. I finally fell asleep.

My mom made me go to school on Friday, even though I begged her not to. Nicole talked about Max for the entire first and second periods. I don't know why, but I wore my Hard Rock Cafe T-shirt from Tijuana that day. In English, I watched them while I attempted to pen tortured poetry. I felt a tap on my shoulder from behind.

"Rachel, right?" he asked. It was Andrew Rogers. I remembered him from "The Name Game."

"Yeah," I replied, shyly. He was cute!

"I'm going to Tijuana for winter break. Is it fun?" he asked. I smiled and shrugged.

"I've never been there, but tell me about it when you get back."

"You got it," he said as he winked.

I knew then that things were going to be okay.

Rachel Louise Moore

Not Forgotten

I would rather live and love where death is king than have eternal life where love is not.

Robert Green Ingersoll

Music and laughter danced in the hot humid air that surrounded the annual summer carnival. A smell of popcorn and hot dogs tickled my nose. I admired him through the crowd. The forest green polo shirt he wore accented his beautiful brown eyes. As I watched him, I silently prayed that fate would make him turn my way. Finally, when the booms and crackles of the fireworks awakened the summer sky, our paths crossed. His name was Brandon.

"You're in my driver's ed class," was the first thing I said to him, later feeling quite embarrassed by my choice of words.

"Yes, I am," he said with a smile. We conversed only for a little while, barely scratching the surface of each other's lives, but as he spoke, his words made my heart dance, and his smile made me go weak in the knees.

Summer turned into fall and thoughts of him were all that filled my mind. We had become friends, acquaintances, even pals, but I wanted more. I wanted Brandon to be my boyfriend. I wanted him to take me out on dates and send me flowers, and I wanted to share that perfect kiss with him as he squeezed me tight in his strong arms. But Brandon was filled with uncertainty at the thought of a relationship. His reluctance kept me awake night after night. I couldn't lose him now; I was too attached.

In time, Brandon's fears vanished, and we became official. Not only did Brandon take me to little Italian restaurants where we'd eat pasta by candlelight, and shower me with ruby red roses that felt like satin to the touch, and kiss me with passionate kisses, but he loved me.

I knew by the way he'd hold my hand gently as we drove around in his truck, the way he'd hug me tight and share his warmth if I was cold, the way his eyes would light up when I'd step outside my front door for an evening out. I knew by the way he whispered, "I love you, Sarah," into my ear on our three-month mark.

Those three months turned into a year. And the year turned into a year and a half. We were what everyone called the "perfect" couple. We were the high-school sweethearts that would marry someday, or so everyone thought. But when twenty months rolled around our relationship reached a rut, and there was no going back. Our tender kisses could no longer generate sparks, the roses didn't smell quite as sweet and the stars that we once saw in each other's eyes just didn't shine as brightly.

Almost two years to the day that I met Brandon, it was time to let him go. The loneliness strangled me when I heard the roar of his truck leave my house for the very last time, but the need to be free was stronger.

My memories of us are so wonderful, and he was a great

guy. Just when I start regretting what I did, I realize that if I hadn't, my memories wouldn't be so sweet. The way it is, now, he will "never be forgotten."

Sarah Strickler

Never Too Late

Last night, as I was searching for some paperwork, I came across a box I hadn't seen for a long time. There it was, at the bottom of a trunk I'd filled with old clothes, books and other junk: my treasured box of letters. Inside were letters from my brother, Remi, written to me when he was six and I was seven, doing a two-month stint for bad behavior at Camp Villa Maria in Wisconsin. Also inside were funny letters from my favorite aunt, Shirlee, written long before she discovered all those fatal lumps in her neck. There were some hysterically sappy love letters from old boyfriends and a bulky, prolific pile of correspondence with my best friend from grade school, Mary Ellen, whose family moved to Arizona when she was in fourth grade, and with whom I long ago lost all contact. At the bottom of the box were a few toys from childhood and this letter . . . from Scott Athens to my sister, Lisa.

Suddenly, looking at that letter I was transported back in time. I remembered a warm, spring day in April, coming home from high school and opening up the giant, tin mailbox that had been dented by a cherry bomb attack the night before. As I looked through the piles of mail—mostly bills for my mom and dad—an envelope fell to the ground—it was that letter from Scott to Lisa.

Scott was my first love. He lived in Leland, Michigan, where our family summered every year, and from the minute I spied him bagging groceries at the Merc, a local grocery store, I was madly in love with him.

Shortly after discovering my dream man at the Merc, I ran into him again at a fishing class my dad had forced my brother and me to take at the dilapidated and aged Town Yacht Club. Scott was there to help old Mr. Peterson teach the class. Mr. Peterson's face looked like a badly used, leathery sock-puppet with a long, brown More cigarette that he never ashed hanging from his flaccid lips. As that oily, sock-puppet mouth slapped open and shut, his long brown cigarette stuck like a permanent, cancerous growth off to the side of his lower lip as he tiredly mumbled out knotting techniques and bait tips.

Mr. Peterson doled out his fishing knowledge while sitting plopped on the floor of a small, battered dinghy. With his freaky cigarette and *special* thermos drink always nearby, his lectures would begin: "All right, now listen up kids. This is how you can remember to tie a good fishing knot." A swig from the thermos and then, with shaking hands, he picked up his fishing line to demonstrate.

"Now, the rabbit goes around the tree twice, then down into the hole it goes, back up the other side, around the tree. . . ." His presentation went unnoticed as we kept our eyes riveted to the impossibly long ash that clung to the remains of his slow-burning More. All the while Scott stood behind the dingy, passing me furtive glances and beautiful, kind smiles whenever I caught him looking my way.

Eventually, we were marched to the end of the short yacht house pier. All eight of the bored fishing-school prisoners stood shoulder to shoulder, our fishing poles in hand, waiting for Mr. Peterson's command to cast. At last the rubbery lips in the land-locked dinghy shouted out the order, and in one collective, spasmodic motion, we jerked back our poles and yanked our scarily whizzing barbed lures behind us while we kept our eager eyes focused on the imagined landing hundreds of yards out.

Two made it into the water five feet ahead; one dug into the wood pier. Four lines got crossed and snarled in the air above our heads, and one dug itself cruelly into my arm. I was in agony—until Scott rushed to my side. From that moment, all pain was forgotten. Scott carefully removed the rusty lure from my arm with needle-nose pliers that Mr. Peterson had clumsily tossed our way along with a comforting, "Aw, it's nothin'." Then Scott pulled off his T-shirt and wrapped it around my bleeding arm.

"Wow! That looked like it hurt!" Scott said, holding my hand as he guided me away from the screaming gang on the dock, leading me to the yacht club stairs and the shanty structure above the beach. I honestly didn't know what he was talking about. I just smiled back at him, transfixed by his lanky, half-naked, manly presence so close to mine. His thin, brown hair fell in front of big blue eyes that looked at me with compassion.

"Hey, you're Lisa Dunham's sister, right?" he asked with a sweet, nervous smile.

"Yes!" I said, blissfully unconscious in my transparent, pink love bubble. *He knows who I am!* I thought, and then with my heart slamming into my chest I looked into his eyes and said in my mind, *I love you!*

"Yeah, I kind of have a big crush on her," Scott gushed. His excited confession hurt worse than any rusty hook could have.

"Ohh . . ." I managed to say, my heart leaking out of my mouth and dribbling down my punched-in face.

"Do you think you could tell her I like her?" Scott

suddenly whispered and then, inconceivably, he blushed.

My arm began to throb. I felt weak, like my knees had suddenly disappeared and the air around me had gone thin. "Sure . . ." I was sacked and ambushed. Stunned, I heard myself agreeing to give Lisa's phone number to Scott. I watched with glassy eyes as he wrote it down on a Merc receipt he pulled from his pants pocket.

Then I watched as the same hands of fate that seemed to have brought Scott to me, handed him over to my older sister. And there she was suddenly, sitting in the sporty, green Jeep in the yacht club parking lot, with her blond hair flickering around her tanned and pretty face and music blasting on the radio. Scott spotted her, too, and practically groaned. Using my injury as his foot in the door he practically carried me over to the car. I don't remember any of their conversation. I sat slumped in the seat next to Lisa, the sad, witless conduit to the start of their summer romance.

For three long months I sat in the shadows, watching their sunny courtship. Finally, the merciful day came when my dad said, "It's time to say good-bye to Lake Leelanau." We packed up all our clothes into large, brown plastic garbage bags and shoved them into the green station wagon with wood paneling, along with two dogs, a parakeet, my mom and dad, my three sisters and brother, and myself. My misery was over—we were finally headed back home to Illinois. As the station wagon passed down the drive and by the lake, my dad sang out a short, melancholy farewell, "Good-bye Lake Leelanau, Land of Delight!" We pulled out of the drive and onto M-22.

"I wish I had told Scott that I loved him," my sister unexpectedly sighed to me as we sped through the small town of Leland and past the Merc. I was floored. I thought they had been telling each other that all summer long!

"You mean you never told him?!" I said, trying to mask

my excitement and welling hope with concern for her love life.

"No. I was afraid to! He never said it to me!" She moaned. I was absolutely ecstatic.

"Now he'll go away to college and think I don't care about him and meet some other girl." She cried to the car window—it cared more about her problem than I did.

"I'm sure that won't happen," I said, as I prayed to God it would. Lisa shrugged her sad shoulders and stuck her chin in her hand, still staring miserably out the window. Then, suddenly whipping around to me, she whispered excitedly, "I'm going to write him and tell him I love him!" With this genius plan, Lisa immediately forgot her sorrows, and I immediately remembered mine.

Oddly enough, all winter long I never heard or saw any correspondence between Lisa and Scott. Eventually, as the snow melted and spring sogged it's way into the world, I had pretty much forgotten my secret, burning first love. Down by the mailbox that afternoon I was looking for a letter from Mary Ellen when the envelope fell to the ground, landing on top of the charred cherry bomb remains. I picked up Scott's letter and quietly slipped it into my folder to read later.

What was I thinking!? I was crazed. Later that night, hiding in my closet I carefully opened the letter. "I MISS YOU LOTS!" Jumped up from the page in giant, capital letters. Then a paragraph about how *much* he missed her and finally, he wrote: "To answer your question, YES! I LOVE YOU!" The "I love you" was capitalized, exclamation pointed and underlined four times.

My absurd dream of winning Scott back for myself was gone, and I was now left holding an opened letter that belonged to Lisa. Briefly I thought of blaming my younger sister, Holly, but I knew Lisa wouldn't buy it. Holly was her biggest fan and would never have done anything to anger her idol. No, Holly was out of the question. Frantically I searched my mind for a plausible scapegoat or way to make the letter look a little less *opened*. I could do neither. I ever-so-briefly thought of confessing to Lisa, but a vision of her fist slamming into my back, forcing my kidney's out through my mouth, put an end to that. Better, I thought in a mad panic, to never, EVER show it to her. In any case, Lisa was at the dizzying height of her Farrah Fawcett look-alike years—she had admirers galore. "She'll never miss one sappy letter from Scott Athens," I rationalized as I hid the crime in the small, brown trunk my Grandpa had made for me when I was six.

There it stayed, eventually forgotten, as was Scott by Lisa—though not without her heart having been badly broken when she never got an "I love you" letter back from him. Eventually, I forgot about my shameful secret, too. And so, Scott's letter lay forgotten yet preserved, waiting and waiting with the Girl Scout knife, the rabbit-fur dog pen holder, and the plastic French dolls and other letters, all locked up in the old, brown trunk.

As I opened the envelope once again and reread Scott's awkward love letter, I remembered all of this, but most importantly, I remembered the shame I felt at having stolen Lisa's first "I love you" away from her. Even though all turned out fine for Lisa back then, and even though I know she would have immediately broken up with Scott that next summer when she saw the horrible Orphan Annie perm he got, it still didn't make it better. The only thing to do was to come clean and send Lisa the letter, even though several years had passed, and hope she would laugh, forgive and forget. After all, she will at least get her first "I love you" back.

Linnea Gits-Dunham

4

LESSONS AND LEARNING

. . . [E]very experience in life enriches one's background and should teach valuable lessons.

Mary Barnett Gilson

My Moment of Truth

Hi, my name is Candice, and I'm fat. No, you did not just walk into an Overeaters Anonymous meeting. I just wanted to get that out, right away. Some people might think it's not politically correct to use such a vulgar term. They'd prefer I call myself some nice euphemism like "cherubic," "voluptuous," or for those lovers of *Xena Warrior Princess,* "Amazonian." However, when you are thirteen years old, stand five feet tall on tippy-toes, and weigh in at 150 pounds, most kids your age don't express your condition in such tender terms. I have been called such names as "Lardo," "Wide Load," and even "Candy, the Candy Terminator, No Candy Is Safe with Her Around."

Ironic, isn't it, that my parents named me after my own Achilles' heel—food? But an ice-cream sundae is no substitute for a social life. Not even when they give you extra sprinkles. There is simply not enough ice cream in the world that could make me impenetrable to the hurtful things kids say about me.

I have always enjoyed the movies. It is a way of buying a ticket to the ultimate escape. Movies are a common thread running through most of my memories. Like the summer my parents sent me to a camp for overweight kids in upstate New York. I hated it. Being raised in New York City, I preferred sterile concrete to tick-infested woods. The only nights I ever looked forward to were movie nights in the old casino house. The spray of light from the old projector mesmerized mosquitoes from across the Catskills. There was always that one rebel mosquito that was strangely attracted to the images on the old, worn-out movie screen. It would dance across the scenes; sometimes it was a mustache, sometimes a beard, sometimes it appeared as a kind of weird growth on an actor's nose. I felt like that lone insect in my own life. I was in the picture, and yet no one in the scene seemed to notice me.

That is what I remember most about my time at Camp Stanley. That, and the way we sat around at night discussing things like Chips Ahoy, Entenmann's and Frito-Lay, as if they were friends back home we longed to see. And, for some, these were indeed their only friends.

I was a chubby toddler and progressed through life expanding ever larger. My size did not go unnoticed by my peers. You would think I would have grown tougher from the years of name-calling. You would be wrong. I enacted the classically wrong reaction every time: I cried. And I cried easily.

My mother would try to console me after school each day. She would lecture me, like a pathetic old football coach trying to boost the morale of his losing team. "They are just jealous of you, honey," she'd recite regularly. "Just *ignore* them!"

But I knew that she was lying to me. I knew that the whole entire school, including the janitorial staff, could not be jealous of me. Yes, even the school janitor had commented about my size.

My free-flowing tears only loaded my enemies' guns with powerful ammunition. Each of their shots hit the mark. Their constant taunts made me less than excited to go to school with each passing day. I was never going to be acceptable to them, and as a result, my self-esteem was becoming nonexistent.

One day, I was watching *Oprah*. She had a show on "Fighting Back." There was a middle-aged guy on the panel. He was obviously losing his hair. He had a black fringe of hair around the back of his head. Then, way, way up on top only a few lonely hairs remained. They were like the lone survivors on a desert island. The man, in an effort to conceal his baldness, let his last few precious hairs grow quite long. With his comb, he could swirl them around his head like a cinnamon bun. He reminded me of a friend of my dad's. He swam at our community pool. Whenever he stepped out of the water, his long top hairs would flop over to the side of his head. The wet strands of hair congealed together and appeared as some sort of love-struck sea urchin, nibbling amorously at the poor man's sunburned ear. His bald head gleamed in the white-hot sun like an SOS. It was quickly noticed by all the neighborhood kids, who would laugh at his expense. But the bald man never seemed to care. He'd just carefully smooth the hairs back into place, suck in his gut and step out of the troubled waters. Maybe he didn't notice those kids and their cruelty. Maybe he didn't care. Maybe he was in denial. Denial must be like a kind of Disneyland for the adult mind. However, I digress. The man on *Oprah* did not deal as well with the criticism he received from his coworkers. He admitted that he had never fought back. He grew those few sad hairs longer, as if he could hide beneath them.

Oprah told him that he had to come out from hiding behind his hairs, that he was a smart man with a lot to offer the world. He should not let these bullies stand in his way. He must confront them. They did not dictate who he was in life.

"You," she told him, "are the only one who is in control of your destiny!"

The whole audience cheered for Oprah. They cheered for the balding man. But most of all, they cheered for the free foot-massager and bunion remover they would receive after the show.

Was I like the balding man? Was I eating my way into hiding? My weight, like his hair, was something I could never hide behind. It was that day that I decided to fight back.

The next day in class my science teacher, Mr. Roster, was leading the class in a lab. Of course Jill and Haley, the popular girls, were chatting up a storm. Mr. Roster looked up quite suddenly. He was annoyed at their disturbance.

"Would you girls like to share what you are chatting about with the class?" asked Mr. Roster.

The whole class turned to watch what would happen next. They were like rubber-neckers around a three-car pileup. I also turned to look. Bad move on my part. Haley's eyes hit mine like a dart hitting its target.

"What are you looking at, Chubbo? Time for another feeding at the zoo?"

Now the whole class turned its eyes to me. As I turned and looked back at the smirking faces something finally hit me. Maybe it was Oprah and the bald man. Maybe it was all those years of abuse, which had struck a final chord inside my very soul. Or maybe it was just the heart-burn I felt from the tuna tortillas they had served for lunch that day in the cafeteria. It doesn't matter. Whatever it was, it was *my* moment of truth. I would not look away. I would not cry. I was in control of my destiny. I would con-front my fears. With fire in my eyes and total conviction on my side, I looked Haley and all the others who had ever hurt me in my life straight in the eyes and said, "Maybe your little friends aren't afraid of you . . . but I am!"

Of course, right away I knew I had said the wrong thing. What I meant to say was, "Maybe your little friends *are* afraid of you . . . but I'm *not!*"

Well, it seems it didn't matter what I said that day. The point is, I stuck up for myself. I didn't run away. Haley and her friends never bothered me again. Maybe it was because they saw the fire in my eyes, or maybe it was because they thought I was totally insane. It just doesn't matter. The important thing is that I confronted my fears, and I was still standing.

That was the day I felt like I was no longer watching the world from the outside looking in. I was no longer that dull mosquito thrashing wildly against the movie screen. I was in this movie now, and I liked the ending.

As told to C. S. Dweck

Perfection

Perfection is a trifle dull. It is not the least of life's ironies that this, which we all aim at, is better not quite achieved.

W. Somerset Maugham

Skinny legs, bigger breasts
Is all they want to see
Tiny waists and thinner arms
The opposite of me.
The pressure to be perfect
Is slowly closing in
An utter suffocation
That doesn't seem to end.
Society is telling me
Beautiful is thin
And if I choose to starve myself
Perfection's what I win.
Shoving something down my throat
Will get me what I want
Bring me closer to that goal

Of a body I can flaunt.
Society is telling us
Beauty is a prize
Measured in the size of your breasts
In weight and clothing size.
But let me tell you here and now
No good will come from that
It seems okay at first
But soon becomes a trap.
A disease that clouds the mind
And believes what is untrue
Believes you're never good enough
No matter what you do.
There is one beauty that I know
It's the greatest prize of all
It's learning to accept yourself
Imperfections, flaws, and all.
The beauty that really matters
Lies in our heart, our soul, our core
Because when you love what's inside
You love what's outside even more.

Brittany Steward

Dear John

It was the last day of school; the last day I would ever walk down those halls as a student. I had a few things to take care of before the rehearsal for our graduation ceremony. I had to return my school library books and pay a shop-class fine from my sophomore year when I had broken Seth's project and was supposed to pay to replace his kit.

I was always clumsy around him, and that time I had knocked over the birdhouse he had made. It had tumbled and shattered at our feet.

We were on our knees picking up the pieces when our hands brushed against each other. I felt the same electricity I had first felt in fourth grade when he grabbed my hand for a Red Rover game.

I looked into his eyes, and he looked into mine. I thought that maybe this time he would notice me. My heart fluttered. I flushed with embarrassment and anticipation. Just an inch closer and he could kiss me.

Seth parted his lips and said, "Hey, why are you all red? It's not that hot in here." I guess it wasn't.

Seth and I had a different circle of friends. His were the

outgoing, athletic, school council, homecoming court, merit scholar type. Mine weren't.

As our class assembled in the gym for graduation rehearsal, I couldn't help but feel sentimental. My mood lifted when Seth sat down in front of me, until I remembered that this would be the last day he would be part of my daily life.

The announcements droned on and on. Yearbooks started circulating for last minute signings. When Seth's was handed to me, I autographed my senior picture and was about to pass it to the next person when the thought hit me. What did I have to lose by telling him now?

I tapped my pen on my teeth while I composed the note in my head. It had to be perfect. My hand shook when I began to write.

Dear Seth,

I have been in the background of your life since elementary school. You have meant more to me than I have to you. I wished that we could have known each other better and spent some time together. I will always remember you and wish you a great life.

Forever,
Cindy

I closed his book and passed it on before I could change my mind. As I scribbled my name in other books, I began to imagine and then to hope that maybe, just maybe, my yearbook would come back to me with a similar message from Seth.

It wasn't until the bus ride home that afternoon, that I finally had the nerve to open my book and look for Seth's picture. In its corner he had written, "To Cindy, whoever you are, Seth."

I can't say that I was crushed. I didn't expect anything more, really. I could've worried about what I wrote in his book, but I guessed he wouldn't know or care who I was, anyway. Still, his terse message did hurt. He didn't have to prove that I was invisible to him.

I was one step away from a "what a jerk" conclusion, but I just couldn't go that far after years of holding his perfect image in my mind.

I was putting my book into my backpack when the guy behind me tapped me on the shoulder. "Sign my book?"

"Sure," I said and handed him mine. I found my picture again and scribbled, "Good luck, from Cindy."

With the whirl of graduation and the activity of early summer days, it was a week before I thought to open my backpack. My yearbook was on top, and I sat down on the edge of my bed to thumb through it. I cringed when I reread Seth's message to me.

What a sorry thing that a guy could just overlook someone, no matter how nice she might be or how much she cared about him, just because she wasn't part of his circle.

It was then that I noticed another inscription. The friendly smile in the picture looked vaguely familiar.

Dear Cindy,

I was new this year. You are the first person I noticed. I've been sitting behind you in English Lit and I looked for you to come in every day. I wished we could've gotten to know each other and spent time together. I will always think of you and remember you.

Forever,
John

My heart sank as I realized the truth. I had done to John what Seth had done to me. I hadn't taken the time to know him, because, well, I didn't already know him. I had dismissed him without really seeing him.

I still feel a pinch of remorse when I remember that moment. Ever since that day, I have tried to notice and acknowledge the people in my daily life.

I had barely taken a thought to scribbling my name in John's book, but his message to me has been written across my life.

Cynthia M. Hamond

What One Boy Can Show a Girl

I was never fat nor was I ever skinny. I always had some meat on my bones, which made me look healthy, not scrawny. But when I entered middle school, the first thing I pointed out to myself was how fat I was.

I came from a small elementary school, where no one wore name-brand clothes and everyone liked to have fun regardless of how they looked. We were not worried about guys or what other people thought of us; we were merely being kids. So middle school was a shock to me. There were so many different groups to hang out with. There was one that was considered "bad," one with girls whose moms still dressed them, one that was really smart, and the one that required name-brand clothes and lots of makeup. Of course I wanted to be cool, have the boyfriends and be a part of the in-crowd.

I would only wear my name-brand clothes, which meant my wardrobe consisted of two pairs of jeans and four shirts. I begged my parents to let me wear makeup, but they wouldn't budge. I tried to hang around the popular girls and win them over by complimenting them on their clothes and looks, but they just looked past me and pretended I wasn't there.

My self-confidence dwindled. I gave up on my popularity quest and soon found myself back with my friends from my previous school. They were great. They were there for me and liked me for me, but I still didn't like myself. I thought I was fat, and no one could convince me that I wasn't. At the beach when all my friends would be playing volleyball in their bathing suits, I would be in my clothes. When we went swimming, I would make sure I had shorts on over my bathing suit bottoms to cover up my thighs. I was no fun to hang around because I was constantly worried about how fat I looked.

At the start of eighth grade I was faced with another issue: boys. I became interested in them and even had middle school boyfriends. But now not only did I worry about how fat I looked, I worried about everything else that went along with my appearance. I became so consumed with my looks that nothing else seemed to matter. Wherever there was a mirror, I was there fixing my hair. Wherever there was a scale, I was weighing myself to see if I had lost any weight. I wasn't worried about grades, family and homework—only me. The world revolved around me and my appearance. My parents were concerned about how I was acting. I was not confident in my body, and it showed.

On the last day of school my class was to take a trip to a local water park. I cringed at the prospect of having to walk around and stand in lines in just my swimsuit. I wouldn't even do that in front of my friends, much less all the guys and other girls in my school. I was dreading it, but I couldn't miss the last class trip. And I'm glad I didn't.

With the help of one very special person, Adam, I was able to open my eyes and see what I had not been able to see for so long. Adam was what all the girls considered a "major hunk." Blond hair, blue eyes and a great body. So you can imagine my surprise when he asked if he could hang out with me and go on all the rides together. Things like that just didn't happen to me, so I was thrilled, to say the least.

We had a blast together. At first I was noticeably uncomfortable with just my two-piece on, but after I realized that Adam wasn't gawking over how "fat" my thighs were or how "big" my butt was, I settled into my skin. For the first time in nearly two years, I was beginning to feel comfortable with my body. Being with Adam gave me the confidence I needed to start appreciating and accepting myself.

The next day, as I was looking through a picture album, I questioned why Adam wanted to hang out with me when he could have spent the day following one of the popular blond girls parading around in her skimpy bikini. Then I spotted a recent picture of a friend and me at school. I looked closely at the picture and studied how I looked. I discovered that my butt wasn't that big and my thighs weren't really that huge. I had always compared myself to girls with other body types, and that only left me feeling sorry for myself. I turned the page and found a picture of my mom when she was in high school. It's one of my favorite pictures because she looks so pretty. I cherish the picture because my mom died of brain cancer when I was in grade school. I compared the picture of my mom with the picture of my friend and me, and the resemblance shocked me. I had always been told that we looked so much alike, but I never really realized it until then. We share the same thick brown hair, the same body structure and the same facial features. I realized that if I can't be skinny and tall like a model, then at least I can look like one of the most beautiful people I know: my mother.

Sarah Erdmann

When the World Stopped Turning

Asking your father about dating is always difficult, especially if you are the son of a strict, religious Filipino immigrant. In fact, bringing up any subject always seemed to be arduous for me. However, dating the opposite sex was not only a topic that was rarely mentioned in my homestead, but it almost appeared strictly taboo. Thus, dating while in high school was not allowed for any of my siblings, and I was certain that my father would not change the rule for me. Even though he had no qualms about grounding his children for disobedience, it was the sheer disappointment from him that we feared the most.

Although any child would normally be deterred by punishment from a stern father, *something* made me pick up the telephone. With two weeks left in my senior year of high school, that *something* made me ask out the most beautiful girl in my school.

My father was raised with a strong moral code. Determined to raise his children with the same values, he pushed us to academically achieve as well as respect his rules. He always felt that romantic relationships were strictly adult in nature, and children were not mature enough to cope with or understand them. Moreover, he felt that children who prematurely participated in romance got nothing in return but distraction from their education, precocious mental stress and, most important, unplanned pregnancies.

We respected that opinion. Well, at least we respected it outwardly. Inwardly, we thought he was *ruining* our adolescent years. Like all other teenagers, we felt the urge to pursue the opposite sex. However, due to my father's quiet sternness and seemingly immobile moral code, none of us children ever had the audacity to ask otherwise.

It was his quiet stance on the matter, as well as my squeamish nature that brought me to the tough current situation. Here I was, on the phone, asking out the most beautiful girl in the school. Not only was I not sure that my father would even let me go, but I wasn't sure how I'd manage borrowing his car for the occasion. With the exception of my older sisters going to an occasional dance or hanging out with a male friend, my situation would be wholly different. To remedy this awkward scenario, my only hope was that this girl would turn me down!

Unfortunately, she accepted my offer. I couldn't believe it! While celebrating my unimaginable joy for having a date with the prettiest girl in the entire school, a sudden eruption of reality caused it to skid to a halting stop. Through my elation, I had completely forgotten about my parent's restrictions. How was I to tell my father about a date? How was I to tell my father I needed his car?

I went to my mother with a cry for help. Being the more sympathetic of my two parents, she was actually *proud* of my accomplishment. For her, the problem seemed simple to solve: we would not tell my father. In my house, the world appeared to turn regardless of my father's participation or foreknowledge. Being a devoted physician, he was constantly consumed by work and study. He was often quiet and reserved. Going out on a date and *merely* not mentioning it would be an easy task to pull off. Although this idea was a little immoral, it certainly wasn't unconventional. My mother had occasionally concealed a bad grade or a speeding ticket from my father. I knew for a fact that the secrecy of my "date" was safe with my mother. Problem solved.

Despite being excited about the plan, I was very concerned about the car situation. My mother drove a minivan, the most uncool vehicle a teenager could drive. My father, however, drove a Toyota Camry. Now mind you, it wasn't a Corvette, but it certainly didn't have a sliding door. The only problem was sneaking the Camry out of the garage. My mother had a solution for that as well. She asked my father if I could borrow the car for a "night out with my friends." He agreed. With both problems apparently behind me, I now could concentrate all of my superpowers on perfecting every other angle of the date. Remember, *she was the prettiest girl in the school.*

All week long I prepared for that Friday night. The movie plans were set. Dinner reservations were arranged. I even had the perfect mix tape for the drive. It was all going as planned.

Friday night arrived quickly. All my anticipation had built up like an orchestra warming up for a concert. Every instrument was in tune, with every musician waiting in symphony. After reviewing my final plans for the night, I went to the garage to stash a dress jacket in the trunk of my father's Camry. As I opened the garage door, my heart came to an abrupt stop. Every muscle in my body went tight, and my stomach wound up like a clenched fist. My eyes began to glisten with tears as I noticed an unnerving absence in my father's parking spot. *The Camry was gone.* My father *had* to have taken it. My brother had already taken the minivan. With no cars left, my heart was broken.

I ran inside and quickly sought out my mother. As fearful as I looked, my mother looked worse. Unaware that my father had taken the car out, she seemed at a loss for words. My father had apparently forgotten about my little *"night out with my friends."* There was no telling when he would return. For once, the world seemed to stop turning without my father.

With time chasing me to the finish line, my father arrived home. Of all times, he had chosen to take the car for a stupid car wash. Upon pulling into the garage, I stood impatiently at the door. I tried my hardest to not look nervous, though the sweat on my brow was close to revealing my secret plan. In no apparent rush at all, my father appeared as calm as ever as he proceeded to clean the inside of the car as well! Steam poured out of my ears. My time was up, and I was about to explode!

I ran back into the house and asked my mother for help. "Remember Mom, don't say anything about the date," I pleaded. She calmly walked out into the garage and spoke with my father. As she walked back into the house, a smile stretched across her face. She told me there was no other option but to tell my father the truth.

"What?!" I screamed in agony. "What did you say?"

"I told him that you need the car for a date tonight," she answered calmly.

"And?" I anxiously prodded.

My mother smiled. "He said, 'I know. Why else do you think I'm cleaning it out?'"

* * *

Although my family often presumed that my father was oblivious to the random speeding ticket or sporadic bad school grade, he apparently possessed a sort of omniscience that ultimately *made us all look foolish.* To this day, we still do not know how my father found out about the date.

Michael Punsalan

Let Me Live

Our greatest glory is not in never falling, but in rising every time we fall.

Confucius

Let me cut my own hair.
  If it looks horrible,
  let me learn not to touch scissors and that hair grows
  back.

Let me spend my money.
  If the shirt's too little and the store doesn't give refunds,
  let me learn to save my cash.

Let me kiss a boy.
  If he thinks it's just a fling and I get my heart broken,
  let me learn that some boys are just that way.

Let me flunk my test.
  If I fail the class and miss the honor roll list,
  let me learn to study more.

Let me miss the shot.
　　If my team loses and I'm on the bench,
　　let me learn to concentrate on the basket.

Let me go out past curfew.
　　If I get grounded and miss that big party this weekend,
　　let me learn to follow the rules.

But most important, let me live.
　　If I learn a lesson,
　　you've done your part.

Jennifer Danley

Happiness

Happiness depends upon ourselves.

Aristotle

I stared at the word I had written at the top of my blank sheet of notebook paper: "Happiness." I was working on a creative-writing assignment my teacher had given the class. We each had to write about a different emotion. That was it, just a slip of paper as we were leaving class. No format at all.

But it wasn't the lack of structure that was bothering me. It was the word "happiness." Anything else I could have handled. Jealousy, I knew that one all too well. I could write pages about jealousy. I could write about my older sister and how she got everything first. Or my best friend, Julie, who always got the guys . . . and the lead in the play . . . and straight A's.

Or pain, I could write novels about pain. Not the kind of pain you get when you break your arm, but the kind that makes your broken heart go into your throat, so that it takes all of your energy and concentration to breathe. The kind of pain that makes you want to scream and sob at the same time. The kind of pain that makes you want to hurt everyone around you because you're suffering and they're not, because they can breathe without feeling guilty and hold a normal conversation without breaking down into fits of tears or rage.

But I was supposed to write about happiness. How could I, of all people, write about happiness?

There was a knock at my bedroom door.

"Hey, um, Sarah?" asked a small voice from the hall. "Can I come in?"

"Rachie," I said to my five-year-old sister, "I'm kinda busy right now. Can you come back later?"

"Um, this is kinda important."

I sighed. "All right, come in."

Rachele came in and sat down on my bed. She looked so sweet and cute, swinging her black, patent leather Mary Janes back and forth and looking around my room. Her baby-doll face was framed by her curly, red hair. "Well, um, I caught this butterfly. . . ." she began uncertainly. "And it's really pretty . . . but I let it go."

"So what's the problem?"

"Well, it was my favorite-ist butterfly I ever had." Rachele wrinkled her forehead and frowned, as if concentrating really hard. "But . . . I had to let it go 'cause Mommy said it would die. And I was so sad thinking about not having it anymore. But I knew Mommy was right, 'cause if I were the butterfly I wouldn't wanna live in a glass jar. And so I let it go." She turned and looked at me.

"Yeah?" I asked.

"Well," she whispered, leaning towards me as if she were about to share a deep, dark secret. "When I set it free, I was glad to see it go. Does that make me a mean person?"

I smiled. "Of course not, Rachie. You were just happy

that the butterfly was free and that it wasn't imprisoned in the jar. You felt relieved."

"You mean I'm not mean?" Her face lit up.

"Of course not!" I gave her a hug. "Now you gotta go. I have work to do."

"What do you have to do?" she asked, frowning.

I glanced at my blank paper. "I have to write about happiness."

"Oh, that's easy," she said and started to leave.

Yeah, real easy, I thought.

"Hey Rachie," I said before she left.

"What?" she turned around at the door.

"What do *you* think happiness is?"

She frowned and tapped her foot on the ground for a few seconds before answering. And then she gave me her answer.

"Butterflies," she said simply. And then she left.

"Butterflies," I said out loud to myself. I thought about our conversation. She was happy to catch the butterfly and happy to see it go. Maybe she was right. Butterflies bring nothing but happiness. Maybe butterflies aren't exactly the key to happiness, but maybe there is something to be said about the simple things in life, things that bring joy, like snow or wildflowers or a sunny day or the smell of pumpkin pie. Not clothes or guys or keeping score or getting the lead in the play or even good grades. None of those things in themselves will *really* make you happy. But the little things, like catching and releasing butterflies, just might.

And with that, I started to write.

Sarah Provencal

Watch Out for That Tree!

Experience is simply the name we give our mistakes.

Oscar Wilde

Missy was absolutely my best friend in the whole world. We had known each other since first grade, and we literally did everything together. We frequently visited each other's homes, we knew each other's families like they were our own, we shopped, we went to parties together, and on and on and on. The interesting thing about our relationship, however, was the fact that the older we got, the more our values seemed to differ. We still enjoyed a lot of the same things, but I was a bit more settled while Missy seemed to enjoy pursuing the world of pretense. She loved being associated with popular people and things, and although she was basically a good person, she had no problem with forcing things to go her way. Perhaps this is why it seemed that her family actually trusted me more than they trusted her. So, on the day that Missy showed up at my house with a huge dent in her father's car, I knew that we were in for an interesting time.

She had banged the car while out that day, and she knew her father was going to have a literal fit. So she stopped by my house in order to concoct a story that would lessen her father's rage. Missy decided to tell him that while in a parking garage, someone must have backed into the car and dented it. My role was to corroborate. Now keep in mind that I had strong objections to lying, and I wanted absolutely nothing to do with the situation. I loved her parents just like my own, and I did not want to be a party to this fallacy that Missy was creating. Nevertheless, after much prodding and a general questioning of my loyalty, I decided that the least I could do was to act as a silent witness. That way, I wasn't actually lying; I just wasn't divulging the full truth.

So an hour or so later, we presented Missy's father with the car and the inquisition began. He wanted to know exactly what had happened, when and how. Missy recapped her concocted story, and I stood there in silent agreement. Then Missy's father decided to do a closer inspection. He walked over to the dented area and started to pull and pound the dent until it gave away. It was at that point that pieces of bark from the tree that Missy had hit fell out. We were both stunned. That was *so* not part of the plan.

Needless to say, Missy was caught in her fabricated story, and I was proclaimed as the "guilty" bystander. I actually think that her parents were more disappointed with me than they were with her. As a matter of fact, I'm not sure if they ever fully trusted me again. It was at that time that I realized how incredibly fragile trust actually is.

Cady Carrington

Self-Esteem

Please treat me well; I am as I'm treated

When I am loved, I can love who I am
When I am cared for, I can care for myself
When I am treated as someone, I can feel like someone

Speak to me, so I may learn to listen
Expose the world to me, so I may see its beauty
Look into my eyes, so I may feel I am seen

If you're good to me, I must be a good person

When you smile at me, I can smile inside
When you let me make choices, I know that I can choose
When you give to me, I can give a bit back

Touch me gently, so I may touch others
Rest my unrest, so that I may learn self-control
Soothe me, so I may learn to soothe

Love me, but give me room to love others

When you treat me as successful, I can learn to succeed
When you respect my dreams, I can explore reality
When you allow my mistakes, I can accept what they
    teach

Teach me diversity of thought, so I may be open-minded
Help me help others, so I may grow to be selfless
Demonstrate your diligence, so I may earn my way in life

Show me how to laugh, so I may laugh with others
Laugh at your shortcomings, so I may accept my own

I am someone and I am loved

Jim Lauer

5

FAMILY

In family life, love is the oil that eases friction, the cement that binds closer together, and the music that brings harmony.

Eva Burrows

The Doctor's Son

I grew up in a small town in northern Vermont. I suppose it's a typical small town—a few houses, lots of trees and a business district consisting of a dozen stores, two restaurants, three service stations and a doctor's office. Like most villages in rural Vermont, Enosburg is a community where neighbors greet each other by name. Even now, although I've lived elsewhere for nearly twenty years, the residents of Enosburg still welcome me with a smile. "Doctor Eppley's son is back," they say.

My parents moved to Vermont when I was still an infant. A soft-spoken man, my father settled quietly into his medical practice. Within a few months the people of Enosburg accepted him as one of their own. Word passes quickly in small Vermont towns. They know good people when they meet them. Around town the neighbors greeted my father as "Doc Eppley." And I soon learned that as long as I lived in Enosburg I would always be known as "Doctor Eppley's son."

On the first day of school, my classmates crowded around me because I was the doctor's son. "If you're anything like your father, you'll be a smart boy," my first-grade teacher said. I couldn't stop beaming.

Throughout the first years of my life, I never tired of letting others know that my father was one of the town's most respected citizens. Somewhere in the midst of my teenage years, however, something changed. I was sixteen years old and the neighbors still called me "Doctor Eppley's son." They said that I was growing up to be an honorable and industrious young man, living an honest life just like my father. I groaned whenever I heard their compliments.

I wondered how I would ever fit in with my teenage friends. Having a popular father worked to my advantage when I was younger, but now that I was in high school my father's good name seemed like an ugly shadow that followed me wherever I went. And so when strangers asked me if I was Doctor Eppley's son I replied emphatically, "My name is Harold. And I can manage quite well on my own." As an act of rebellion, I began to call my father by his first name, Sam.

"Why are you acting so stubborn lately?" my father asked me one day in the midst of an argument.

"Well, Sam," I replied, "I suppose that bothers you."

"You know it hurts me when you call me Sam," my father shouted.

"Well, it hurts me when everybody expects me to be just like you. I don't want to be perfect. I want to be myself."

I survived my last years of high school until finally I turned eighteen. The next fall I enrolled in college. I chose to attend a school far from Enosburg, a place where nobody called me "Doctor Eppley's son" because nobody knew my father.

One night at college I sat with a group of students in the dormitory as we shared stories about our lives. We began to talk about the things we hated most about our childhoods. "That's easy," I said. "I couldn't stand growing up in a town where everybody always compared me to my father. Just once, I'd like to be known as someone other than 'Doctor Eppley's son.'"

The woman sitting next to me frowned. "I don't understand," she said. "I'd be proud to have a father who's so well respected." Her eyes filled with tears as she continued, "I'd give anything to be called my father's child. But I don't know where he is. He left my mother when I was four years old."

There was an awkward silence, and then I changed the subject. I wasn't ready to hear that woman's words.

I returned home for winter break that year feeling proud of myself. In four months at college, I had made a number of new friends. I had become popular in my own right, without my father's help. My parents marveled at how much I had changed.

For two weeks I enjoyed being back in Enosburg. The main topic of interest at home was my father's new car.

"Let me take it out for a drive," I said.

My father agreed, but not without his usual warning, "Be careful."

I glared at my father. "Sam, I'm sick of being treated like a child. I'm in college now. Don't you think I know how to drive a car?"

I could see the hurt in my father's face, and I remembered how much he hated it whenever I called him "Sam."

"All right then," he replied. "The keys are in the kitchen."

I hopped into the car and headed down the road, savoring the beauty of the Vermont countryside. I drove a few miles and then stopped at a busy intersection in a nearby town. As I stepped on the accelerator my mind was wandering, and I failed to hear the screech of brakes in front of me. I only heard a thud as I reacted too late.

The woman in the car I had struck jumped out of her

vehicle unhurt. "You idiot!" she screamed. "Why didn't you look where you were going?"

I peered through the windshield and surveyed the damage. Both cars had sustained serious dents.

I sat there like a guilty child as the woman continued with her barrage of insults. "It's your fault," she shouted. I couldn't protest. My knees began to shake. I choked back my tears. The woman's words came so quickly that I didn't know what to do. "Do you have insurance? Can you pay for this? Who are you?" she kept asking. "Who are you?"

I panicked and without thinking shouted, "I'm Doctor Eppley's son."

I sat there stunned. I couldn't believe what I had just said. Almost immediately, the woman's frown became a smile of recognition. "I'm sorry," she replied, "I didn't realize who you were."

An hour later, I drove my father's battered new car back home. With my head down and my knees still shaking, I trudged into the house and handed the keys to my father. I explained what had happened.

"Are you hurt?" he asked.

"No," I replied solemnly.

"Good," he answered. Then he turned and headed toward the door. "Harold," he said as he was leaving, "Hold your head up. There's no need for you to slouch."

That night was New Year's Eve, and my family attended a small party with friends to celebrate the beginning of another year. When midnight arrived people cheered and greeted each other with laughter. Across the room I saw my father. I stepped toward him. My father and I rarely hug. But recalling the day's events, I wrapped my arms around his shoulders. And I spoke his real name for the first time in years. I said, "Thank you, Dad. Happy New Year."

Harold Eppley with Rochelle Melander

My Favorite Professor

One father is more than one hundred schoolmasters.

George Herbert

My father was not a quiet man, and when it was his turn to drive the carpools of my childhood, we weren't going to get much time to wake up slowly.

"Top o' the morning," he bellowed, a Jewish baby boomer from New York, pretending to be Irish as he opened the doors for me and two of my friends.

"And the rest of the day to you," we groaned the response we had been instructed to on so many occasions.

He taught constitutional law at the university, and his energy instantly made him a popular professor. They loved how he once instructed a class on the first day of the baseball season dressed in a New York Mets uniform, a wad of chewing gum bulging from his right cheek. They loved how, after class, he would engage in conversations about their lives, their food preferences and their favorite sports. They loved how he cared. Three graduating classes named him Professor of the Year.

Friends and family look at me and smile.

I am the spitting image of him, they say. I have Julian Eule's mannerisms, his face, his sense of humor, his initiative, his enthusiasm, and on and on and on, to which I can only reply, "I hope so."

There was a time when I didn't quite know how special my father was, but then a time came when I realized it. I had gone to bed angry after some argument with him. I was young, probably in elementary school, and don't remember what it was about. But I do remember his response.

After the argument, I could not fall asleep. Minutes, then hours, went by. Music, then call-in talk shows, then news blared from the boxy clock radio on the night table near the head of my bed. And still I couldn't sleep.

Around midnight, my father finally came in.

I didn't say anything. He motioned for me to slide over, sat at the side of my bed and turned off my radio. And then, he began to tell a story he had read once in the newspaper.

There was an actor who always spoke of how close he had been with his own father. The two had always had a remarkable relationship. One night, though, after a slight disagreement, they left each other's company angry, refusing to even say a simple "good night" to each other. Later that night, the father died.

The son had no doubt that the love he had for his father was both known and equally returned, and yet he had to live with the memory that he and his father spent their final moments together upset, arguing over something presumably meaningless. They had not said "good night" to each other on their final evening together, and this stuck with that son for the rest of his life.

As it has with me.

I hugged my father tightly and told him I loved him. He

told me the same and from then on, no matter how late I came home, no matter how frustrated I was, I never again went to bed without telling him, "Good night, I love you."

Indeed, my father was a brilliant storyteller. Yet of all the stories, cancer was the biggest. Cancer had been like war stories for my father, something he had survived when I was too young to recall, something he was proud to have defeated. Suddenly, in the summer before my senior year in high school, I learned that my father was going back to war.

It didn't seem fair, but that was not the way he chose to look at it. That was never the way he chose to look at things. When I was just a toddler, he was given an 11 percent chance of surviving a battle with cancer. With these statistics in mind, the important things in life were separated from the trivial ones. He wanted nothing more than to see his two young children grow up, a privilege denied his own father, who died of heart complications three years after my father's birth.

Eleven percent. A death sentence waiting in the wings. It amazes me that he could live with that. But he made a vow to appreciate life for all of its joy. When he beat the odds, my father kept his promise. In watching him, I learned how to appreciate life. He taught me not to get mad at the little things, saying, "Is this worth losing a day of your life to stress?"

It was a life where every day was valued, every moment treasured, every person appreciated. A life where he made sure he was where he wanted to be, with the people he wanted to be with. But after almost fourteen years of remission, my father spent a beautiful California summer evening in an ugly hospital bed, my mother by his side.

"How can I be upset when I was given the past fourteen years as a gift?" he asked. Those years, he told me, had been the happiest of his life, and if he had to die, he was more content this time.

I wasn't content. I found I needed him to remind me not to lose sight of things. He was the hand on my shoulder, calming me down without any words.

One night, during that summer, my mother called from the hospital. She was tired and wanted to go home to get some sleep. My father needed to stay. He had lost some blood, needed a transfusion and wanted someone to keep him company for the rest of the night.

I took a radio, a sleeping bag and a pillow and set off for the hospital at 10 P.M. My father smiled, glad to see me as I entered the room. I motioned for him to slide over, sat on the side of his bed, and we talked.

During the past fourteen years, there had been nothing left unsaid, so nothing specifically had to be spoken during those moments. We just sat there and enjoyed each other's company.

As the new blood entered his body, the life returned to his face. By midnight, the radio was blasting. We sang along to every song we knew and faked those we didn't. Down the hall, a door closed. At six in the morning, the transfusion was complete, as was our pajama party.

I set off for home content, knowing that in an hour my mother would settle herself in the same spot I had occupied all night.

Exhausted, I was halfway out the door before I remembered. I turned back toward his bed, bent down and kissed him on his cheek.

"Good night, I love you," I whispered.

Brian Eule

Uncle Jerry

Everyone has their own special gift. In some it is speech, in some, silence. The world has need of small perfection as well as great achievements.

Anonymous

I was probably twelve or thirteen when I first heard the word "retarded" applied to my Uncle Jerry—and it was Jerry who used it. He had always been a part of my life. He stayed with us during the summer, and we saw him frequently during the rest of the year. He was my mother's youngest brother, and he talked "funny," with the nasal honk of someone with a malformed palate. He sounded fine to me. We had recently moved, and our new house was farther from my grandmother's, with complicated bus transfers. In my innocence, I asked Jerry when he was going to get his driver's license so he could see us more often. He was in his early twenties and worked as a dishwasher. His hands were cracked and red from the harsh detergents, but he was a good worker, my mother said. A responsible and reliable worker.

"I can't get a license." He looked down and rubbed those red hands together.

"What do you mean? You just take this test and then you get it."

"I can't because I'm, you know, retarded."

Well, I had heard this word before, and it certainly applied to some people I had seen. My mother was a scout leader for a troop of boys with Down's syndrome, and I had been on a bowling outing with them. But Jerry was like a regular person to me. Sure, he was hard to understand, but so was my grandmother with her French accent. He could read, he could tell very funny jokes, he could carry the heaviest furniture, and he loved to hike and ride his bicycle. He wasn't very good with money, that was for sure. But I wasn't good at math, either. Jerry could never figure out how much the bus fare was, even though he took the same route every day. He compensated, though. He got on a bus, held out his hand with lots of change, and the bus drivers, who knew him well, would just take what was needed.

Did this make him retarded? Retarded was drooling and limping, wagging tongues and strange behavior. It wasn't Jerry. I wondered on that day, when I was barely a teenager, who had told him he was retarded. Who had fooled him into thinking he couldn't do anything he wanted to do? So I went to my mother and asked her why Jerry couldn't get a driver's license.

"Jerry can do lots of things, but getting a driver's license is beyond his abilities. He reads, you know that, but mostly comics and *Mad Magazine.* Passing the written test for the DMV is more than he could handle. He knows that. He's okay with it."

This made me mad, somehow. How could he be okay with it? My mother had always said that I could do anything I wanted, if I just set my mind to it. But here she was, limiting my beloved uncle, the uncle who could lift me like I was a feather and swing me around, who could make me laugh like nobody I knew, and who had many, many friends. Everyone loved Jerry. He was smart in so many ways. Why didn't other people see that? Why should that keep him from doing anything he wanted?

When I was about fifteen and studying for my own driver's exam, and Jerry was still washing dishes, I realized that I had passed him by. I was now smarter than he was. According to the definition in some psychology book somewhere, I suppose he was retarded. But I refused, even then, to acknowledge that label. Jerry made a full life for himself. He went backpacking, took train trips to the Grand Canyon and made even more friends.

Jerry died when I was in college. When he was an infant, the doctors had told my grandmother that he would probably not live to be a teenager. My mother always said that Jerry's body wasn't quite put together all the way. He had an invisible line that started in his head—where the gaps in intelligence struggled to understand math and the world—and went down through his eyes—which never focused well and needed thick lenses—to the roof of his mouth that never quite came together—and finally through his heart—which struggled for thirty-six years and finally gave up trying to coalesce. But that heart was as full and rich and strong as anyone's I have ever known. If friendship and the capacity to love and laugh are the marks of intelligence, my Uncle Jerry was a genius.

Mary Shannon

New Beginnings

My sister and I weren't exactly what you would call close. I was three years younger, and I thought she walked on water. Everything she did was perfect, and I wanted to be just like her when I grew up. If she wore her hair in twin braids with a pink clip one day, the next day I wore mine exactly the same way. I used to follow her and her friends around, begging to be included, but there isn't much room in a thirteen-year-old's life for a pesky ten-year-old sister. As a result, over time, my worship of her became indifference. We were strangers living in the same house, eating together but never communicating.

So when she sat me down last year and told me she'd be going to Israel to study abroad for ten months, I wasn't too concerned. I figured I would get to wear the clothes she left behind and use her CD player. That was the only way I thought her leaving would affect me.

That first night after she left, I sat in my room and tried to do homework. I couldn't shake the feeling that something was wrong, something was missing. The house was *too* quiet. No Tova's CD player and no Tova's voice giggling on the phone with her friends. Sitting there, I realized just how different it was without her in the house. Even though we didn't always speak, I had felt safe just knowing she was near.

I cried that night. I cried over all the years we had wasted trying to live our own lives and ignoring each other's. I cried that I couldn't even give her a hug before she boarded her plane. But as the night wore on, my tears changed to tears of calm, tears of new beginnings.

I picked up the phone and called her halfway across the world. I waited for her to pick up, my doubts growing with every second.

"Hello?" Her voice sounded as though it came from nearby and not Israel.

"Hey Tova. It's me, Sara. I just called to tell you I love you." My words came out in a rush. I knew that if I stopped in the middle, I wouldn't have the courage to continue. "I know we aren't as close as some sisters, but that doesn't mean I'm not missing you a ton."

For a long time there was only silence on the other end. Finally she spoke. "I've been sitting here, all alone, thinking about you guys back home," she said. "Your voice makes me feel as though I'm right there with you." And before she hung up she said, very quickly just as I had, "I love you, too."

I'm counting down the days until my sister returns home, so I can give her the hug I never gave her when she left and say, "I'm so glad to have you home."

Sara Ronis

When It Counts

*O*ther things may change us, but we start and
end with family.

Anthony Brandt

My brother and I are only a year apart in age. When we were little, people would ask if we were twins. We lived in the mountains and only had each other for a long time, so we weren't just brother and sister, we were best friends. I was the artist. I came up with ideas. He was the scientist. Whatever ideas I came up with, he found a way to make them work.

Then our parents divorced. He went to live with my father, I with my mother. Sometimes he visited us, sometimes I visited them. But it got weirder each time. He had friends I didn't know because he was going to a different school, and it wasn't really cool to hang out with his sister who was a snob and a brain. Then there were my friends, who thought he wasn't cool because he wasn't in sports or in the Honor Society. By the time I was thirteen, we'd stopped hanging out altogether. I think the only time we ever spoke was at Christmas, and it was all very formal and awkward, like he was a complete stranger instead of my little brother.

Finally, my high school graduation day came. I had been accepted to a major university three thousand miles away. I'd had big plans on attaching a U-Haul to the back of my beat-up Mustang and driving cross-country. The problem was there was no one to go with me. I was more than happy to go alone. I didn't need anybody. But my parents conferred and decided that my brother would have to be my travel companion.

Needless to say, we were both furious with the idea. The last thing he wanted was to spend a week in a car with someone he barely knew and drive three thousand miles to a college he could care less about. The last thing I wanted was to spend a week in a car with someone I barely knew and drive three thousand miles with a baby-sitter when I was more than capable of taking care of myself. But it was settled. So two weeks later I packed the car and the U-Haul and drove across town to pick up my brother. He flopped into the passenger seat and stared out the window. Neither of us really spoke for the next six hundred miles unless absolutely necessary.

Then fate stepped in. We'd already had several minor arguments about music, speeding and stopping. The last one, though, had been a bit more heated. It was getting dark, and I wanted to stop for the night. He thought it was stupid to lose that much time. Eventually I agreed to drive for another two hours just to end the argument. But I was mad. There he was, not speaking, making me listen to his idiotic music, making me drive when I didn't want to, and rolling his eyes every time I wanted to stop for a bathroom break. This was supposed to be *my* trip! I didn't want him there in the *first* place!

I was so busy debating him in my head that I stopped

concentrating on the road. Suddenly, a strip of shredded rubber from an eighteen-wheeler in the road flashed into my headlights.

"Look out!" my brother shouted.

I shrieked and swerved. The U-Haul and my car jackknifed, and we went flying into the shoulder. Thankfully, we were on a stretch of highway with only two lanes, pastureland on both sides of the road and not another car for miles.

When everything stopped moving, we sat there in stunned silence, only the sound of the car engine and my heartbeat in my ears. Then I started shaking and crying.

"Oh God! Are you okay? Are you hurt? Are you okay?" I demanded slightly hysterically. I didn't even know if *I* was hurt. All I cared about was that I might have hurt my brother.

"No—I'm cool. I promise. No damage, see," he held up his hands and smiled through his color-drained face.

"Oh God, I'm so sorry! I'm so sorry," I repeated again and again.

He just held my hand and kept telling me everything was fine. I think he was a little unsure about whether I was going to have a nervous breakdown right there in the car. Then he did something he used to do when I would get upset. He made a joke.

"Come on! That was awesome! Are you kidding?? Let's do it again!" he grinned.

Reluctantly, I smiled a little. But he was relentless.

"No seriously! If I'd known there would be near-death experiences on this trip, I would've been way more psyched to go!"

This provoked a slight giggle from me.

In the end, after several more comments and a few silly faces for my benefit, we were both outright laughing.

"All right," he clapped his hands together decisively,

"Let's see if we're spending the night here tonight."

We got out, inspected the damage and spent the next two hours unhitching and re-hitching the trailer (which, unfortunately, also required some unpacking and repacking) and rocking the back tires of the Mustang out of a small ditch.

By the time we were back on the road, we couldn't stop laughing and talking about the whole scenario. I even admitted to him why I hadn't been concentrating, and he admitted he should have taken the shift since he was the one who wanted to drive at night. We crashed (the sleeping kind, not the dangerous vehicular kind) at the first motel we came to and promptly overslept.

Over the next six days we stopped at the Carlsbad Caverns and the Grand Canyon (which neither of us had seen). In the end, he did most of the driving, and I did most of the navigating. Already I was back to coming up with the ideas, and he was finding ways to make them work. When we arrived, he even helped me get settled.

The night before I had to drive him to the airport to fly home, we were sitting at Denny's, making jokes and reminiscing. We'd talked a *lot* in those last few days. I'd found out so much about him I never knew: things about school, friends, girlfriends, even my father. Suddenly, I was crushed. I couldn't tell him because it was just too "girly." But I had my little brother back, my long-lost best friend . . . and he was leaving in a few hours.

Life is never as perfect as the movies. I never told him how much I loved him and missed him. But I hugged him for the first time in more than five years before he got on the plane.

I couldn't wait for Christmas, even though it was months away. But I found a perfect present. It was a wall map of the world, complete with pins. We decided at the Grand Canyon that, when I graduate, we're going to backpack together and mark all the places we go. Hey, I may have great ideas—but I need someone to help me get there. And . . . maybe to drive at night, too.

Heather Woodruff

No Longer an Only Child

I thought my parents were crazy when they announced over dinner one night that I was going to have a brother or sister in about nine months. Being fifteen years old and in high school, I figured I was out of the woods and free of siblings. Well, that wasn't the case.

My mom and dad had divorced when I was three years old, and several years later, my mom met a wonderful man named Randy. They got married, we moved out to the country on a hog farm in rural Illinois (yes, I was officially a farmer's daughter), and things were going fairly smoothly. A week after their wedding, I went to Japan for a study-abroad program, and when I came back a month later, I had a newly decorated room waiting for me. It didn't take long before I was calling Randy "Dad." I loved him dearly, and he treated me as if I were his own daughter.

I always considered myself a fairly well-adjusted teenager, and things were going just fine for me. I was an only child and never had to go without anything, so you could say I had it made. About two years later, the big announcement that a baby was on the way left me feeling, well, not really feeling anything. I wasn't mad, upset or happy; I was just feeling neutral about the situation. I always wanted a little brother or sister, and now I was finally going to get one. However, I was at a point in my life where I was used to not having siblings, had learned to entertain myself, and was perfectly content with being the center of attention at every family function.

The next several months were filled with chaos as we prepared for the new addition to the family. My idea of a new addition would have been a deck and a pool or even a new car for my sixteenth birthday, but I'm referring to the little bundle of nightmare that would soon be living in my house. I knew things were going to change, but I had no idea the emotional roller coaster my mom would be on during this time. One day, Dad drank the last Diet Coke and I thought she was going to kill him, then the next moment she would be the most pleasant person on the planet.

My mom's two older sisters, Aunt Dorothy and Aunt Lynda, threw her a wonderful baby shower with all the trimmings. To my surprise, I also received presents, including a gift basket with earplugs. My family was very concerned about how I would feel once the baby was born, so they were putting forth extra effort to make me feel loved, and they showered me with attention. All of my friends were excited for me. In a way, I think they were looking forward to me experiencing the aches and pains of being an older sister.

The next few months went by rather quickly, and before I knew it, one summer morning in June my mom was taken to the hospital. I was visiting my Aunt Lynda in Missouri when we got the call that my mom was in labor, so we loaded up the car and drove to Illinois, hoping and praying that we wouldn't miss the big event. I remember it like it was yesterday. We stepped into the hospital at 12:03 P.M., which was the exact same time my sister, Bekah, was born. I saw my dad coming out of the delivery room, and he was glowing. Everything seemed to be going just fine when all of a sudden they were wheeling my mom in a mad dash to the operating room. She had some complications after the delivery, and what was supposed to be a time of celebration now became a life-or-death waiting game. My first instinct was to hate the baby, since I felt it was all her fault that this happened. I had my mom to myself for fifteen years of my life, and now it looked as if she was going to be taken away from me forever.

As soon as I saw Bekah for the first time, those feelings of hate went away, and I saw her as a helpless being who had no idea what was going on. At first, I didn't see what all the fuss was about. She looked like a raisin with hair and couldn't do anything. But as I continued to look at her, I could see that we possessed some of the same features, and I started to think about what kind of person she would be five years from now. I imagined all the things we could do together and how much I loved her already.

Everything was touch-and-go for about a week, but my mom pulled through, and soon it was time to go home. Our family was very supportive, and everyone took turns in shifts coming out to our house to make sure we had meals and to help take care of Bekah. My mom was somewhat bedridden because she was still recovering, so it was comforting to have family around.

I look back now, and I find it hard to believe all of this took place about thirteen years ago. My sister and I are very close, and I see her as an extension of myself. I think about the future and how we will be a continual source of support for one another. It's hard to believe that at one time I dreaded her existence. Now I can't imagine life without her.

Jessica Wilson

My Other Family

It's four in the afternoon and I am heading out to yet another of my best friend Angie's family get-togethers. This time it's Mother's Day.

I really hate this day and Father's Day, too. These are two of the most dreaded days for me. I can't get my arms around these "family holidays." Those people with parents complain about them. The ones without them wallow in stories of the past.

Angie constantly complains about her mother's nosiness and her grandmother's pickiness. All of these mundane complaints drive me crazy. I live in a foster home, where people come and go. My adoptive mother died a few years ago and my adoptive father several years before her. I now live with one of my foster sisters, her new husband, my little brother and several foster brothers and sisters. I feel far apart from them in many ways.

No one has a baby album of me or infant stories or knows when I started crawling or knows whom I look like.

I have a trinket wrapped for Angie's mother, a picture of all of us under a covered bridge. I spend my holiday vacations with them in Vermont. I play the part of "the other daughter," to fulfill a need I have to belong to something other than my foster family.

I go downstairs, brush my hair and listen to my foster sisters at the kitchen table. They, too, are sad. They are relishing times gone by with their mother, my adopted mother.

"Remember when Johnny was born?"

"Remember when I ran away?"

"Remember how mad Mom was when we snuck out?"

I listen from the bathroom door and feel a pain shoot down my shoulders to my heart. I know none of these stories, and wish I had my own.

I never really got along with my adopted mother. I came to her when I was four, and I never felt that close to her. A hard-working woman, she had six children of her own, whom she raised pretty much alone. My little brother had a great connection to her. Having come to her when he was an infant, he knew nothing else, and she doted on him all day long.

I was close with my adopted father until he passed away just a few years after I was adopted. He was always a great comfort to me. He was probably the only person who never said an unkind word to me. His memory has been a security blanket for me during my teenage years.

Angie's father beeps the horn outside my house as I finish brushing my hair and doing my makeup. In all the years I have known them, they have never come to my front door. Maybe they are afraid of something that is outside of their norm. But, it is nice to keep our "families" separate. It gives me a secret retreat and my own little place to go when everything else seems unwelcoming.

I grab my gift and hop in the car. Angie's mother smells like Elizabeth Arden's Red Door perfume, and her father has a mysterious scent I can never pinpoint. Angie sits in her Ralph Lauren tailored jeans and distinct conservative blouse. Her bright pink toes shine through her new sandals.

This is nice. We are eating at a restaurant on the north shore, where I don't fit in at all, but I smile anyway and enjoy the panache. The waters of the sound are behind us, and the smells of rosemary and garlic rise from our hot plates.

Angie and her parents talk about other Mother's Days, with grandparents and even great-grandparents. They tell me how silly Angie was as a baby and how hard it was at first to be a parent. How Mother's Day takes on a whole new meaning when you become a parent. I sit quietly and laugh and tell a few of my crazy foster-family stories and concentrate on my potatoes. They are firm yet soft, like my heart.

After lunch we go to Angie's house to meet up with her aunt and grandparents for dessert. Her house is always so cheerful. The light blue couches always smell of lilies. Nothing has changed since grammar school except for maybe a moved picture or a new quilt. It is solid, quiet and comforting. I am envious. I smile through coffee and then head home. I only live two blocks away so I decide to walk and take some time to think. I pass the large yellow house I always wanted to buy. I pass the gardens of the pretty college girl, Anne, and eventually end up at my brick and aluminum house.

In the yard is my brother, redheaded and crazy with youth, and my foster sister and her husband. People are coming and going. And they stop me and say, "Phyllis . . . remember when you . . ."

And we all laugh; laugh so hard the sky can hear us. And for that moment I am all right.

Phyllis Anne Guilmette

She's My Sister

He was twelve years old and going on sixteen. He gelled his hair into spikes and wore his pants with the crotch below the knees. He listened to rap music, watched MTV, and generously bestowed on me the nickname, "Sister C."

Yet when I looked at my brother Matthew, I kept expecting to find the little kid he once had been—the sweet, eager boy who used to drag me outside by the arm, begging me to play football with him or to help him build a clubhouse or to catch salamanders in the creek. That Matthew had always looked up to me. I had been his hero, his big sister and—despite our age difference of several years—his best friend. Now everything was changing.

These days, instead of our usual hikes through the woods, Matthew spent his time indoors, talking on the phone. He refused to dive after the football when we played catch for fear of getting grass stains on his designer jeans, and he hollered at me whenever I bopped him playfully on the head, because how dare I mess up his perfectly sculpted hair.

Of course I had always known he would grow up eventually—I just hadn't expected it to happen overnight.

Matthew was becoming a teenager faster than I thought possible. It was tough facing the fact that I was no longer the center of my brother's universe, and I worried about where I fit in this new life of his.

I discovered the answer during the spring of Matthew's seventh-grade year. That was when the kids from my brother's small private school attended a weeklong outdoor education camp. I had always been involved with Matthew's school, and because I loved both the outdoors and kids, I volunteered to chaperone.

On the very first day of camp, I was playing catch with Matthew and some of his friends. We were tossing my brother's football back and forth when some older boys— older than Matthew, at any rate, a few around my age— sauntered over and began snatching the football in midair.

These boys were obviously part of the "in" crowd here at camp. They dressed like teen pop stars and strutted around like they owned the place. It wasn't long before they had joined my brother and his friends, starting up a competition to see who could throw the football the hardest.

A year ago Matthew would have stood quietly to the side, not sure how to handle himself around "cool" guys like these. But not anymore. Now, my formerly shy kid brother jumped right into the action, showing off exaggerated football player poses, playing the part of the goofball and making everybody laugh. I could hardly believe the change.

For the rest of the week I barely saw my brother. During meals he sat at the most crowded table in the cafeteria, the one packed with young teenagers sporting the latest styles and laughing loudly. Not only that, but my brother was usually the center of attention, making pyramids out of water glasses and blowing straw wrappers at all of his buddies. He was the wacky kid everybody in camp knew and loved. As for me, I quickly became known as

"Matthew's big sister."

I was happy for him; I really was. For the first time in his life my brother had more friends than he knew what to do with. But a part of me resented being cast aside like an old shoe. I was the one who had taught Matthew how to blow the wrappers off of straws. I had taught him to play football. I had been with him for every major moment in his life until now, and suddenly it was as if none of that mattered.

Or so I thought.

Then, on the last evening of camp, Matthew ran up to me as I was heading back to my cabin. "Chrissy!" he called out. "We're gonna play football! You have to come!"

I blinked in surprise. "Are you sure you want me to?" I asked. "I won't embarrass you?"

"Not unless you stink up the place," he replied, but he was smiling. "It doesn't matter. Just play."

I followed Matthew to the football field. All his cool new friends were there waiting, and when they saw me, they laughed. "I thought you were getting a real player!" one of the guys exclaimed. "Why'd you bring a girl?"

"She's my sister," was Matthew's reply. "And she's really good!"

"Hey, girl!" another boy laughed. "Do you know what this thing is?" He held the football two inches from my face.

"Yeah." I grinned and jokingly shoved my fist in front of the boy's nose. "Do you know what this is?"

A few of the guys snickered, and we were able to get on with the game.

As bad luck would have it, I wound up on the opposite team from Matthew. Still, I wanted to score a hundred touchdowns to prove to my brother that his faith in me wasn't misplaced.

Unfortunately, I never got that chance. The guys on my team simply refused to pass the ball to a girl. In fact, they wouldn't let me anywhere near it. That football game might have been the most frustrating I'd ever played . . . had it not been for Matthew.

As soon as he realized what was happening, he began to stick up for me. He shouted loudly over at his teammates.

"It's a good thing they're not throwing the ball to my sister or we'd be losing big time! She's wide open during every play!

"Hey, if you hadn't pushed in front of my sister she could've gotten that kick return and made a touchdown! Lucky for us you're not letting the fast person touch the ball!

"At least my sister isn't guarding our good players or we'd never even score!"

Over and over, throughout the entire game, my brother stood up for me in front of all his new friends. As badly as he wanted to be one of them, and as important as it was for him to be cool, Matthew proved that I was even more important. "She's my sister," he had said proudly. And the awesome thing was that he was still saying it, even though I couldn't even try to score a single touchdown. He claimed me even when his friends laughed.

That night I realized that I no longer had to worry about losing my brother as he became a teenager. I didn't have to worry about ever losing him. Because even though our relationship might change over time, it would always be strong.

That night Matthew proved that no matter what, he would always care about me, and on that night I had never been prouder to be called his sister.

Christina Dotson

Everything Is Possible

Everything is possible. How many times did my mother tell me that?

She could say that. She had never tried to get a hit off Mongo, the fireballing left-hander from Morristown, or attempted to get 100 percent right on one of Mrs. Bach's spelling tests. Mrs. Bach always put in a couple of tricky words that were actually spelled the way they sounded.

We were sitting on the front steps of our old farmhouse one warm summer night. This is something my mother and I did a lot when the mosquitoes would allow it. We had no air-conditioning, so it was a little cooler on the steps, and I guess we just sat there waiting for my father to build us a front porch—a place where we could sit and watch the world go by. Dad never did get around to that because he was too busy milking cows.

The steps were a great place to talk. We would listen to the birds getting in their final songs before darkness fell. We would listen to the frogs and toads romancing their mates. This particular night, we watched a large airplane fly overhead. We wondered where the occupants were headed while we sat on our steps.

"I sure would like to fly in one of those things someday," I said.

"Everything is possible," my mother replied.

Ha! A lot she knew about it. Neither my mother nor my father had ever set foot in a plane, let alone flown in one. It was then that I saw the fireflies blinking along the edges of our yard. The flashes of the lightning bugs demanded that they be watched.

"Get the jar!" ordered my mother enthusiastically.

I got the large jar from my upstairs bedroom. It was a jar meant for collecting and holding insects. It was equipped with a lid with air holes poked into it in order to make the fireflies' short stay as comfortable as possible. We would normally observe captives for only a brief time before releasing them unharmed. I presented the jar to my mother for her approval.

"Let's catch some fireflies!" she said.

We chased and we caught. My mother was much better at chasing than she was at catching. We laughed a lot. The fireflies may have done some laughing, too. Who knew? After a bit, I had caught a number of the elusive fireflies. I placed the jar of captured fireflies near the steps we sat on. The jar glowed in the night. Mom and I smiled. We watched in silence until another airplane flew over, its lights blinking across the dark sky.

"Yup," I said, "I'd sure like to fly in an airplane one day."

"Everything is possible," my mother said once more.

"Do you really think that's so?" I asked as I picked up the jar and prepared to release its luminescent prisoners.

"How can someone holding a jar full of stars believe that anything is impossible?" asked my mother.

So whenever I feel like I can't do something, I remember the fireflies.

Al Batt

Grandpa's Gift

Grandpa Louie was quite positively the most respected and well-known man my young eyes had seen. His knowledge of what seemed to be everyone in town was spectacular. Growing up, I watched him answer every question with references, intellect and backing and thrust his love upon each and every person without any need of the love being returned. His volunteer coaching career spanned nearly fifty years, and children were his passion. Loving others was certainly his calling.

But Grandpa Louie didn't do as he did for the return of love, and when he was given a gift, either in thanks or for any certain gift-giving occasion, he frequently had trouble accepting it. I remember it being nearly impossible to purchase anything for him.

One Christmas, while I was still very young, I decided that I wanted to be able to give each member of my family a gift. Being the age I was, I didn't have much money of my own. Most of my gifts were handmade. But Grandpa's I bought. It was a red glossy key chain that simply said "Grandpa." I do not recall how much or how little I spent on the silly little gift, but I was quite proud. One can only imagine how disappointed I was when Grandpa opened it with his characteristic half scowl, nodded at me and then set it aside. This was just his way, but I was too young to understand how every present could not be means for celebration!

Years passed and somehow I never saw Grandpa's keys or the key chain. He kept them in his pocket, and I was too afraid to ask what had happened to the little red Christmas gift. But I always looked for glimpses when he would arrive at our house with a car full of groceries as a surprise. He brought fruits and vegetables for my mother, ice cream for me and licorice for my brothers. Each time I looked, though, his keys were in his pocket or somewhere out of my sight.

Grandpa grew older, and with time his health declined. His mind and ability to tell stories, however, refused to do the same. One day he seemed worse than ever before, and we quickly took him to the hospital. He had horrid cramps in his legs and had pneumonia. After being checked out, he returned to our family farm to recover. My father took me aside and asked if I would be able to help Grandpa regain his strength at the gym. By this point I was working at a local health club and had dedicated myself to bodybuilding. I gladly accepted the task.

The following weekend Grandpa still had not regained his health, but I visited him nonetheless to talk to him about our personal training sessions. Grandpa sat up in his chair with a tube in his nose, unshaven. I had never seen him unshaven or dressed in such shoddy clothing, since appearance always was important to him. Something wasn't right, but Grandpa smiled anyway. He told me that he heard I was going to be his personal trainer, a thought I beamed at. Then he proceeded to tell me that I would need to pick him up—me, who had just turned sixteen—since he could not drive, and that I should use his car. Then he offered his car to me when he died. I was emotionally torn. I could not imagine my life without Grandpa in it. He then reached into his pocket, brought forth his hand and advised me to go get acquainted with the vehicle. In his hand shined a set of car keys accompanied by an old gray key chain.

Grandpa went back to the hospital later that morning. He slipped into a coma he never came out of. Later that night he died.

The mourning quickly funneled through my family to all in the community. Hundreds upon hundreds showed up for the funeral.

And me? I drove to the funeral in an old, beat-up Mercury, courtesy of Grandpa. At the steering column dangled my own set of keys, with an old gray key chain attached firmly. If you looked closely enough you could still see the little red specks of paint that had clung on all of those years where the word "Grandpa" used to be.

It was the first present I ever gave Grandpa, and the last one he ever gave me.

Cazzey Louis Cereghino

A New Coat

If there is one thing that growing up in the Midwest instilled in me, besides my insatiable craving for red meat, it is a love for football. I was born and raised in Cleveland, Ohio, and spent most of my impressionable childhood years rooting for the Cleveland Browns during the '80s. In those years, the Browns were referred to as the "Cardiac Kids," seemingly destined to always come one drive, fumble or interception away from a championship victory. Thousands of fans would travel over an hour through inclement weather to arrive at the dingy yet beloved Municipal Stadium and root for their heroes. I was one of them. Back then, my room—like so many of my friends'— was a shrine to Browns football. The walls were plastered with banners and posters of Ozzie Newsome, Bernie Kosar and my favorite player, Webster Slaughter.

Late in the 1987 season, I went with my dad to the nearby mall so he could buy a new coat. We didn't have a lot of money, but my mom convinced my dad to replace his old coat, which had some pretty sizable holes it. I was only eleven, but my memory of that day remains vivid. It was lightly snowing when we arrived at the mall. The parking lot was plowed, but the lines were still buried under the snow. My dad did an extremely crooked parking job next to an uneven row of crooked cars. The minute the car came to a resting stop, I was out of the door and racing up to the mall entrance, leaving my dad trailing behind. As I approached the familiar tinted glass doors, one of them swung open and a huge figure came through it. The man was wearing a black jacket and sunglasses instead of a brown jersey with the number 84 printed on it, but I immediately recognized him. It was Webster Slaughter.

My heart began pounding, and I felt my ears go flush. I could barely contain my excitement as the man approached me. I looked up at my hero towering in front of me, and in a shaky voice said, "You're Webster Slaughter, right?" He stopped in midstride just as he was passing and glanced back. "Yeah. Are you a Browns fan?" he replied. I think I startled him as I began to rattle off at the mouth at a hundred words a second. I proceeded to tell him I was a *huge* Browns fan and that he was my favorite player. He smiled but began to walk away saying something about being in a big hurry, which I didn't hear because I hadn't stopped talking. Desperately, I yelled to his back for an autograph, but he made no sign that he heard me and briskly kept going. As fast as he had emerged, he was gone.

I felt a hand on my shoulder and looked up to see my dad. I wondered how long he had been there. "Who was that?" he asked. When I told him, he looked back up and squinted his eyes at the parking lot, but I knew Webster was already gone. I could feel my dad looking at me, probably for some details of the chance encounter, but I said nothing. As we approached the men's department, he finally asked me what had happened. "Nothing really. He was in a hurry. I just told him he was cool," I blurted back. My dad gave me a concerned look, usually reserved for times he suspected I was about to do something to embarrass him. He dug into his pocket, pulled at a crumpled bunch of bills and handed me a few dollars. He told me to go play at the arcade while he picked out a coat. I grabbed the money and wandered off. About a half an hour later, my dad came for me and we headed home. Once there he opened the shopping bag in his hand. He told me he had a surprise and reached into it. "After you left, guess who I ran into?" he said with a smile on his face. I just stared blankly. "Webster Slaughter came into the store and said he saw me with you. He asked where you were and I said you were at the arcade. He said he went back to his car to get this for you, but you were gone." He pulled his hand out of the bag and in it was a glossy photo of Webster Slaughter signed, "To my greatest fan." I was so overjoyed I almost cried. I grabbed the picture and bolted up the stairs to my room. Proudly, I placed the signed photo on my dresser. I just sat on my bed almost in tears and stared. It's hard to describe what I was feeling. Then I noticed something on the side. I looked closely at it and saw it was a small tag labeled $30. My first emotion was anger that I had been tricked. I stomped downstairs and yelled for my dad. There was no answer. Then I heard the sound of the shovel out front and went to the window. I stared out of the frosted pane at my dad, shoveling the walkway. He was wearing the same old coat with holes in the sleeves and back.

I thank my dad for the unacknowledged sacrifices he made for my siblings and me. I still have the picture of Webster Slaughter, but now on my dresser sits a picture of my dad and me.

Peter Lim

Dreams Inspired by Dad

Dad can celebrate a humiliating loss on a golden
    September afternoon
Curled up in the corner of the car, I am sulking
The window is cracked, air rushing over the odor of
    sweaty shin guards
Perspiration shimmers on my forehead, limitless with rage
The buzz and crackle of Dad's oldies music flirts with my
    sour mood

I turn to Dad, and the laughter in his eyes bewitches me
In a flash, disappointing experiences are forgotten in our
    unspoken moment
We dream as friends
Just the two of us

We chatter endlessly, free to be ourselves
I teach Dad the lingo, who is babeworthy, what is new to
    wear
I dramatize my dislike of school, outspoken against use-
    less knowledge
But Dad helps me discover the power of that knowledge

Each assignment is a beautiful achievement, a gilded
   cloud of hope
His words dance like slow-falling snow
Gifts a beloved father gives his child
Acts of a father's undeniable love

Emily Peck

My Brother, Ben

Each handicap is like a hurdle in a steeplechase, and when you ride up to it, if you throw your heart over, the horse will go along, too.

Lawrence Bixby

When my brother was born he looked different from other babies. The doctors told my parents he had Down's syndrome. Everybody, including my parents and relatives, started crying. I was only three at the time, so I wasn't sure what Down's syndrome was, but I knew it wasn't good. I also knew that I finally had the baby brother I wanted, even if he wasn't perfect. The doctors said Benjamin might need help doing simple things such as walking, talking, eating and interacting with people. I was told I would need to be extra careful with Ben, and that I might someday have to stand up for him and protect him. Of course, none of these warnings fazed me; I knew from the second I laid eyes on him that I loved him.

As Benjamin and I got older, we were always together,

always helping each other. After Benjamin learned to walk, we wanted to get him to jump, run and move around. Since Ben liked to follow my lead, his therapist or Mom would have me do the exercise first, and then Ben would try to do it. That procedure worked better than just anybody showing him how to move. Following me was Ben's way of saying he loved me.

A few years ago, I went away with some friends for the day. About five of us were just sitting in the van, and we started talking about our siblings. My friends were saying how stupid their siblings were and what they did to agitate them. I hadn't said anything; I was just listening in amazement. I had never thought there were brothers and sisters that just didn't get along. Suddenly I said, "I love my brother."

I said "love" proudly because it was true. All my friends thought I was a little weird, but they all knew Benjamin and how sweet he was. I was glad I told my friends I love my brother. He's the best little brother, and he loves me right back.

I would describe Ben as a very cute little nine-year-old boy that would do anything for anybody. If people tease him because he has Down's syndrome he doesn't scream and call them names. Instead, he tries even harder to become their friend.

There are no second thoughts in my head when I hear people making fun of Ben. I go right up to them and explain that Ben has Down's syndrome and that life isn't as easy for him as it is for us, that if you give Ben a chance he'll be the best he can be at whatever it is you want him to be.

I think Ben is perfect just the way he is. I will always love Ben, and he will always love me, no matter what.

Donata Allison

Some Service

My father was the hardest-working man, and he loved to give orders: what to eat, how long to stay up, even when to shower. After a long day's work, he always stretched out in his throne-like recliner, making us take off his socks and shoes. "Give me some service," he would say.

When I was sixteen, he brought me to the restaurant where he waited tables. It was Thanksgiving Day, and he didn't even bother to tell me where we were going. He just told me to slap on a pair of black slacks and a white dress shirt and get in the car. When we got to the restaurant he handed me a jacket and bow tie, telling me—not asking me—that today I would start to work.

All the waiters were surprised to see me come in wearing a busboy's outfit. I mean, they had seen me in the booths as a kid, eating dishes of ice cream. They swirled all around, plates stacked along their arms. The customers all looked wealthy and important, the men dressed in suits, the women wearing mink coats and tons of makeup. Each table was clothed in a sparkling white tablecloth. I just knew I was gonna spill things on all these people's laps.

An old, gruff Chinese man, the head busboy, showed me

the layout of the kitchen and the dishwashing section, a flat metal table stacked with dirty plates. He flung the dirty utensils, forks and knives, with fury into this gray murky basin of water. Some of the utensils first ricocheted off the wall. There was no way I was going to copy his style.

I cleared dirty dishes from the tables into a bus box of my own, learning to balance it and not to set the box on the floor. I barely knew the menu, but toward late evening my father made me go over to a table of customers—"a party"—and take their order. "Does the lasagna have any onions in it?" the lady asked, frowning into the menu. "I'm very allergic to onions." Allergic to onions? I didn't know there could be such a thing. My father overheard, and he told the woman, "Yes, it has onions. Take the ziti instead." I managed with the rest of the order and served the food— ziti for the woman and broiled salmon for her husband.

Soon I was working part-time as a waiter. My protective father made me suspicious of everyone, the other waiters, even the customers. "Pick up the money the second you see it, before someone else puts it in his pocket." Most of the other waiters were over seventy years old. Roy had tattoos on his forearms from his days in the Navy. Mad Diego used to work as a shoe-shiner in Panama. And Walter, the slowest waiter, was still hoping to be an actor, performing poetry for strangers in the subway.

With his broad smile, my father was the customers' flat-out favorite. They were demanding, but he knew how to take care of them, and they kept on coming back, lining up at the door even when the other waiters had open tables. My father would introduce me to them: this one's a dentist, a lawyer, a wheeler and dealer in real estate. I was never really sure if he was telling me that one day I would have such a job, or if he wanted me to recognize them in case someday he couldn't be there to take their orders.

His shift went from 2 P.M. to midnight. After 8 P.M. the

other waiters went home, and he worked alone, covering the entire restaurant. On many nights over the years, even while I was in college, he would call me for help if it got too busy. I'd drop everything, grab my stuff and race to the restaurant. "Hey, the bull pen made it on time!" the cashier always joked as I rushed through the door.

Maybe it was all those long hours and being around so much food, but my father's health got worse. He gained weight, had trouble sleeping and was often on antibiotics.

One day when I was off from college, my father called me from work. I groaned, knowing my free day would be ruined. "Can you come to the restaurant fast, and bring me a fresh white shirt? Size seventeen." He hung up. I went there quickly. But when I got there I found him in the shadows of the back room of the restaurant, pale and ashen.

"Why'd you need a white shirt?" I asked him, "Yours got dirty?" And then I saw his shirtfront and stopped; it had a dark red blotch spread across the front of it. "Are you all right?" I asked. He just shook his head softly. I told him to go home. "I won't let you work like this." I went into the locker room and put on the shirt myself, gathering his pencils, waiter jacket and checkbook. Worried that I would not be able to handle the station alone, my father wouldn't leave until my mother finally came with the station wagon to take him home.

Somehow I managed by myself with my father's customers. I found out later that he did not go to the hospital until nighttime, when he woke up coughing blood. Even then he insisted that he was just vomiting some beets he'd eaten. My mother had to practically drag him to the ambulance.

Those doctors saved his life. It turned out that a growth was putting pressure on his esophagus. Hooked to an IV in intensive care, he was too weak to sit up or sip water or even have family come see him. I couldn't believe this man, who had taught me to swim in the waters of Coney Island, would ever be anything other than invincible. After all, he was the strongest man in the world.

I visited him at night after work, the bow tie stuffed into my back pocket, my white shirt and black pants smelling of the restaurant. I went upstairs through the maze of corridors and florescent lights. My mother had arranged it with the staff so that I could see him after hours. After a bunch of false starts, when I thought this person lying down, white and weak, must surely be my father, I arrived at his bed. His appearance was so abrupt and sudden. There he was.

He opened his eyes immediately. He shook his head a little, as if to make some sort of comment on the situation like, "Me in bed, can you believe it?"

And then I leaned over. I leaned over and kissed him on the cheek, my ribs pressing into the metal rails of the bed, because I knew I loved him, and because he was still alive, and he would get better. We would all make him better, my family and the doctors and everyone. And I kissed him because I never kissed him enough; I probably hadn't kissed him in years. "I love you. I took care of all your customers," I whispered to him, and kissed him again. And then I heard a beep and then another. The beeps were coming from the machine he was hooked up to, its monitor showing the lines rising higher and higher to the point of a mountain. The sounds of his pulse.

Eli Shoshani

My Father's Truth

My father says that when he was a little boy, he saw a French farm wife chop off a chicken's head. Dad says the chicken ran around for a while before the farm wife picked it up. He says that the air that day was sweating, and the chicken looked as if it were sweating, too. My dad says that a plucked chicken looks like a harried banker—all thin and scrawny and miserable.

When my dad was in his late teens, he saw the race riots in Chicago. He says that he and a black friend of his climbed on top of a roof to watch the people protest. He saw men pushing cars over, men punching each other, men screaming like shrews. He saw white and black men glare at each other, ashamed of their own fear and each despising the other for it. He says they tried to kill each other in the dank Chicago streets. My dad tells me that fighting people are sly snakes, and he warns me to stay away from them. He says that when a man is in the company of snakes, sooner or later he will get poison spit in his eye.

My dad was twenty-three when he went to Thailand. He says that the children there try to sell the GIs pencils at an equivalent of five American dollars. Most GIs buy the pencils because the children look as if they're starving and could use the five dollars. He says that he would visit orphanages and that all the children went barefoot. He would bring crackers with him, and the children would line up perfectly and hold out their cupped hands for a cracker.

My dad is no longer a little boy in France. He doesn't live in Chicago, either. And he never went back to Thailand to buy five-dollar pencils. My dad teaches art to children, who mostly don't appreciate it. He can't tell them about the orphans in Thailand with no shoes. He can't tell them about the fear he had when the rioting scarred the streets. All he can tell them about is Picasso or Rembrandt. But he can tell me what he knows to be true. And I can remember.

I probably won't become a harried banker, and I might even see Chicago's streets. Maybe I'll end up in Thailand buying a five-dollar pencil from a barefoot girl. Either way, I'll at least have some truths to go by, and my father will have done his job well.

Rianna Ouellette

6

TOUGH STUFF

Character cannot be developed in ease and quiet. Only through experience of trial and suffering can the soul be strengthened, ambition inspired and success achieved.

Helen Keller

Don't Stop the Dance

Christy Gonzales killed herself in the spring of our senior year.

She was beautiful. She played volleyball. She was homecoming queen.

Everyone was more than shocked. She'd always been so happy, so popular and so active in extracurriculars. She had so much love and light. She always signed her name with a heart above the "i" and included her middle name, which was Valentina.

Why she did it is a human mystery, but the obvious reason given was that she was heartbroken because her boyfriend—some sophomore, no less—dumped her.

I remember the silence in our homeroom class—except for the sounds of people crying, boys and girls, jocks and nerds.

As the hour wore on, Nick Denver, the quarterback, quietly spoke to Fred Gregory through his sniffles.

"Remember," Nick said, "when Christy punched me in the face at the seventh-grade dance?"

They both started to laugh, softly. Nick had been making fun of her, and she lost her temper and gave him a sock straight to his nose that started him bleeding.

He was shocked, but recognized he deserved it.

I could imagine Christy doing something like that. Although she was the sweetest person in the world, she had so much fire—she lived so in the moment of her feelings and emotions.

In English class, freshman year, we'd read the other's stories aloud to class because we were too scared to read our own.

She'd let me cheat off her geometry test my sophomore year. We'd both been caught.

I'd once had a secret romantic view of suicide. I thought that it would be nice to have everyone miss me, to have my name forever bound with the tragedy of a depth no one could fathom. I imagined the kind of silence in the classrooms, the people sobbing in the halls. I imagined how people I didn't know or barely knew would try to remember every detail—what I had said to them, what I had worn the last day.

She had worn red the last day. At lunch the last day, she had said she was tired of always getting the Tater Tots, tomorrow she was getting fries.

I could not have imagined a better funeral for Christy with the heavens outpouring rain like tears. The entire town was there, mourning.

I just kept thinking about how we all kept on going but Christy's life stopped.

When I want it all to stop, I remember that you can't dance without a body, and you can't cry without eyes, and you can't have the luxury of feeling when you aren't here.

I wish she could have loved herself when she didn't feel it from anyone else.

Simone Would

When Daddy Died

Filled with the frenetic restlessness of my fourteen years, I impatiently stood in my parents' kitchen listening to the drone of their conversation. *Hurry up, hurry up,* was my sole thought as I beat an accompanying tap with my foot. The bus would be arriving at the corner stop any minute, and I was tired of listening to chatter about doctors' appointments and chest pain and shortness of breath. My main goal was to get to school on time and avoid a detention slip.

I couldn't wait any longer. "Bye, Pop," I called out. Totally out of character, my father was lying in bed while I tore through the house grabbing my jacket, lunch and bus fare. Mother was making Daddy a cup of tea when I hesitated at the door. It was the first time in my life that I could remember not kissing him good-bye. Oh, well. No time for a kiss today. Gotta go. My friends were waiting. He'll be here this afternoon. I'll kiss him then.

Besides, Daddy, at age fifty-four, was a strapping five feet, eleven inches. He was a railroad engineer working long, unorthodox hours on his daily train routes. He led the life of the rails, playing cards at the station house with the rest of the crew until his next "run." Sure, he smoked unfiltered Camel cigarettes, but so did most of his friends and coworkers. He was usually the first one on the dance floor, whirling my mother around in a dizzying polka, stopping long enough to quench his thirst with a beer.

In between his extended train trips Pop tilled and weeded his garden, coaxing abundant crops from the earth. The back porches of the neighborhood were filled with the fruits of his labor, and if the neighbor lady were home, he'd stop by for a cup of coffee and a good joke. Everyone loved to see his big smile.

So, on that cold February morning, I didn't give it much of a thought when I naively decided to exit without my usual hug and kiss. There was nothing to worry about. Besides, my father had promised to refinish a piece of battered furniture he'd picked up at the salvage yard. His workshop in the cellar was outfitted with the lifetime collection of a man who saw beauty in wood and castoffs. A favorite comment of his after a trip to the dump was, "Look at this beauty. Why, just a little sanding and it will be as good as new." Our home was filled with little beauties.

His lesson to look beyond the outer shell of a piece of furniture also included the people we met. A particularly grouchy salesclerk was excused with, "Well, her husband is sick. She has a lot on her mind." He didn't let other people's bad moods ruin his day.

As I ran into the brisk air I called over my shoulder, "See ya later!" But the guilty nagging of unfinished business bore into my conscience. I tried to relieve the ache by calling home at the end of the school day. Daddy was about to drive to the doctor's office for his appointment, and he'd see me when I got home. Absolved, I went about the business of a high-school freshman.

Something was very wrong when I got off the bus at the end of my road. I could see a black stretch limousine parked in front of my house—the kind of car only the funeral director in town drove. I tried to run on rubbery legs, but no matter how hard I pushed myself, it felt like I was going in slow motion. Breathlessly, I flung open the kitchen door and stopped in my tracks. My mother's face told the story. Next to her, the mortician began his technical explanation of what had happened. I couldn't hear for the blood rushing into my ears. The only sound was an empty roar.

The next few days were tearless and raw. I sat in the back of the funeral parlor looking at the body of my father in the casket. *I'm only a kid! He's not supposed to die yet! My friends all have their fathers. He's too good and too young. It isn't fair.* I spiraled into my empty core and knew that life as I knew it was over.

There was no rushing out the door now. I didn't care about school or my friends. Burning into my brain was the memory of the lost moment, words never spoken and the hug never felt. Time was the enemy, and it overwhelmed me as the clock ticktocked through the night. Hour after hour I heard the chime until dawn viciously invaded my room. I was in no hurry for the day's events.

I wouldn't allow the tears that were pushing against my eyes to fall for fear that I'd be unable to stop the torrent. The pain that saturated every pore of my body prevented me from hearing or seeing anything but my father. I wanted to be invisible, to be with Daddy. Who would come to my concerts? My graduation? My whole being screamed, *I need you! How could God do this?*

The hours, the days, the years after my father's death were blurry and turbulent as I foolishly tried to escape reality. Attempting to fill the aching void in my heart with the empty promises of a fast life delivered only trouble, and time did not heal my wounds. I was too busy being angry about my loss, but the day came when my grades couldn't fall any lower, when there were no more parties, when my dearest and oldest friends stopped calling, when I couldn't look at myself in the mirror without shame, and the dam of tears broke.

For the first time, I mourned the death of my father, allowing emotion to wash over me. I cried for the loss of my childhood, for the way things used to be when my father was in our home, for the good times never to be realized, but most of all, for the person I had become. I felt like I could never be normal again.

Powerless, I called on the God of my childhood, and the healing began. The simple act of asking for help was the first step of a long and difficult journey. Daddy's death lost its sting as my rebellious, destructive existence became a new life filled with self-discipline and responsibility. There were many times when I felt like a jigsaw piece that didn't fit into a puzzle, but eventually that feeling left. Gratitude stepped in and took its place.

I had known pain. I learned to know joy. Finally, I had become my father's daughter.

Irene Budzynski

Life Is a Gift

Difficult times have helped me understand better than before, how infinitely rich and beautiful life is in every way, and that so many things that one goes worrying about are of no importance whatsoever.

Isak Dinisen

My hands trembled as I let the phone fall carelessly on my unmade bed; this had to be a mistake. There was no way Gray could be dead!

At that moment, everything in my life seemed insignificant. How could anything else matter when my best friend—someone I had known, trusted and loved since eighth grade—was gone forever? I looked down at the clothes I was folding and saw Gray's national soccer team jersey lying on my bed. My whole body froze. *How could this be true?* I wanted to cry, but I was in complete shock.

It took a month after Gray's death before I was emotionally ready to visit his grave site. It was a cold Sunday afternoon and the rain bounced off the pavement as I stared at my muddy black boots. The fifty feet from the car to the grave seemed like fifty miles. I looked around at all the different tombstones and flowers, and I thought about just how many people must have done exactly what I was here to do. They had all endured the pain of visiting loved ones who had passed away. Tears streamed down my face as I began to walk toward my best friend's grave. My legs felt like they weighed one hundred pounds each, and my stomach twisted into a knot so tight that I thought I was going to be sick. I did not want to look up and see his name written on the temporary headstone. I wanted to savor my last moments of hope that he would come back.

The rained turned into a downpour, and it was cold enough that I could see my breath. I did not feel a thing; my entire body was numb. I shut my eyes, hoping, praying this was all some horrible dream. When I opened them, I was still in the cemetery, blurred by the shield of tears that covered my eyes. Taking a deep breath, I glanced up to the sky and made one last desperate wish that I would wake up from this nightmare. Then I slowly turned my eyes downward and looked at his name written on the headstone, the fresh hay laying over his body, the wilting flowers with water dripping off their petals and splashing into the soil covering his casket. The moment I saw his grave, I finally stopped fantasizing that he would come back, and the reality sank in that I would never again see my best friend. I knew this was good-bye, but I could not leave. I did not want to walk away; I yearned to stay by his side forever. I stood there and let my mind drift to all of our experiences together, from the time we fell in love to our first real fight. The memories came in crystal clear torrents.

"Do not tell him that I like him! Pinky swear?" I told my best friend Falon in eight grade. I was in love. He was taller than all the other boys and had shoulder-length blond hair just like Taylor Hanson, from my all-time favorite band, Hanson. Sure enough, by the end of the day Falon had told him how I felt. Word was now out that I had a very serious crush on Gray. Every time we passed in the hallways, my cheeks would turn a soft pink. I had no idea what was happening; this was definitely not like me. I never liked guys; I was always "one of the guys." My friends would try to get me to talk to him, but no words would come out. Then our eighth-grade dance made all my dreams about him come true. Gray dedicated "All My Life" by KC and Jo Jo to me and asked me to dance. I was on cloud nine. We dated for about three weeks and then broke up. (In middle school, a week was considered a long-term relationship.)

After we got through the soap opera breakup, Gray and I were inseparable. Even distance did not hurt our friendship. In the tenth grade, Gray was offered the opportunity of his lifetime; he was asked to be the captain of the United States Junior National Soccer Team. He had to move to Florida to attend a special training center. He frequently traveled to tournaments in Italy, China, France and other locations throughout the world. Despite his distance and hectic schedule, he was there for me during all of my most difficult hours, and he always took the time to call with encouraging words.

I'll never forget the time I spent the night at Falon's house in tenth grade. We were lying in bed talking about our past relationships, teasing each other about our old boyfriends and laughing for hours. It was around 3:30 A.M. that morning, and right as we were about to drift off to sleep, Falon said something that will stay with me forever. "LP, you know that Gray loves you more than anybody ever will. You are lucky to have such a good friend." At the time, I didn't think much of this statement, as I took our friendship for granted. I never recognized just how lucky

I was to have a friend that I could call at any time of the night, who would talk with me until I fell back asleep. Only now, in his absence, do I realize what an incredible friend and person Gray truly was.

Just two months ago, I approached Gray for advice, as I had frequently in the past. I was caught in a dilemma, debating whether or not I should transfer to Appalachian State University. Gray's words were simple and wise; he told me to follow my heart and that, no matter what, he would always be there to support and guide me. I then asked if he knew that I loved him, and he told me that he never doubted it. If I only knew that this was the last time I would talk to him, I would have driven to Furman and spent the entire night with him! However, I know I can't live regretting the past or wishing I had done more.

I have learned to cherish every moment I have with the people I love. I take time to fully enjoy life, and I try to appreciate each minute I am given on this planet. I did not "lose" Gray. He is still my best friend, only now he is guiding me from above. I can talk to him every night and know he is listening, and I still see him in my dreams. Gray was my angel on earth, and now he is my angel in heaven.

Lindsay Ann Parker

My Mother: Her Depression, Her Strength

I grasped my blanket in one hand and my doll in the other as I reluctantly pushed open my parents' bedroom door. I shivered as I stepped into the dim, frigid room and tiptoed to the side of their bed. A single arm cautiously reached from the bundles of blankets and sheets and sorted through the countless bottles of medication on the nightstand. "Oh, hi baby . . . do you want to come lie down and take a nap with Mommy?" I crawled into the king-size bed, snuggled up next to her warm back and laid with her for the next couple of hours. This was the most contact I'd made with my mother for many years of my life. I thought that all families functioned as mine did. It took me several years of frustration and confusion to understand that my mother suffered horribly from depression.

As I began making close, personal friends in school, they shared the details of the relationships with their mothers with me. I realized I was missing out on something wonderful with my own mother and began suggesting to her that we spend more time together. She would continuously find an excuse or dilemma that would hinder her from going out with me. She would then proceed to her bedroom to take medicine and go to sleep for the remainder of the day. I remember sitting in my room crying so many nights because I could not make sense of her broken promises and refusal to spend time with me. It broke my heart to know that she would rather sleep than spend time with her own daughter.

My mother's behavior soon came to affect my entire family. My father would constantly question and quarrel with my mother, not understanding her illness. He built his entire life around pleasing her: cooking her favorite comfort foods and making sure I never made a single noise while she was sleeping. Why did my father put up with my invalid mother all those years? Adopting my mother's ways, my sister began sleeping all day, only coming out for meals or to log on to the Internet. The way things were going, I felt like I was the next in line to be plagued by this disease. So I kept myself active and hardly ever spent time at home. The only way I could face the fear of becoming depressed was to distance myself from the people who were most likely to cause it.

The culmination of my mother's battle with depression came when I was a senior in high school. It was an early Saturday afternoon, and I had just returned home from band rehearsal. I could sense that something was wrong the moment I unlocked the front door. I heard the shower running in my parents' bathroom, which seemed odd because my father was working in the front yard, and my mother should have been asleep. As I cautiously walked toward the bedroom that adjoined the bathroom, the sound of someone weeping rushed to my ears. My stomach dropped. I was afraid to go in because of what I might find. I carefully opened the bathroom door to find my mother huddled in the corner of the running shower, fully clothed and sobbing uncontrollably. I rushed outside to tell my father. For reasons I still do not understand, he became angry and stormed inside, shouting at her that he didn't have time for this and to get out of the shower and dry off. We called her psychiatrist and he immediately admitted her to the mental institution wing of Baylor Hospital under a suicide watch. I was in denial about how critical my mother's condition had gotten and explained to all my friends that she had hurt her back and had to stay in the hospital for a couple of days. Visiting my mother behind the secured doors of the institution was the single most difficult thing I've ever had to do.

Wounded and hurt, my mother watched as I could not meet my eyes with hers. I sat across the cafeteria table from her, barely making conversation and fidgeting my fingers. I did not want her showing me the macaroni art that she had created earlier that day in "craft therapy"; I needed her to give me a long, safe hug and tell me that everything was going to be all right. I trudged out the hospital doors that day wondering what my life would be like if my mother had actually followed through with her intended plan. It terrified me.

After her short visit to the hospital, my mother became dramatically healthier. It was not because of any prescribed medication or therapy session; it was because she realized that she did not want to spend the rest of her life in so much emotional pain. We sat down together after the hospital released her, and she attempted to explain to me what was going on inside of her mind and body. She felt that she had nothing to live for and did not see any point of going on. But as she was crying helplessly on the floor of the shower, she saw me standing there and found a reason to go on. She called me her "angel" because, in a sense, I had saved her life. After all those years, I finally understood my mother's pain.

My mother and I have a bond today that surpasses everything that happened in the past. I love my mother more than anyone in the world, and I am so proud that she has overcome her depression and is the remarkable mother that she is today.

Laura Pavlasek

Take Back the Night

For most of my life, I kept all my feelings bottled up inside, and I wouldn't allow myself to acknowledge any anger or pain. I thought that by ignoring the pain, I could somehow avoid experiencing it. What I didn't realize was that I would eventually have to deal with all the emotions I suppressed. Over time, it became increasingly difficult to hide my problems, and I desperately needed someone in whom I could confide. Thankfully, my parents sought counseling for me, and this was the first step in what has become a long, harrowing journey.

For the past four years, I have been striving to conquer my depression and end the mental and physical torture I inflict upon myself. I have begun talking about an issue from my childhood that caused a great deal of anger and self-hatred: sexual abuse by an extended family member. Initially, it was difficult to speak about such a painful time in my life, but the tremendous support I've received from family and friends has made an immense difference. I can't even begin to express the sense of relief I felt once I disclosed this painful secret; it was like an enormous weight was lifted off my shoulders.

As a victim of molestation, I have carried a large burden of shame.

There is something very healing about the words: "It was *no*t your fault; it is a horror that *no one* deserves." Once I realized how much this insight helped me, I decided I wanted to talk with others who had been through similar traumas. When my mom informed me of a candlelight vigil in New York City to speak out against sexual crimes, I immediately decided to attend. Although I looked forward to participating, nothing could have prepared me for the life-altering experience I would have.

Even though it's been almost two years since I participated in that momentous event, I still think about that night. Recently, while looking through some old journals, I came across the following entry. As I read it, I began to relive the evening I took part in, an amazing event appropriately called "Take Back the Night."

Dear Diary,

I have to write about the unforgettable time I had tonight! At 8:30 P.M., I took a train into Manhattan and then a cab to Greenwich Village.

When I arrived, I was overwhelmed by the amazing scene. The entire area was blocked off, and a huge circle of women sat on the soft earth below. I found a spot among the crowd and took a deep breath. On a small platform set up for this event, women took the stage to share their stories of abuse. I was also surrounded by a multitude of T-shirts, each designed by a victim of sexual crime. Small shirts represented childhood abuse, while larger ones symbolized trauma that took place later in life. These shirts displayed such comments as "It wasn't my fault," "Love and hurt," and "Rape kills."

Repeatedly, my eyes welled up with tears that

refused to fall. I was numb from the pain, inundated with shame as I rocked back and forth in fear. I wanted to scream and cry, but I was too embarrassed to do so in the middle of the crowd. When I could no longer hold it all within, I ran inside the bathroom and sank to the floor, sobbing. A few people asked if I needed help, but I could not respond; their voices seemed far away. Eventually, I picked myself up, grabbed a few tissues and headed back outside.

When I returned to the rally, volunteers distributed white candles for our march through the Village. Women of all ages stood together. We screamed the chants, "Wherever we go, however we dress, no means no and yes means yes!" and "All colors, shapes and sizes, this is the power that rises: take back the night!" As we stormed through the dark city, our unity illuminated the crime-filled streets. Police officers walked beside us, and people came out of clubs and restaurants to see us and listen to our message. I held my candle high in the air and felt a strong sense of purpose. In my mind, I was telling the person who hurt me that he had taken too many years of my life, and I would no longer grant him that power.

I left the Village just after midnight. Even though I am exhausted both emotionally and physically, I feel an immense sense of activism and accomplishment. It was moving to see such a shocking number of people who have endured this pain. Their stories and our common bond have inspired me to continue speaking out! This evening, there were many different emotions amidst the crowd: agony, despair, anger, etc. However, there was one feeling that shone through all of that darkness as a powerful beacon of light: hope. It was a hope so strong and plentiful that everyone could take as much as they needed and store it in their hearts forever.

Life is about giving and taking, and this evening I was able to do both. I let go of the burden and shame I have always felt, and I embraced a new sense of peace and self-worth. I took the power of my future back into my own hands. I recognized that I must no longer live in the shadow of the past, and I refuse to spend one more day of my life as a "victim." The time has come to open my eyes and acknowledge what I am, always have been, and always will be: a survivor.

Lauren Nevins

The Unexpected

Life is an adventure in forgiveness.

Norman Cousins

In September of the year I turned nineteen, my parents drove up unexpectedly one Sunday afternoon to my college dorm. My mother sat down, quietly sniffling, while my dad, truly uncomfortable, cleared his throat, paused for a moment, and told me that they had received a letter from the Social Security Administration.

The letter said that Daniel Frazier—*and for a moment, a heartbeat moment, I couldn't remember who he was*—had died, and I was entitled to Social Security benefits. *Oh yes, he used to be my father. Well, my birth father. I don't even remember him.*

A part of me stood in the corner of the room quietly watching as this surreal scene unfolded. The person who I regarded as my true father, who had raised me from a child—my stepfather—was telling me about Daniel Frazier's death. Another part of me was summing up what I felt at this moment, which was nothing—no sorrow, no sadness. Only a sense of melancholy that sometimes comes over one when reading a stranger's obituary. Despite the chaotic thoughts scuffling around in my head, all I could think was that this isn't how I thought it would end. I always thought I would see him again, at least once. This was the second and final time I had lost him. He left my mother, my six-year-old sister and two-year-old me, promising to be back in two weeks—walked out the door and never looked back. When I turned six, my mother married a man who happily took on an instant family, and when our family grew through the addition of a baby brother, my sister and I happily spoiled our little prince.

But always, my thoughts would return to this missing man. I had wildly conflicting views on exactly how I should feel about Daniel Frazier. For a long time, I hated him. Despised him for walking out our front door and never looking back, never calling. I sometimes thought that perhaps he would silently be watching us at school or home, ashamed to show his face, lurking around the edges of my life, interested in how I was growing and my emerging chrysalis personality.

But the saddest thing is that I really have no memories of him. My sister recalls holding his hand and walking with him on a rainy October evening, the streetlights reflecting off the water-slicked streets. They stopped at a large building, where he pointed to one of the windows and said, "That's where your mommy and baby sister are." And that is as much as she can recall. But at least she has *something*, a bonafide picture captured in her heart. I find myself envious of her for that small glimpse.

My family had such an authentic core of sheer love that it was outside my understanding that someone of such looming importance to me could simply not care. Well, he didn't. Care, that is. But what was not apparent to me when I found out about his death was how unspeakably troubled his life was. Only years later did the details of his life emerge.

My mother's most hidden fear was that he would reemerge to haunt the lives of my sister and me, and only because he had died did she reveal some of his past. It turns out he had, for years, been manic-depressive, undiagnosed and untreated during their marriage. My mother found out that he died alone in a hotel room after taking an overdose of sleeping pills.

I know truth is often blurred in interpretation and no one knows what anyone's final, most intimate thoughts are before exiting this world. But I want to believe he achieved some sort of redemptive grace before he died. Only lately, as I've gotten older, can I understand how utterly terrifying his world must have seemed. The chasm between him and a normal life must have seemed incalculable. How defeating it must have all been. With the added, overwhelming responsibilities of parenthood, he simply unraveled. All semblance of reality sloughed off of him, and during his last few years, he evidently lurched between medicated and nonmedicated crises. He had no friends, no family, no one to hold his hand at the end of his life.

It's taken me a long time to be able to write these words. And only after I went through some troubled times in my own life did I begin to comprehend his pain. I found myself understanding how he could walk out that door and not look back. And not call, not write, not be part of our lives. He had nothing left to give, except his own grief and madness. I'd like to think he knew this. So, as my sister and I talked about him last weekend, we realized that we forgave him for leaving us. We had finally stopped looking for the reasons why he went away.

He will always be the first man who broke my heart, but today as I write this, I can finally accept him with all his flaws.

Julie Lucas

A Struggle to Be Me

You, yourself, as much as anybody in the entire universe, deserve your love and affection.

Buddha

I'm sitting in the dark on my bedroom floor. The musky scent of incense is lingering in the air and Fiona Apple is droning softly in the background. I'm crying without knowing it, and my wrist is bleeding from the razor I've just dragged across it.

I'm a cutter.

That was no particular day. That was four years of my life.

Freshman year was the beginning of a very long struggle with depression for me. I'd never been good at vocalizing my emotions or expressing pain verbally. Instead, I'd act out by doing things that generally made the situation worse. When I got nervous or anxious, or scared and angry, I'd overreact to the situation because I just didn't know what to do with my feelings.

When I entered high school my freshman year I was thrilled because I could make a new start and leave behind my glasses and braces from middle school. I could start anew without my former label of "geek."

But old habits die hard. I was painfully shy and intimi-dated by the thin blonds who played sports and got drunk on weekends. I wanted to be those girls, but I didn't know how.

Instead, I found a new role as an outcast who rebelled against everything those thin blonds stood for. I spoke out against Catholicism in a Catholic school. I joined the liter-ary magazine while they played field hockey. I dyed my hair purple while they bleached their roots.

And I hung out with other outcasts who rebelled with me.

My mom calls them "that bad crowd" that I used to hang out with. We smoked pot and skipped school func-tions. My best friend and I often hid in the parking lot smoking cigarettes instead of going to mass with the rest of the school. And it made my embarrassment and shame so much easier when hiding behind rebellion, purple hair, and pot.

But at night, lying alone in my bed, the pain washed over me until it was unbearable. All the insults I'd ever received, every rejection, every stupid thing I'd ever done came flooding back. A voice in the back of my head called me stupid and worthless. But I had no idea how to vocal-ize the pain I'd been hiding.

And that's when the cutting began.

The first time, it was just an experiment. To see if it made me feel better. And it did.

I can't explain the feeling of relief it was to pour out my misery and punish myself. But it wasn't just about pun-ishment. I needed people to understand that I was silently screaming for help.

I never purposely showed my scars to anyone in order to receive attention, but something like that is bound to get noticed. And it did.

My mom took me to psychiatrists to get me on

medication, but for someone who was so used to rebelling, I couldn't stand to be told what to do. Cutting was like an addiction that I was terrified to get rid of and if medication would make me stop, I didn't want it.

I went through many different therapists and anti-depressants. I wanted to be happy, but I wasn't willing to give up my pain. Being depressed and shameful was the only way I knew how to be. What I really wanted was just to be like those thin, beautiful blonds, but it seemed like an unattainable goal.

By the end of my sophomore year, things were the worst they'd ever been. And to top it off, my parents told me they were separating. That summer was the turning point of my depression.

I spent the whole summer stoned with my friends. My parents would try to control me, and I'd run away. And then my boyfriend broke up with me because I cut myself after I'd fought with my mom on the Fourth of July. And a month later, my parents caught me smoking weed, and I had no choice but to deal with everything.

I spent the next nine months in drug treatment and group therapy. I was finally forced to work through issues without hiding behind my scars or drugs. And anytime I cut myself I had to talk about it in therapy. It made me work on verbalizing my pain and figuring out why I did what I did.

I made a vow that I would be who I wanted to be. I vowed to figure out who I was. And it was really the start of a new life. I can't say I am confident with who I am 100 percent of the time, but I have realized that I can't do everything on my own.

I still get depressed, but I have stopped the cutting. For the first time in a long time, things are better than I could ever have hoped.

Lizzy Mason

The Bully

He rages from within, his eyes fixed in a stare,
Anxious for a fight, with whom he doesn't care.
His heart is filled with anger, his fists clenched in a ball,
Eager to ruin someone's day, as they hurry down the hall.
Who shall be his victim, there are many he can choose,
The girl with braces on her teeth, the kid in school who's new.
To him they're all the same, how he longs to make them
    cry,
And as the anger builds within, his classmates scurry by.
And then he sees around the corner, the shortest boy in
    class,
Should he be his victim, he wonders when he teased him
    last.
He doesn't quite recall, he really doesn't care,
His choice is finally made, because the boy is there.
So he calls out nasty names, as the boy dares to hurry by,
A boy who's done nothing wrong, just merely wondering
    why.
Why he's being teased, why won't anyone step in?
He's terrified of fighting back; there's no doubt he'd never
    win.

And there stands in the doorway, a teacher in plain view,
Who merely shakes his head, for what else can he do?
He's simply there to teach, the boys aren't in his class,
Teasing is a part of life; it's a phase he knows will pass.
So the bully is the victor, his place has well been earned,
The lesson no one taught him, is one he'll never learn.
To a teacher, he's merely trouble, to the kids he's to be
    feared,
To his alcoholic father, he's a mistake and wasted years.
He's headed for a jail term; his life cannot be saved,
His problems are his own; his path to crime is paved.
So there he stands so angry, his back against the wall,
Begging for attention, by making others small.

Standing on a corner, traffic whizzing by,
He yells out to the world, angry clouds roll through the
    sky.
His displeasure is apparent, his fists clenched so ever
    tight,
Who shall be his victim, on this fast approaching night?
There are many he can choose from; they all deserve his
    rage,
To him the world's just an act, he longs for center stage.
And then he spies that tired old man, with groceries in his
    hand,
At last he's found his victim, he proceeds without a plan.
He calls out angry threats, as the old man stumbles by,
One who's done nothing wrong, just merely wondering
    why?
Why he's being cursed at, why won't anyone step in,
He's terrified of fighting back; there's no doubt he'd never
    win.
And there stands in the doorway, a grocer in plain view,
Who merely shakes his head, for what else can he do?
The man is not his father; the boy is not his son,

Words are nothing more than that, the boy's just having
    fun.
So the bully is the victor, his place has well been earned,
The lesson no one taught him, is one he'll never learn.
To the grocer he's merely trouble, to the old man he's to be
    feared,
To his alcoholic father, he's a mistake and wasted years.
He's headed for a jail term; his life cannot be saved,
His problems are his own; his path to crime is paved.
So there he stands so angry, his back against the wall,
Begging for attention, by making others small.

Drunk and with a shotgun gripped within his hand,
Hidden in the shadows, by a station where he stands.
He watches cars pull in and out, customers walking to and
    fro,
Staring past their faces, as they rush past him on the go.
Who shall be his victim, on that robbery barely planned,
There are many he can choose from, their lives so close at
    hand.
His heart beats out in anger; his brow is damp with sweat,
He has to win this game; the rules have long been set.
He sees her through the window, of her bright and shiny
    car,
The easy perfect target, his plan will take him far.
He hurries to the car door, he forces himself inside,
The shotgun near her head, as she begs him for her life.
But they are merely words; they do not faze his ears,
Her life is unimportant; he mocks her many tears.
And somewhere in the struggle, her screams pierce
    throughout the air,
She is just another victim, why, because she's there.
And there stands in the doorway, a mechanic in plain
    view,
Watching as the man drives away, what else can he do?

The girl is not his daughter; the boy is not his son,
He could not risk his own life, to stop a stranger with a
     gun.

The papers showed his picture, his face glorified across
     the screen,
To the world he was a loser, to himself he'd found his
     dream.
For at last somebody noticed, the boy with all that rage,
At last he found an audience, there from center stage.
So the bully was the victor, his place had well been
     earned,
And the lesson no one taught him, someone else was
     forced to learn.
For somewhere in the world, the shortest boy in class,
Stands there on the corner, watching everybody pass.
His anger overflowing, poison in his heart,
Getting even for his torment, seems the perfect place to
     start.
And elsewhere on the sidewalk, creeps a feeble man,
For his own protection, a weapon in his hand.
Watching every single person, who quickly passes by,
His heart no longer frightened, he's no longer asking why.
For inside he knows the answer, as does the smallest boy
     in class,
Words ignite an anger, whose meaning may not pass.
But perhaps the biggest lesson, that stands out from the
     rest,
Has been forced upon a mother, who wonders what lies
     next.
As she stands there at the gravesite, where her only
     daughter lay,
Wondering about the horrible events, that led her to that
     day.
What caused a child so young, only sixteen years of age,

To be filled with so much anger, to internalize such rage.
That he would kill her daughter, so young and full of life,
Didn't anyone ever take the time, to teach him wrong
   from right?
To his father he was nothing; his life at home was fear,
And from his drunken father, came a message very clear.
Words that wreaked their damage, that no one cared to
   see,
The day a good-for-nothing boy, became what they said
   he'd be.

Cheryl Costello-Forshey

My Own Thing

Wooden sticks slapping against each other, sharp metal blades cutting through snowy ice and heavy-metal music blaring from the PA system . . . It's like my very first hockey game remains with me wherever I go.

My father had just been diagnosed with cancer; his life and that of my family was thrown into complete flux. I was thirteen years old, and I couldn't grasp that my dad's time on this earth was growing short. There was no fathoming it.

For more than thirty years he was a teacher—he taught science to his classes and life to my sister and me, two jobs he would pour his heart and soul into. Two jobs he was holding on to ever so tightly because he could feel them beginning to slip away.

At the center of my relationship with Dad were sports . . . baseball, basketball, a little football . . . but never hockey. That was, until his school offered a class trip to see the New Jersey Devils.

When Dad first mentioned the idea of going, I was apprehensive. "Hockey? Really? Hockey?" By the time the ticket reservation deadline arrived, Dad had convinced me.

When that cold night in December fell upon us, and the hour of departure neared, my father was alas too ill. His mind said "try," but it could not deny his weakening body's ultimate wish to remain in bed. The sense of normalcy he was hoping to provide with this outing was escaping him just like everything else. With a look of mortality in his eyes he said, "I'm sorry, Son. I just can't make it tonight." And perhaps even worse, he continued, "Your mother will take you. . . ."

And so I stepped onto a bus filled with a group of impassioned, anxious high-school boys . . . and what felt like a thousand suspicious eyes turned toward my tiny frame. "What is this awkward kid doing on our bus with his mom?" they whispered among each other. A good question, really . . . it was the very same question that was running through my own mind as I slouched in the bus seat next to my equally shy mother. All of a sudden I couldn't wait for this night to end.

Somewhere between the suburbs of New York and the swamps of New Jersey a much older, intimidating high-school freshman turned toward me and asked the most obvious question on the face of the earth. "You don't go to Ramapo, do you?" I was too nervous to reply . . . my mother intervened, "This is Neil, Mr. Katcher's son. It's his first hockey game."

"Oh," responded the boy. "Where's Mr. Katcher?"

"He's not feeling well tonight," my mother replied. The boy nodded and got really quiet for a moment . . . as if he knew about Dad's condition.

Within moments he started a new conversation, this one about hockey. For one night he would act as a substitute.

As we entered the arena, a shiver passed through me. A sense of excitement was filled with the smell of hot dogs and beer. I was in the Meadowlands. The Brendan Byrne Arena.

As the game began to unfold a few tiers below our discounted seats, my bearings and my instincts began to kick in. I was in the world of sport. Questions started flowing from me. "What's icing? What's off-sides? Who's that guy, he's good." I needed to understand this game, and my new mentor was always ready with the knowledge I craved. The game was the fastest, most enthralling sport I had ever witnessed.

I learned that I was watching the underdog New Jersey Devils getting dominated by the big burly Philadelphia Flyers . . . the game flooded through my blood and into my very DNA. Midway through the game there was this one play . . . a defining moment, hour, day in my life. One of the Flyers, maybe it was Peter Zezel, Rick Tocchet or even Tim Kerr, made a spin-o-rama move. With the puck sitting on the blade of his stick, this Flyer made a 360-degree maneuver past a Devil and then fired a shot past a flailing goaltender into the rippling twine!

As the red siren light behind the goals spun, I jumped to my feet. . . . My mentor tugged at me, "Kid, don't cheer for them. They're the enemy." Lost in the game, I replied, "Did you see that?!!"

Upon returning home, I ran as fast I could up the thirteen creaky, carpeted steps to my parents' bedroom. I called out, "Dad! Dad!" At first there was no answer until I realized he was in the adjoining bathroom. I went right up to the door and knocked, "Dad? Can I come in?"

"No . . . how was the game?" he managed to reply. I must have talked his ear off through that bathroom door. I talked as much as he's probably heard me talk in my entire thirteen years. The last thing I said was, "What team do you root for?"

"The Rangers," replied Dad . . . after all, fandom was not something one chose in our family, it was passed down from one generation to the next, like an heirloom. And so,

from that moment on, the Rangers became my team . . .
and the game of hockey seemed so magical that it could
stop time itself.

Over the next five years my father would fight for his
life, my family would fight to remain a family . . . and my
heart would find its shelter in a 200-foot by 85-foot arena.
Inside that space, every season and every game became a
reason to dream—if for just a few hours at a time.

Recently, my father lost his battle with cancer, but even
as I grow toward adulthood, hockey remains my beacon of
hope. And it was that one chilly December night in the
swamps of New Jersey that showed me that my father's
spirit would continue to teach and comfort me . . . even in
his absence.

Neil Katcher

Staying Strong

Walking through a quiet field on a dewy morning, you spy a wild horse. Slowly you walk up to him, and to your delight he doesn't run away. He lowers his head for you to pet and then motions with his snout for you to climb on his back. You ride away, hair and mane blowing in the wind behind you. You hear a voice, quite faint. You cannot tell what it is, but it is getting louder . . . louder . . . louder.

You awake abruptly from a relaxing sleep to the sound of your mother yelling, "Come on, we've got to go!" You wipe the gunk from your eyes and roll over to look at the clock. Seven A.M. It's time to leave for chemotherapy. You really don't want to go, so it is a struggle, but you make yourself get out of bed. Making all of the lovely "I'm not really awake yet" noises, you drag yourself to the bathroom. It is almost a ritual now, with no thought really involved. You step out of your clothes, turn on the shower, wash, step out of the shower and dry off, all the while wishing you were still asleep. You find your most comfortable clothes and put them on haphazardly. You're only going to the hospital, so who cares what you look like?

"We're going to be late if we don't leave right now!" you

hear from down the hall. Walking down the hall you realize your stomach is growling and remember that you have
yet to eat anything. Guess you'll just have to ask Mom to
stop somewhere; what a pity.

You're in the car now, reclining and squinting to see
through the sunlight in your eyes. You get your breakfast,
and after eating, you perk up a little bit. Forty-five minutes
later you arrive at the hospital clinic. Parking is an adventure in itself, so you get Mom to drop you off at the main
entrance. You're not quite in the mood for battling blue-
haired ladies for parking spaces.

As you enter the clinic, the first thing you notice is the
smell: doctors, latex gloves, saline drips and disinfectant
spray. After checking in, you scout out a nice seat to relax
in. After settling on a brightly colored plastic couch, you
realize that it is incredibly cold. Good thing you remembered to bring a sweater. You wrap it around your
shoulders and wait for your mother to arrive. Once your
mother returns from the parking lot battle, your nurse for
the day comes into the waiting room.

"You ready?" she asks. "Oh yeah, you know it," you reply.

She leads you to the check-in room where you are
instructed to stand on the scale. Oh boy, it looks like
you've gained two pounds since last week, so you make a
mental note to lay off the Twinkies from now on. The
nurse takes your blood pressure and asks what medicines
you are taking. You recount the oh-so-familiar list once
again. You think they could at least remember twelve
medicines from last week. She takes you into the "access
room." You climb up on the lovely examining table, all
covered in disposable paper. Lying back, you lift your
shirt to reveal the semipermanent IV that is under your
skin, located right below your bra line. This is more com-
monly known as a venaport, or to other patients as "the
poison-control center."

You peel the Tegaderm off the area on and around your port, wincing all the while, as it pulls out the little hairs on your stomach. Taking a tissue, you wipe off the Emla cream that had been applied earlier to numb the first two layers of skin. You watch as your nurse puts on her latex gloves and begins the procedure. She opens her "kit" and arranges everything the same way she does every week. Three syringes, the access needle and betadine—all waiting to be used.

She walks over to where you are lying and begins. First she uses a giant cotton swab soaked in alcohol all around your port. Following this, she swabs you three times with betadine, each time with a new swab so that she won't counter the disinfectant. Once again she swabs your port with alcohol and then waits fifteen seconds.

She prepares the needle and asks, "Are you ready?"

"Go for it," you reply.

You have done this so many times before. Still though, right before she presses the needle through the skin, your stomach clinches. You take a deep breath, close your eyes, and exhale as the needle goes in. A sense of relief comes to you; it didn't hurt this week! Your nurse places two cotton squares under the "butterfly" part of your port (the area up against your skin) and places a sheet of Tegaderm over the entire thing. She then screws a syringe into the tube attached to the needle, which is now in your port, and takes some blood. Now she takes a syringe of saline and slowly pushes it into your port; you ask her to do it faster because you want to get a head rush. After the head rush, she flushes your port with heparin. You begin to taste it inside your mouth as she pushes it in, and it doesn't taste good.

You are sent to a back room with chairs, TVs, VCRs and a wide variety of board games. You choose a seat, and your nurse hooks your port line up to a fluid drip. Some time passes, and the doctor arrives to examine you. He makes jokes while prodding you and feeling for lumps and bumps. Then he asks you the same questions he asks you every week: "Have you been nauseated? Have you had headaches? Back pain? Diarrhea? Constipation? Blood in your urine?"

All to which you answer a quick "No, no, no, no, no and no." He says you're looking good and to let him know if any problems arise, and then he leaves. A little while later your nurse returns with a copy of your blood counts. Your ANC (absolute nurtaphil count) is over five hundred, so you can receive your chemotherapy. Yippee for you!

Your nurse gives you a small push of Zofran, so that the chemo doesn't make you throw up, and then she hooks your port up to the bag of chemotherapy, or as it's more fondly called, "poison." You find it ironic that the nurse must wear special super-thick gloves to handle the bag of chemotherapy, yet they are pumping it into your body. You watch as the liquid runs through the IV line . . . slowly making its way closer and closer. Still tired from getting up so early, you doze off to the quiet sound of the IV machine pumping . . . pumping . . . pumping.

You awake suddenly to the sound of an alarm going off. The nurse comes into your room and messes with the IV machine, pushing buttons, and then the alarm stops.

"It looks like you're all done! Let's go de-access you."

You willingly obey, anxious to get home and lie back down. Already you are feeling the chemotherapy's effects on your body, and all you want to do is go back to bed. You lie on the table in the access room once again and peel the Tegaderm off from your port, again ripping out the little hairs on your stomach. The nurse puts on her latex gloves once again and flushes your port with some saline and heparin. Now it is time to take the needle out. She gets a good grip on the needle and asks you to take a breath and hold it. You do as she says, and as you hold your breath, she quickly pulls the needle out. You let your breath out, relieved that you finally get to go home. She places a Band-Aid over the port and says she will see you next week.

Your mother makes an appointment for next week while you stand there looking like you're about to fall asleep. Mom goes out to get the car, and you wait in the main waiting room. After about five minutes you walk out to the garage area and see your mother pulling up. She brings the black van of comfort, waiting to take you home to your bed. Climbing in, you sigh—your life is so different from everyone else's, yet so much the same. You remember with a smile that this will all be over soon, and then you drift off to sleep.

Deiah Haddock

A Step Toward Healing

I look at my reflection in the bathroom mirror and think, *Will I be missed if I die? Do I really have a purpose in this superficial world?*

"Hurry up, Yaa, you're going to be late for school again!" my mom screams from downstairs.

I take my bag and head for school. I sit in class and listen uninterested as my first-period teacher rambles on about the speed of light. Lately I have lost interest in everything including after-school activities. My mind is consumed with the hopelessness of ending my life. I look at the teacher and curiously wonder if she can detect the grief in my eyes.

At school, I don't belong to any specific clique. Even though I am a cheerleader, I don't really hang around with them anymore. I don't belong with the drama students despite the fact that I am in the drama club, or the computer kids even though I like learning about computers, not even the Goths, although I listen to heavy metal. I simply can't bring myself to be with a particular circle of individuals. I just walk around the hallways, occasionally stopping to chat with some "friends." I don't even have a best friend. At lunch, I sit and listen to people talk and sometimes even try to participate in the conversation so no one will be suspicious of my sudden change in behavior.

After cheerleading practice, I go home, up to my room and cry and cry because I don't understand where this feeling of depression is coming from, and it's overwhelming. I listen to sad songs because I feel better when the pain is directed somewhere else. Every night, before my mom comes home, I wash my face to hide any evidence of tears because I know how hard she works and the last thing she needs is to worry about me. We always eat dinner together, and during that time I assure her that my health, classes, school and everything in general is fine.

She always says, "Yaa, I know high school can be tough, and if anyone or anything is bothering you, you can talk to me and let me know."

It's every time she says these words that I open my mouth and try to tell her about what I am going through, but I am so convinced that she will never understand it and that no one will ever understand me because I don't even understand myself.

Late one night as I lie in bed, I look up at the ceiling and think of the many ways to end this misery. I finally come to the conclusion of ending my life. As is customary with those who've decided to kill themselves, I decide to leave my mom a suicide note.

I start with the words "I am sorry," and I continue writing, listing my reasons, my everyday sadness and my lack of interest in everything. I tell her I love her and it's best for me to do this and that we will meet up in heaven someday. As I begin to fold the letter, I realize what I am about to do, and I'm not scared; in fact, it's comforting to me. Then I think of my mom. I realize I am her only source of hope and happiness in this world. I realize how much pain she will go through. She tries so hard to make me—her only child—happy. My father left us six months ago to get married to another lady. I cry when I see my selfishness, cry some more when I reread the letter out loud. I collapse on the floor. Maybe death isn't the road to regaining my happiness. Because I remember there was a time in my life when I was happy. I sway my weary body as I cry. I wipe away my tears and head to my mom's room. I knock on the door.

"Yaa, is that you?" her tired voice asks.

"Yes, Mom," I respond. I start crying as I walk toward her.

"What's wrong?"

I tell her everything. She cries and hugs me, and I feel relieved.

After that night, we sought help together, and I met a lot of kids in my same situation, and I understood how much better life could be. Ending my life was not the solution to my freedom and happiness. Talking about it, no matter how hard, was a giant step toward healing.

Yaa Yamoah

Unbreakable Bond

My mother always told me that I was my "father's daughter." By that she meant that we looked alike and shared similar traits—Dad and I were both stocky, intellectual, quick-tempered and funny. Being the firstborn and only child for nearly seven years, I developed a strong bond with my father. We would rub each other's feet and be goofy together, and he always told me that he loved me and that he was proud of my academic performance and artistic endeavors. We understood one another and sensed that we were always on each other's side.

Dad had always been a healthy and energetic man. He had a big appetite, lifted weights and rarely got sick. With his dark hair, green eyes, olive complexion and round belly, he was an image of vigor and joviality. His temper, humor, outspokenness and hearty laugh made him a powerful presence.

Dad was diagnosed with hepatitis C during my freshman year of high school. Doctors told him he had contracted the liver-eating disease as a teenager and that it had lain dormant in his body up until then. The doctors also said Dad would need a liver transplant to survive.

Dad's deterioration was rapid and heart-wrenching. His skin grew pale, he lost about seventy pounds, his physical activity was drastically restricted and his diet was altered. His barely functioning liver caused him to be in pain most of the time. Toward the end of Dad's battle, the toxins produced by the liver caused encephalitis, which made him an incoherent insomniac who could barely control his own actions. He died on April 27, 1998. My grandfather died from cancer two months later, leaving my mom orphaned and widowed—and leaving me with only one parent and one grandparent.

I never thought I would be able to handle life without Dad. His death was a tragic event in my world—but it was not the end of it. I think about Dad every day, and I am still trying to work through my emotions three and a half years after the fact. Nonetheless, I have managed to go on with my life. Writing about his death is the ultimate testimony to that statement, because I have aspired to be a writer since I was a small child. I know that by actively pursuing my dream, I am doing what Dad wants me to be doing—I am going after what I want in life. It saddens me to think there are so many events that he did not and will not get to participate in; he never saw me graduate from high school, and he will not be there to walk my sister and me down the aisle when we get married. But even if he cannot be there physically, I know that he is always with me. Every beautiful sunset that I witness and every piece of good fortune that I am graced by reminds me that I have angels watching over me, and there is one in particular who is always whispering, "I'll go wherever you will go."

Lauren Fritsky

False Hope

Hope, the patent medicine
For disease, disaster, sin.

Wallace Rice

My sister smiled when the doctor pronounced that she would die. Of course, her smile wasn't a reaction to what she had just heard—she was only a baby then, completely incapable of understanding the fate that would befall her. An innocent giggle escaped her lips, and my heart broke.

The night before, we had received a call from a technician at the Yale-New Haven Hospital. The message he had left had been cryptic, revealing only that Lindsay had Canavan disease. What was Canavan disease? The technician had no idea, and even my father, a physician himself, had never heard of it. Now, here we were at the hospital to speak to someone who could decode those frightening words.

The walls echoed medical chatter from the hallway and the room reeked of formaldehyde, while the mahogany conference table and upholstered pearl-white arm chairs tried uselessly to disguise the fact that we were, indeed, in a hospital. The geneticist's nametag read "Sharon Pearl, M.D.," although I'm sure that the chair color was just a coincidence. She sat with her legs crossed and her elbows on the table, hands clasped in front of her. Her fingers did not twitch or tap but remained firmly locked, giving the impression of someone who is so used to bearing bad news that it no longer fazes her. Directly across the table sat my parents, bracketed on either side by my sister Samantha and me. In the secure cradle of my mother's arms lay Lindsay, barely three months old, with a wisp of blonde hair falling about her forehead. She and Dr. Pearl were the only ones in the room who appeared relaxed— she for knowing too little, the doctor for knowing too much. The rest of us were tense; my father wrung his hands, my mother gripped his knee, and Samantha and I exchanged worried glances. Dr. Pearl cleared her throat.

"As you already know, urine tests have indicated that Lindsay suffers from Canavan disease." She stressed the word "Canavan," as though saying it put a bad taste in her mouth. She went on to explain its origin: the inheritance of a recessive allele from both parents. The parents in question nodded in understanding, but their eyes reflected both the impatience to hear the prognosis and the fear of bad news. Dr. Pearl's next words ended the impatience but confirmed the fears.

"Children with Canavan disease face immediate and constant deterioration, including blindness, difficulty chewing, difficulty swallowing, loss of head control and profound mental retardation. They are never able to walk, speak, or feed themselves. . . ." Here she paused, and for the first time, I saw a glimpse of compassion in her eyes. Hopeless compassion.

" . . . and they seldom reach the age of ten."

The silence was deafening. I thought that I might vomit

all over that nice mahogany table. Pins-and-needles numbness took over my extremities, thankfully, or I might have lashed out and hurt someone. Possibly "Dr. Pearly White" and her lovely matching chairs. Possibly myself.

Years (or perhaps minutes) later, I regained enough internal composure to look around and gauge everyone else's reactions. Samantha, only eight, wore the confused and helpless expression of a lost puppy. My father stared directly at the doctor, his eyes wide but glazed, and I knew that he was seeing nothing. My mother, usually so cool and composed, had already broken down; her eyes were squeezed shut and tears were carving their way down her cheeks in black mascara rivers. Her mouth was twisted into a sorrowful grimace, and I thought that her noiseless sobs might choke her. It was only at this moment that I noticed Lindsay, the cause of all this muted mayhem. She was completely oblivious, and she was smiling. The smile began at the edges of her cheeks and reached up to her enormous grey eyes. They were creased at the corners from the smile and framed with unusually long lashes. Her pupils were slightly dilated and sparkled with life but stared straight ahead, not moving to focus on anyone or anything. It was my first clue that the doctor was telling the truth.

My father was the first to break the silence, as he coughed, blinked and addressed the doctor. "Is there any treatment? Is there any cure?"

"I don't want to raise any false hopes. There is nothing. Nothing can be done for her. She'll only be a burden to your family until she dies. I can recommend some good institutions where she'll be safe and happy. There's nothing that you can do." She stood up. "I can also recommend some support groups. I'm sorry I had to be the one to give you this terrible news," she concluded, and with a polite nod, she left the room.

Dr. Pearl was my first glimpse into the pessimism that all too often accompanies knowledge. To imagine putting my beautiful sister in an institution until she died of a seizure, or choked on her own saliva, or even passed away in her sleep. To even consider the possibility! To be Dr. Pearl and put forth the suggestion!

Clearly, I wasn't the only one shell-shocked. As soon as the door shut, a communal sob-fest burst forth in the room. After ten minutes of hugs and kisses and wet cheeks, we all simply stopped and turned to my father.

"There's got to be something," he said. "I'll find it."

He tried; God knows he tried. The very next day, he cancelled his office hours and hid in the medical library at Danbury Hospital, searching desperately for information on any sort of treatment. The war-weary look in his eyes when he stumbled in the door late that night revealed his lack of success. Still, he didn't give up—Lindsay needed help, and she was going to get it. He—*we*—wouldn't stop until she got it.

After his failure at the library, my father took a new approach. Utilizing his connections as a medical professional, he began calling colleagues, asking if they knew anyone who might be able to help. Each colleague told him something like, "Well, I have the name of this neurologist . . . but I doubt that it will amount to anything. Just go home, get some rest." Rest? Hah! So my father would call the neurologist or researcher or scientist—and oftentimes find himself on the other end of a dead phone line. "Canavan disease?" said Dr. Branson, director of a leading research institute. "Forget it." Click. "It's a pie in the sky," declared a geneticist from a government regulatory agency, "You're wasting your time."

Each night, as we lay in bed, Samantha and I could hear my father's footsteps on the stairs, increasingly heavy by the day. "Any luck?" my mother would whisper, always cautious of waking Lindsay. "Not yet," he would reply, "but there's a researcher at the University of Pennsylvania that I have to call tomorrow. . . ." Always optimistic, always filled with hope. I dreaded the day when my father would walk in and say, "No luck, and I have no one left to call," and we would be forced to admit that the words of Sharon Pearl, M.D. rang true: "I don't want to raise any false hopes."

' We were lucky: that never came to pass. After searching the globe for a researcher whose hope matched our own, we found Dr. Mathew During and Dr. Paola Leone working at Yale, the very university at which Lindsay had been diagnosed months earlier. After all those locked doors, we had finally found brilliance and compassion tied together in a small sliver of hope. Their lab was currently working on gene therapy for Parkinson's disease, but During and Leone agreed to convert their research into gene therapy for Canavan disease. Lindsay was beautiful, they agreed. They, too, had hope.

Today, Lindsay is ten years old. An age that Dr. Pearl— and many others—believed she would never reach. Only a year and a half after her grim diagnosis, she became the first person in the world to undergo gene therapy of the brain. She has undergone the same treatment thrice more, her condition improving markedly each time. She sits in a wheelchair and cannot speak or feed herself, but she can smile. She can laugh. She can indicate when she is thirsty, or full or tired. And she lives at home, with her family, where she belongs—not in some cold, antiseptic facility devoid of love and feeling and happiness. Devoid of hope.

I live every day with hope; the emotion that allows us to always look for the sun behind the clouds. Hope has prolonged Lindsay's life, and more importantly, her quality of life. What if we had listened to the "experts" who told us to stop trying? What if we had lost all hope?

Dr. Pearl's words about false hopes have become a sort of running joke in my family. Who can define what hope is "false"? Our hope in Lindsay fills our days and nights; without it, we would simply be automatons robotically taking care of a woebegone child. Without hope, we would be lost. We cannot be afraid of it. There is no such thing as false hope.

Molly Karlin

7

OVERCOMING OBSTACLES

The only use of an obstacle is to be overcome. All that an obstacle does with brave men is, not to frighten them, but to challenge them.

Woodrow Wilson

My Worst Enemy

Self-pity is our worst enemy, and if we yield to it, we can never do anything wise in this world.

Helen Keller

He used to look at me like I was the most beautiful girl in the entire universe. He often gazed at me, the corners of his eyes wrinkled by a sweet grin on his lips, and would tell me I was an angel who had swooped down from heaven just for him. There were many moments in our relationship when I convinced myself that Brian and I were destined to spend our lives together. When he looked at me with his adoring eyes, I felt, for the first time ever, like I was beautiful.

When I was with Brian, I was at peace with myself. Unfortunately, things were not so tranquil without him. My self-esteem was terribly low, and by the time I was seventeen, I was painfully aware this was a serious problem. Instead of solving the problem, I opted to hide it and pretend like I was perfectly content with myself. I let Brian give me the love that I couldn't give myself. I didn't want him to know that my reflection was my own worst enemy. I didn't want him to know that I spent nights crying because my hips were too wide and my thighs were too fat. I didn't want him to know that the girl he loved didn't love herself.

"Emily, you're amazing," he would whisper softly, tickling my ear while my heart threatened to burst from happiness.

As the months wore on, my lack of self-confidence began to show through. Brian would say, "Emily, why don't you wear that shirt?" And I would argue, "It makes my hips look too big." He would shrug, as boys often do when they can't understand the reasoning of a female mind, and the subject would be dropped. The problem was, moments like that began to show up more and more often in our relationship, and Brian started to get frustrated.

"Emily, you're beautiful! Why do you have to get so jealous? You know I love you!" And even though I knew this, every time I saw Brian talking to other girls, my mind instantly feared he had finally realized that I really wasn't as gorgeous as he had thought.

"I can't deal with this anymore," he announced one day. "How can you love me if you can't even love yourself! I love you for you. But you have to find out what it is that makes you so scared of who you really are. You have to stop being so negative about yourself." He left after that, and I was stuck, all alone, with my own worst enemy.

In time, I realized my relationship with myself is just like a relationship I share with anyone else. In order to make it better, it was necessary to nurture it. Just like I spend time with the people I love, I had to spend time with myself. I had to learn and grow and hold my own hand instead of slapping it away.

Of course, it took me many painful months to discover

this truth. I took the breakup really hard and verbally bashed myself time and time again. Ironically, I was punishing myself for not loving myself. I actually believed that I was a plague to society who didn't deserve to live on the same earth with loving and accepting people like Brian. When I looked in the mirror, I absolutely despised the person with the puffy, red eyes and unwashed hair who stared back at me.

Developing self-acceptance was a process that occurred slowly, but gradually I began to smile at my reflection. Little things like a guy in chemistry calling me cute, shopping for clothes that were more fitting and flattering, and discovering new interests and talents contributed to the foundation for my whole new perspective on me. Giving myself a hard time hurt me. Accepting and loving myself nurtured me. I began to feel more energetic, and I was excited about even the smallest things. It's incredible how my worst enemy turned out to be my best friend once I made some humble yet necessary changes. I can honestly say I like myself now. And I've got a feeling things are just going to keep getting better.

Emily Starr

The Sound of My Father's Voice

I have never forgotten the sound of my father's voice as he knelt by my bed with his back hunched, his head craned low and his hands resting on his lap. It's his story-telling voice that I remember—a voice that dropped a note or two but still managed to rise above the murmuring noise of the fans that scattered the hot air in the room. Slow, even and controlled, my father's voice, his presence, filled the room and diffused itself just as the single bulb from the brass lamp cast a dim glow of light over his face.

Growing up, I was always known as the kid with the fun father, the tall dad with the raspy voice and funny African accent who was always willing to throw me on his shoulders or wrestle me to the ground. It was my father who brought my best friend, Chris, and me to car shows, who took us to basketball games, coached our soccer team and, on occasion, took us fishing. In my father's mind, the future took precedence above all else, which is why he was always there, at every soccer game and outing, track-ing and mapping my every move. It was never really a matter of where I was, so much as where I was going. For my father, the purpose of the present was to point the way to what lay next. "What," he asked me nearly every day, "do you want to do when you grow up?" I began following the stock market in second grade as a way of giving him an answer. My father would come home and I would tell him how the market had done. "Up fifty points today, Dad." "Down thirty yesterday." Where the market actually *went* I never knew, and still don't to this day. I knew though that it went somewhere, and that my knowing mattered significantly to him.

When I entered high school things began to change between my father and me. I suddenly became known as the kid with the mean father: the father who barged into high-school parties, disrupting the flow of alcohol in order to pull his son out and take him home. "Not while I'm around," he had always said every time I broke a rule. "Not while I'm here." His presence was almost omniscient, amazing in its ability to trail me around every corner and stand within earshot of every word.

My father and I had what would be the first in a series of small fallouts during those first two years in high school. My friend Chris and I had both suddenly found ourselves thrust into a world where being "cool" meant skipping classes and staying out late at night despite how much work we had to do. When Chris's father left him and his mother our freshman year, I followed him out night after night as he searched for solace or comfort away from home. My grades began to slip, and my father said he couldn't understand what was happening. When I came home late one weekend after another, he would look at me and say that he didn't know who I was anymore or where I was going. He began to grow angry. I began to grow angry. "I won't wait for you to mess up," he said to me one night. "That won't happen while I'm around." This was tough love for him. This was my father telling me openly, directly and honestly that he would never let go of everything he had raised me to believe, everything he himself believed, if I were to fail myself. When my best friend, Chris, and I were caught skipping class, I could visibly see the anger in his face for the first time in my life. "Don't you know what it took for me to be here?" he asked me as we walked out of the principal's office. Didn't I know how much my mother and he had sacrificed to come to this country? Didn't I know how much was thrown away in the name of hope to bring me to where I was now? "Everything," he would say, "everything has been for you kids."

By then, though, I no longer feared his presence. We were beyond that now. He seemed distant and far removed from the world I was in. *How, I thought, can he possibly understand all that is happening in my life?* His words were still there though, as was the voice he had once used to read to me. No longer intimidating, they stood now as the hallmark of our relationship. They reminded me of what we had once had, and what I wanted to have again. I began to look at my face in the mirror every night after I came home, and I knew that my father was right. I didn't recognize the reflection staring back at me.

In the middle of my sophomore year of high school, just before Thanksgiving, Chris ran away from home. His mother came to our house looking for him. She was tired and desperate and on the verge of tears. Before she could finish telling me her story, my father walked into the room with his coat on and his car keys in his hand. He had already heard all that he needed to hear. "We'll find him," he said, as he put his arm around me and walked to the car.

My father and I drove around Chicago for over two hours that night looking for Chris. My father asked me how I was doing, and all I could muster up the courage to say was, "Fine." He asked me what I thought had happened to Chris in the past two years to bring all of this about and all I could say was, "I don't know."

It was below freezing that night, as it is during most Chicago winters, and we both knew that if Chris were here, we probably wouldn't find him, and that even if we did, he probably wouldn't come with us. Truth was, he was out there, and I was with my father, and no amount of pleading or begging would bring us together.

Driving that evening through the nearly deserted streets of the west side of Chicago, I couldn't help but constantly turn my head to stare at my father sitting behind the wheel of the car. I found it strange that he should be driving me again to pick up a friend. I knew then, perhaps clearer and better than ever before, just what he had meant when he had said, "Not while I'm here." I knew then, too, that had he not been there all those years, sitting by my bed or behind the wheel, then I wouldn't have been where I was now, and that he, more than anything else, was the larger-than-life portrait that framed the backdrop through which I viewed the world. I must have thanked him for driving me that evening, for being there, just as I had thanked him a thousand times before for doing just that.

When we returned home that evening Chris had already found his way back home by himself. His mother called to thank my father. He told her that Chris was like a second son to him, and there was no need for thanks. Years later now, I can see that my father's search for Chris was also a search for me, and that in the end, I also found my way back home that night.

Dinaw Mengestu

Watching My Brother Ride

Brothers don't necessarily have to say anything to each other—they can sit in a room and be together and just be completely comfortable with each other.

Leonardo Di Caprio

In the year after my father died, there was nothing I wanted more than a trophy. I was twelve, and the hope of placing a trophy on my dresser woke me up in the middle of the night. All of my friends had trophies, from soccer and football, from raffle ticket sales and BMX races and chess tournaments; one friend even had a trophy in the shape of deer antlers because he'd shot a thirteen-point buck. Any of those would have elated me; I believed they would have given me back something my father's absence had taken away. The problem was that I had no skills or talents that would yield a trophy.

My older brother, Alan, had shelves of trophies. He had some from Little League, but most came from horse shows. Before my father died, he had bought each of us a horse. Mine was a pinto pony that I named Colonel because of a white star on his shoulder; Alan's was a quarter horse, fourteen-hands high, named Otis. He ran the barrels and did pole-racing, and when Alan kicked Otis's sides and hollered for him to come on, they were nothing but run. Colonel always wanted to follow, and I could feel him gathering power and speed in his gallop, but I was afraid of falling, so I'd pull on the reins and we'd lag behind. Really, this is a story about my brother.

After my father died, my mother rarely went to the stables where we boarded the horses. In fact, she really didn't go anywhere. She cut back on her hours at work and stopped going to play bridge. Mostly she stayed in her room. Alan ran a lot of errands for her and cooked our meals and paid our bills with money he made waiting tables.

This was also the year I started smoking. And I was spending time with the crowd at school who set fire to bathroom trash cans. I liked the feeling I got from being around everything I'd been told to stay away from; if I was scared to let Colonel burst into a run beneath me, I wasn't afraid to cut class and play video games at the mall. I liked that after I back-talked a history teacher, girls suddenly knew who I was. I liked the new music I listened to, the way I'd learned to spit phlegm onto the ceiling. I appreciated the depths to which my grades dropped. I enjoyed hanging out with kids who, like me, had no trophies and couldn't care less.

My brother didn't like this behavior, and when the worst of my report cards arrived in the mail, he rode with me into the pasture and interrogated me. To all of his questions—What do you think you're doing? Who do you think you're fooling? Why are you throwing everything Mom and Dad worked for down the toilet?—I answered, "I don't know." And the truth was, I didn't know. I was adrift, floating away from everything I'd known.

He started picking me up from school, denying me the opportunity to carouse with the smokers and bullies, and we drove to the stables to ride until night fell. Through all of this, I still loved riding, still found comfort in being around Colonel, but I hated being made to ride. After a week of forcing me to spend my afternoons exclusively with him, I took a self-righteous stand and told Alan that I refused to be chaperoned like this. I listed all the ways I thought he was treating me unfairly, and he let me work myself into a fury. When I'd exhausted all of my angles, Alan said, "I entered you in the horse show. It's in two weeks."

I was stunned, appalled and incredulous. I was thrilled, but I didn't let on. I huffed, "Why?"

He was cleaning Otis's hooves. Without looking at me, he said, "You want a trophy, right?"

The next week is a blur in my memory. Although I hated to admit he had such sway with my emotions, Alan's implied challenge completely refocused my attentions, my loyalties. Suddenly, I thought of nothing except strategies for running barrel events faster. I distanced myself from the smokers and bullies. When Alan picked me up after school, I asked him to drive faster to the stables. By week's end, Colonel and I had lit upon a new rhythm and we rode hard and fast, the way I'd always watched Alan ride. The night before the junior rodeo, I could already feel the trophy in my hands, the promising weight of its dignity; I could see my reflection in that golden angel's breasts.

Alan had entered me in four events, and in the first three, I floundered. My nerves sizzled in my knees, and I made mistake after mistake. I was on the verge of tears and in the full throes of anger, furious with Alan for subjecting me to my own shortcomings, with my mother for venturing back into the world to watch me fail, furious with my father for dying, furious with myself for being my pitiful self.

The last event was running poles, and to everyone's surprise, I didn't do half bad. My time was nowhere near the fastest, but seemed solid enough to secure me seventh place, the last place that would receive a trophy. Colonel and I watched the other riders. Before the last competitor, I was still in seventh. My mother smoked cigarette after cigarette, while Alan casually set out to find a Portapotty. I asked how he could leave at a time like this—I couldn't stop smiling—but he just shrugged and said, "When you have to go, you have to go."

The last rider started off badly, missing a pole that would have to be circled before the run was over. The trophy was as good as mine. Then the rider hit his stride, and the second half of his run was flawless and breathtakingly swift. My heart stalled.

He'd finished two-tenths of a second faster than I had. He'd knocked me out of seventh place; he'd taken away my trophy.

But this is, as I've said, a story about my brother.

When he found me after the last rider, he claimed not to have heard the judges announce the time that had beaten me out; he claimed that I'd heard incorrectly, that I was misremembering my own time. I thought he was making light of my situation, and I stormed off. How could I have not heard the right time, how could I have thought I'd ridden slower than I had?

When the announcement came during the awards ceremony, I was sitting under a mesquite tree, imagining ways to ingratiate myself back into the crowd of smokers and bullies, the kids who'd never wanted a trophy. I was only half-listening to the announcer, so when he called my name—and Colonel's—his voice didn't really register; it was a voice from a dream, the voice of a ghost. He said I was in seventh place, that I should come claim my trophy. He called my name again, like a question this time. "Donald Keyes, you out there?" None of this seemed real. For a split second, I thought the voice was my father's.

I can still remember running toward the corral as if my life depended on it; I can hear and feel my boots hitting the hard dirt of the arena, can hear the crowd laughing gently as they applaud; I can see Alan and my mother clapping, my mother wiping her eyes, my brother giving me a smug thumbs-up. I can remember wondering how I could have made the mistakes Alan had cited—hearing the wrong time, underestimating my own score—and I can remember letting those mistakes go, releasing with them some of the pain that came from losing my father, some of the anger I had toward him for leaving us, some of the anger I had at myself for being so angry with him.

I've always known that I didn't win that trophy, just as I've known that the reason the judge handed it to me had everything to do with Alan. I don't know where he went during that last rider's turn, but I suspect he ducked away to the judges' booth and somehow convinced them that awarding his little brother a trophy was maybe one of the most important things they would do in their lifetimes. I imagine he did whatever he had to do, no matter what the cost.

My brother had faith in me. He knew what I needed when I didn't. He reached out and cared for me when I was more trouble than I imagined. He taught me how to ride and how to live. And for that I say, thank you. Again and again, thank you.

Don Keyes

So Afraid to Change

I was seventeen years old. I had just graduated in the top ten of my high-school class. I had a lot of friends. I had a scholarship to attend Johns Hopkins University. I had a girlfriend and a great family.

And when the time came to leave for college, to say good-bye to the place I had always called home, I lost it. I lost it the night before leaving, saying good-bye to my friends. I lost it in the car during the eight-hour drive to Baltimore. And when we actually got to the campus, I lost it completely. There was no way I was going to make it as a college student, not at Hopkins, not anywhere. I needed to go home. I needed to go home *now*.

My dad disagreed. At first. But eventually, after several hours of discussion back at the hotel room my parents had originally booked only for themselves, it was decided. I would take a leave of absence. The school understood and told me that my acceptance and scholarship would be held for me if I ever wanted them. But I had no intention of ever taking them up on their generous offer. What I wanted to do was go home and be eighteen forever.

My girlfriend was surprised to get the call that I had

come back. She seemed more concerned than happy. Probably the right response.

Briefly, everything returned to the way I had remembered. I was back home and nothing had changed. I was still eighteen; I still had a girlfriend; I was still with my family. But then my friends started to leave for their respective colleges. Soon, there weren't as many people around to hang out with, and the phrase "You need to get a job" was being thrown at me from all directions.

On a random drive through my town's shopping plaza, a horseshoe-shaped strip mall, I saw a "Help Wanted" sign in the window of an everything-for-a-dollar store. I stopped in and asked to see the manager. Her name was Jean. She had bangs teased way up above her forehead and popped her gum incessantly. She smelled like a bowling alley.

"You're not going to college?" she asked.

"No."

"That's fine. I never went to college. Just makes you stuck-up anyways."

"Yeah."

"So you'll be working five days a week, six hours a day. Your big jobs are mopping the floor and unloading the trucks that come with deliveries."

"I've got the job?"

"Yeah, you got the job, college boy. We'll start you at $4.25 an hour. That's five cents more than what we could legally pay you."

So it was done. Thirty hours a week. $4.25 an hour. Before taxes, a grand total of $127.50 every week. I started the next day.

The first truck arrived at 10:15, fifteen minutes after I had punched in. The second truck came at 1:00. The third truck came at 3:00. By the end of the day I had unloaded almost 12,000 pounds of cut-rate merchandise. I had earned $25.50.

The days wore on. There were many frustrating aspects to my new job, but the one I remember most is how angry I would get when the water in my mop bucket got dirty before I had finished cleaning the floor. One day I just stopped mopping. Jean threatened my job if I didn't return mopping to my daily duties. I made excuses. I hid. I built a small room, deep within the piles of recently delivered boxes. I would read in my little fort. That was where I read *Lolita* and *Catch-22* for the first time.

About a week after our mop confrontation, Jean was fired. Turns out she had been "borrowing" merchandise from the store to furnish her home. About thirty seconds after I'd heard of Jean's dismissal I walked into the storeroom and wheeled my mop and bucket into a closet. I closed the door and never set eyes on them again.

In late October, the regional supervisor made a surprise visit to our store to see how we were doing without the services of a manager. She pulled me aside as her visit was coming to an end. "You're a smart kid, right?" I wasn't sure how to answer so I just nodded. "Well, a smart kid who works hard could really go places here." I wasn't sure if she was joking. "Talk to me in about six months, I might have an assistant manager position opening up in one of our other stores. You could be making one and a half times what you're making now." In six months, I could be making $6.40 an hour. The prospect left me underwhelmed. "Oh," she continued, "and see if you can't find a mop and clean up this floor. It's filthy out here."

On Halloween, my girlfriend broke up with me. She called me after taking her little brother trick-or-treating. She asked me to meet her, that we needed to talk. When I pulled up, she was waiting for me on the curb. She was dressed as a pumpkin. An orange felt globe covered her body from shoulders to thighs. Her head was painted green.

By early November, my posture was noticeably worse. I rarely smiled, and even on those days when I didn't work, my clothes still smelled like cut-rate potpourri. I was down. It seemed like everything I had loved about this town, about being home, had changed. Then one night I got invited to go sledding. I lived outside of Buffalo, where snow in November is not an uncommon occurrence. I snuck onto the local country club grounds, where the best hills were located, with some friends of mine who were enjoying their senior year of high school. Surrounded by the exceptionally clear and chilly night, all they could talk about was college, the people they would meet, the parties they would go to, the chance to finally get out of this "tiny, stifling town." I listened to them for almost an hour. I started thinking about the way Hopkins's campus had looked when we drove up for the first time. I saw the students unloading vans and U-Hauls. A beach volleyball court had been built in front of one of the dorms. Flyers on the trees had announced upcoming parties and concerts. That was all there. And I was here.

And I was jealous.

It shocked me. It was then that I realized I had changed. I had been trying with everything I could muster to hold onto that time of graduations, friends and girlfriends, trying to hold off the future as long as I could, without even realizing that I had been changing the whole time. I'd let some ties drop away, others had come undone. And now I was jealous of my high-school friends. I wanted their future, the same one I had put on hold.

It was time to act.

The next morning, I met my dad in the dining room. "Dad," I said, "you think you could call Hopkins and ask about me heading back there this January?"

He smiled, didn't make a big deal. "I'll see what I can find out," is all he said.

Two months later, my father and I were taking that same route that had proven so problematic in September. The eight-hour drive seemed to take forever, and I'd be lying if I said a little of that old fear, that longing for the past, didn't come back. But every time it did, I thought about that night in the snow. I felt the rush of excitement that came with thoughts of starting a new chapter in my life, with new challenges, and the fear faded away. As we drove through the backwoods of Pennsylvania, we passed by a faded old sign on rusted posts, maybe from the previous fall, maybe from the Great Depression, advertising "jack-o-lanterns next left." I smiled and pulled a map from the glove box. We only had about a hundred more miles to go.

Chris Sullivan

Tear-Stained Eyes

As they called Flight 309 for boarding, my boyfriend
Scott and I said our final good-byes. He gently touched
my face and kissed the top of my head, his little way of
saying everything would be okay. Instantly, I was flooded
with memories of tossing popcorn at each other while trying to stay awake during late-night movies and the endless afternoons spent in my room listening to music. I
couldn't believe it was coming to an end.

Again, the annoying voice echoed over loud speakers in
the crowded airport: "Flight 309 now boarding; please
bring your tickets to the front desk." In my mind, the
announcement was saying, "Donya, give him up! Forget
your three years together and all the sacrifices and hard-
ships that came along with it. Just let him go." We
promised we would always love each other, and then
Scott turned to leave. With that, the one person I ever had
true feelings for was gone.

I watched him walk down the hallway thinking maybe,
just maybe, he would turn back. Then I saw his plane take
off, extinguishing my last glimmer of hope. A lump filled
my throat, and I began to push my way through the

crowd, but I could no longer hide my tears. I used to think it was so easy to "be strong" because I had never before experienced a real reason to cry. As I slid through the revolving doors and stepped out into the pouring rain, I was overwhelmed with sadness and regret.

I drove down the abandoned highway blasting my favorite CD in hopes it would drown out the silence of his absence and cheer me up; of course, it didn't. So many thoughts raced through my mind. *Does he know what he means to me? Does he understand how much this hurts? Does he know that I still love him as much as I did the day we met? Is he thinking the same things right now?*

I pulled into my driveway somewhere around midnight. (I really wouldn't know; it's hard to see through tear-filled eyes.) I climbed the stairs to my room and lay face down on my unmade bed. It was the first time I ever cried myself to sleep.

The next morning, I awoke to the sound of my mom cooking breakfast downstairs. I noticed the mascara stains on my pillow and could only imagine how my face looked. Pulling my hair into a ponytail, I stumbled into the bathroom to wash my face. It was so hard to look at myself in the mirror. I felt like the three years I poured into our relationship were gone. I felt as if the other half of me was missing. I felt . . . empty.

What was wrong with me? Every time I closed my eyes, all I could see was Scott and images of the times we shared. There wasn't a single person who knew me better, and I couldn't stand the thought of starting over. Would this feeling ever go away?

I couldn't help but wonder what Scott was doing at that moment. I walked into my room and immediately grabbed the box of keepsakes from the last three years: pictures, letters, poems, ticket stubs. I turned on my music and went through every item, start to finish.

A month went by, and I still felt the same. I wished with all my heart that I could talk to him, just once. However, along with our promise to always love each other, we also had agreed to not keep in touch. At the time, we had thought it would be best for us to just move on. Now, I wasn't so sure we had made the right choice.

As my dad and I sat in the living room later that night watching reruns of *Saturday Night Live,* the doorbell rang. I placed the bowl of popcorn on the coffee table and walked to the door. To my complete surprise, I found Scott standing in the doorway, with a flower in one hand and a suitcase in the other. I can't even begin to describe all the emotions I felt at that moment. Before I knew it, the questions were pouring from my lips, "Why are you here? Are you back for good? What made you change your mind?" Taking my hand, he replied, "This is where I belong."

"What about college?"

"We'll work it out. Let's just talk for now. I've really missed you."

Donya Brown

Bike Ride

A sister is one who reaches for your hand and touches your heart.

Unknown

One of my teachers once asked my class what our favorite memory was. I vaguely remember that we were studying self-esteem, and as a discussion prompt, my teacher asked for the moment in which "you felt the best, you felt that you had the world in the palm of your hand." Some described prestigious awards; others described winning a tournament. My answer, however, invited giggles and hesitant smiles. Why? Because I felt the best when I first learned how to ride my bike—at thirteen. I didn't mind my classmate's stares and snickering, because I knew there was more to the story.

My sister and I shared a typical sisterly relationship: we couldn't *stand* each other. Or, to be honest, she couldn't stand me. I hero-worshipped her. Her taste was the epitome of glamour, her personality the definition of cool. My clothes were mysteriously inclined to look like hers, and even my words tended to mimic those I heard from home. Many times, I even wanted to *literally* follow my sister, whimpering every time I was barred from attending movies with her. Needless to say, I was a brat and an annoyance to her. Any sort of conversation we had usually degraded to fighting, and try as I might, my sister had an extra six years worth of insulting vocabulary (which meant she usually won). After a while, I stopped trying to impress her and learned to be totally indifferent; perhaps the silent treatment would get more approval. I was wrong. We soon fell into a sad pattern—I avoided her, she ignored me, and deep inside, it hurt. So that's how it was between us. Indifferent or hostile, she was only a sister in name. I truly believed that we would forever be apart, two housemates without conversation, two strangers without warmth. And nothing more.

I still remember the day I learned to ride a bike. I had received the bike that Christmas, which was great, until I realized I had no idea how to ride it. My mom had long since abandoned any attempt to teach me; I had proved to be a panicky, frustrating student. I took it upon myself to learn, a little bit each day, but to no avail; I couldn't ride my bike, and on that fateful day, it was no different. I was coming to the end of my daily one-hour torture, and I was so frustrated that I threw my bike aside and began to cry. I guess that was what caused my sister to come outside. At first I was skeptical and tense, as I thought she would begin to tease me or at least burst out laughing. She did neither. I hunched my shoulders forward and turned my face away, but she gently picked my bike up and motioned me over. That was the beginning. She fearlessly held my hand while the tears dried on my cheeks; she steadily held my bike when my feet faltered. She never once let me fall. And for three hours—three wonderful, blissful hours—we learned to ride my bike. No shouting. No fighting. No arguing.

That day I learned that my sister was human—how else could she have been my teacher? I've seen those TV shows with doting siblings, and I've always longed for that perfect harmony. That was the day, however, I had a taste of what real sisterly intimacy could be like. She saw through my weakness; I saw her compassion. I got off my bike that day empowered, and instead of blind admiration, I now had a newfound respect for my sister and for myself. She was both humbled and exalted before my eyes. My sister walked away quietly that day while I showed off my new skills for my mom, and I did not see her the rest of the day. Perhaps she felt something, too.

The day I learned to ride my bike proved to be my bridge from a snotty, naive little brat to a wiser younger sister. It was a life-changing experience, not a miracle. We still occasionally have our random spats and bitter rivalries, but since that day, it's been easier to get along because we have an unspoken respect for each other. The day she taught me how to ride my bike, she ceased to be a bully and became my sister.

And nothing more.

Esther Young

Silence Is Tiring

Courage is the first of human qualities because it is the quality which guarantees all others.

Winston Churchill

"Brittney and her sister, Cari, shall reside within the custody of their father," announced the judge.

"You know what that means," my eight-year-old older sister whispered to me as she adjusted her bony bottom on the court bench. "We have to move again." Pretending to understand, I looked at her with wide eyes and a smile that masked my pain.

But I didn't understand. I didn't understand the questions the judge had asked me. I didn't understand why my mother told me to say one thing and my father told me to say another. I didn't understand why it hurt so much to be a five-year-old.

Eventually my pain subsided. I protected myself from the hurt by keeping my feelings bottled up inside. *Why express myself?* I figured. My voice always seemed to be drowned out by the demanding nature of my father, the desperate cries of my sister and the constant tears of my mother. There was no room left for me. I felt separate, silent, alone and disconnected from the chaotic world that was my family.

Silence is tiring; I carried my feelings around for many years. The only means of expression I knew was through my writing, but this was a voice I kept secret.

During my freshman year in high school, my sister and I were due for yet another court hearing to determine our future custody arrangements. I was frustrated by the exhausting rituals of these custody hearings, and I decided to finally speak my mind. I wrote a letter to the judge and expressed the rage I felt for my opinion being ignored throughout the years. He listened to what I had to say and responded by saying my sister and I did not have to appear in court. This was a huge turning point for me. Not only did I have a voice, but this voice could actually effect change.

By speaking up I got what I needed. Of course, I have since learned that's not always the case. Sometimes we speak and we aren't heard or we aren't given what we need. Either way I am happy to hear my voice and to no longer have to carry all my feelings inside. I'm much lighter now and far less tired.

Brittney Shepherd

Bat Mitzvah Blues

Courage doesn't always roar. Sometimes courage is the quiet voice at the end of the day saying, "I will try again tomorrow."

Mary Anne Radmacher

At age thirteen, I had my bat mitzvah. I was always the youngest kid in my grade, so I had already spent a year going to everyone else's bar and bat mitzvahs. They were all pretty much the same: the girls would be dressed in ruffly floral dresses, the boys in their first new suits. Each kid would give a short speech and would chant or read the prayers over the Torah. Afterwards, the rabbi would take the kid aside and talk to them quietly for a few moments. We always wondered what was said, but no one ever revealed what was said to him or her. The service would end the same way it always did, and then the real fun would start. The reception. Either at a hotel function room or in the social hall of the synagogue, these always ended up being the same, too. A catered lunch, a DJ, a birthday cake and embarrassing speeches, and games and dancing for the kids. Everyone from Hebrew school and regular school would be there. Sometimes there was a theme; there were always goody bags.

After a long year full of weekly tutoring sessions with Cantor Einhorn, and torturous study sessions at home in my room, it was my turn. My whole extended family descended on our house. Family friends I hadn't seen in years sent me presents and savings bonds. I had two beautiful new outfits to wear: a black and white skirt and vest suit to wear to the Friday night Shabbat service, and a black dress with hot pink and black ruffles on the bottom with a pink flower attached to the chest that I would wear on Saturday. My aunt Frieda had brought me two pink scrunchies that matched the dress, and I planned to wear them both.

Saturday morning I woke up and felt very nervous. I ate breakfast and washed up as if it were a regular day. I got dressed. I stood in front of the mirror staring at myself. In my dress, black stockings and shoes, with my hair pulled back in a hot pink scrunchie, I thought I looked awesome. I sighed, grabbed my coat and my binder and went downstairs. My family oohed and aahed and snapped some pictures. We drove to the temple and went in. Downstairs, we sat in the front row of the chapel. The pews were full of my family members and friends and other congregants. The morning was a blur. I dutifully read along in the prayer book, stood up and sat down with everyone for the important prayers. I was so nervous. I dreaded the moment when I was called up on the bimah.

Finally the moment arrived. I walked up on the bimah, my head down, clutching the binder tightly. I sang out the prayers over the Torah. I didn't miss a word, and I thought it sounded pretty good. Rabbi Zecher held the Torah scroll aloft. She rolled the Torah out on the podium, and using the pointer, she found the place where I was to begin reading. I took the pointer from her hand and stared down at the tiny, hand-lettered text. I knew my portion by heart, but suddenly the words would not come out and the letters started to blur and swim on the parchment. I didn't know what to do. Everyone's eyes were upon me. I tried to say something but couldn't. I was overwhelmed with a feeling of embarrassment. To make it worse, I started to cry. No one said anything. The rabbi put her arm around my shoulder and walked me off the bimah, into a little room behind the chapel. She handed me some tissues and asked me what was wrong. What was wrong? I really didn't know. I just knew I couldn't do it, couldn't go out there and read my Torah portion. And I certainly would never be able to face any of those people ever again. For a few minutes, the rabbi and my parents tried to calm me down. I had never gotten stage fright before. It seemed cruel that I had it now. After what felt like forever, I dried my face as best I could. I took a deep breath and let it out. It rippled through me. At this point, my eyes were red and puffy and my hair had pulled free from its scrunchie. I swiped at my eyes again, and then I was ready. All the way across the bimah, I stared straight ahead, not wanting to look at the people sitting in the pews, not wanting to look at the cantor and the other rabbis who sat waiting. I adjusted the microphone. I sniffed. It sounded loud. My voice was shaky, as was my hand holding the pointer. I blinked my eyes and focused on the words drawn in precise calligraphy on the scroll before me. To my relief, the words came. I read the portion straight through with few mistakes, my voice wavering at the start but growing more confident as I went along. When I was done, the Torah was returned to the Ark. Everyone smiled. I read my speech, my voice still a little raspy from crying. The rabbi pulled me aside for the secret chat. I won't tell anyone what she said, but it made me feel good.

Before I returned to my seat in the front row of the chapel, I got a round of applause. I was surprised: in all the bar and bat mitzvahs I had been to, no one had ever clapped before.

Rachel Moore

$\overline{8}$

GROWING UP

We grow because we struggle, we learn and overcome.

R. C. Allen

Moonlight Drives

It was a 1982 Ford Mustang, the deep, sexy color of blood. My older brother had bought it with his share of the money from my father's life-insurance policy. He'd seen an ad in the paper, then that evening he offered the owner half the asking price. An hour later, the car was parked in our driveway. This was how my brother conducted business, like a grifter.

I was sixteen, and by my mother's decree, we were supposed to share the car. My portion of the insurance money was in an account I couldn't access until I turned eighteen, so she only allowed Alan to buy the Mustang if he promised to teach me to drive. When I saw the car that first night—Alan had already named it Phoenix and referred to it with feminine pronouns—my imagination soared. I saw myself driving to school and spiriting my friends on weekend road trips; I coasted on the moonlit beach, as Erin Wells, whose deep green eyes turned my knees to puddles, sat in my passenger seat. At sixteen, keys to a car are like keys to a vault where the answers to youth's most confounding riddles are stored; getting a car meant getting a life, and by that, I mean, getting the girl.

But Alan never threw me the keys. In fact, for most of the first month, Phoenix sat with her hood open in our garage. Although she ran with such power that I found myself clutching my seat belt when we went for parts, Alan wanted to make adjustments. Most surprising was his decision to reverse the gear configuration in the transmission—first became fifth, second became fourth, etc. If someone tried to steal Phoenix, he'd rigged her to stall and strand them.

I worked at a miniature golf course, as did Erin Wells. She tied her yellow work shirt in a knot above her belly button, and she could make holes-in-one on every green; when our boss gave his weekly lectures about the register continually coming up short, she didn't cower like the rest of us; she threw raucous parties whenever her parents left town. Though we worked together each afternoon, I'd never been invited to a party.

Eventually I started sneaking the Mustang out at night and taught myself to drive the backward gears. After a few excursions, Phoenix rarely stalled. Within no time, my midnight cruises lasted hours on end; I sped through abandoned streets and past my friends' houses, past Erin's. But I never stopped. I liked the freedom of driving alone, just as I liked the promise of having cracked the code to my brother's gear configuration; I liked knowing that he didn't know what I knew.

I'd sworn to myself I wouldn't tell anyone, yet soon enough, I spilled everything to Erin. We were organizing the putters. I told her how my brother had haggled for Phoenix and how he reversed the gearbox, how I'd been stealing the car every night. "She purrs like a kitten," I said, because Alan had said that. I expected Erin to swoon, for her eyes to brighten as she begged me to whisk her away. Instead she said, "I guess that also explains the $100 missing from tonight's till."

A week later, Phoenix wouldn't start. Alan had driven her earlier that afternoon, and she'd run perfectly, but she wouldn't turn over when I cranked the ignition. I thought I'd flooded the engine. The same thing happened the next night, then the next and the next. Alan drove every day and never mentioned any problems, but when I crept into the night and tried the keys, she wasn't getting juice. I feared he'd learned about my moonlight drives and had loosened the battery cables or removed a spark plug, but everything under the hood looked good. Soon, though, Phoenix started giving Alan trouble. It happened once when he took me to work, then twice more when he tried to leave. Eventually she always started, but she became less reliable. When I asked Alan what the problem might be, he shook his head and sulked into our house. The next morning I expected to find him diagnosing the trouble, but instead he was perusing the classifieds. He wanted to sell the Mustang and buy an import. My stomach turned; it was as if he'd said we were euthanizing our dog.

I wondered if my drives could have done in Phoenix, if somehow I'd been doing something so terrifically wrong that her engine just threw in the towel. I decided that if the car didn't start tonight, I'd confess to Alan. He'd be furious, but at least he might be able to save her.

All of this occurred to me during the boss's larceny lecture, and although I'd not paid strict attention, I gathered the register had been short $200 this week. He was livid; he was sweating and veins showed on his forehead. He ranted and paced in the concession area, while the workers—there were six of us—sat at orange tables. We were watching the clock, waiting to go home. Then the boss said, "And guess what? I know which one of you it is."

My heart stuttered. For a split second it crossed my mind that he'd accuse me—though, of course, my only crime was borrowing Phoenix—but my real anxiety came because I, too, suddenly knew who the thief was. Erin was chewing a straw, uncharacteristically eyeing the clock more urgently than any of us. She wore new, expensive Reeboks, and she looked about to cry. As with the doomed Mustang, I wanted to save her.

So no one was more surprised than Erin—not even the boss or me—when I cleared my throat and said, "I'll pay it all back."

"Now you have to find another job," Alan said driving home. Somehow I'd thought he'd applaud my chivalry, but he couldn't believe I'd done it. "And she let you get fired? Sounds like a real catch."

That night Phoenix still wouldn't start. I tried for an hour, then went inside and waited, then returned to try again. I turned the key, pumped the accelerator, but my heart wasn't in it. I'd already resigned myself to the fact that the car was a lemon. She seemed no different to me than Erin—they were just dreams. And dreams, I'd started to learn, were best left untouched; in daylight, they fizzled and stalled; they left you stranded and got you fired. Maybe that night—at the golf course, then later in the Phoenix—I changed. Maybe I wandered from innocence into adulthood, into a world where a dream and $2,000 will buy a broken-down car, but I didn't feel that then. I felt younger than I'd ever felt in my whole life.

"There's a switch under the seat," Alan said suddenly. He was in the backseat, and he scared me half to death.

My hands started shaking. When I spoke, a quiver came into my voice. I said, "There's a what?"

"There's a toggle switch under the driver's seat. When it's flipped toward your feet, it cuts power to the engine."

I reached down, half-expecting a mousetrap to snap on my fingers. But there was only a small switch, flipped forward. Alan said, "I thought you'd figure that out, too, but

I guess not. Maybe there's still a few things your older brother can teach you."

"How about women?" I asked. "Can you teach me about those?"

He laughed a little and said, "Let's start with odometers."

And at that moment I realized Alan *was* proud of me, proud of what I'd done at work and proud that I'd taught myself to drive. He was complimenting me the only way he could, as a brother. We were more alike than either of us knew—sons of the same parents, boys who'd lost the same father—and Phoenix gave us an opportunity to follow our dreams.

"I have a suspicion we'll start seeing more of this Erin," Alan finally said from the backseat, "so you'd better show me where she lives." It took a moment to understand he wasn't moving into the driver's seat. I'd never driven with him in the car before, and an exquisite fear rushed through my body. But that passed, as everything does, and I reached down and flipped the kill switch. When I turned the key, I still expected the engine to fail. She didn't, though. She came alive without so much as a single cough, and driving with my brother that night was like nothing I'd ever known; it was as if I'd been born again, given wings to fly from the darkest of ashes.

Don Keyes

365 Days

I was popular for exactly one year—all through eighth grade, to be exact. The irony of my popularity was lost on no one, particularly me; after all, I had spent the first few years of middle school labeled a complete dork, among other not-so-nice things. How was I instantaneously catapulted from the crowd everyone tried to avoid to the crowd everyone wanted to be in? There was only one explanation: fate.

The first day of gym class that year we all sat around on the dusty floor listening to guidelines for the dress code, the rules of good sportsmanship and the expectation of enthusiastic participation. (Yeah, right.) I fell into a bit of a daze as our teacher droned on and on, until she stated that it was time to assign locker partners. Everyone began glancing around covertly at the girls sitting around them, wondering whose smelly socks would be next to their own for the next ten months.

She read off the pairs, one by one. They were randomly picked, and therefore no one could accurately predict how much they might suffer from the results. When the gym teacher read my name, I closed my eyes and waited. The name that followed was that of the most popular girl in my grade. My stomach dropped. I would have rather been assigned to the most unhygienic of partners than someone so pretty, so well-liked—and who was such a snob. She turned around and glared at me, clearly expressing her own disgust with the cruel hand destiny had dealt her. I sighed heavily, anticipating that this year would be no easier than the last.

But I was wrong. The fact was that although I wasn't stylish, I was kind; and though I was not gorgeous, I had a good sense of humor. And contrary to my own first impressions, my partner was actually quite intelligent and fun to be around. As a result, the stifled conversations my partner and I shared for the first few weeks ("Are these your socks or mine?") slowly developed into discussions on the pointlessness of floor hockey, what the cafeteria food was *really* made of, and whether our English teacher was actually crazy or just trying to keep us interested in her lectures.

As different as night and day, the two of us somehow became close. Thus, I became popular by association. From that point on, I never spent a single song against the wall at dances, and I was at the mall every weekend. Though I didn't make the cheerleading squad (I still maintain the auditions were rigged—I could cartwheel with the very best of them), I spent each football game in the stands surrounded by people who had never seemed to notice me before. I had gone from being virtually invisible to someone people wanted to be seen with—in a matter of weeks.

Undoubtedly, popularity had its benefits. It was a relief not to be called names anymore, and it was a comfort to feel as though I belonged. The year flew by instead of dragging on forever, and soon we had graduated, spent a summer at the pool and were starting our freshman year of high school. I walked in with my friend at my side, certain that we were automatically in. What I found, however, was that with many more students, there came many more groups and cliques who were just as popular as ours. People did not necessarily accept you just because you were admired in middle school. As the first weeks went by, I found myself struggling to keep up and doing things I didn't feel comfortable doing in order to keep my social status. It didn't take me long to realize that the social scene was no longer for me, so one day I did the unthinkable: I sat at a different table for lunch.

The people I sat with that day became dear friends for the next four years, and they are still my friends today. They liked me simply because of who I was, not because I could get them invited to parties or introduce them to the hottest guys. I always felt comfortable with them, and their support encouraged me to broaden my horizons. Instead of cheerleading, we joined the choir. Instead of hanging out at the mall, we planned picnics in the park.

Their admiration was sincere—and reciprocated.

Three hundred sixty-five days of popularity had taught me to recognize what was artificial and fake. Years of being "just another girl" taught me that true friendship is found in unlikely places and that sincerity beats popularity hands-down. It is better to be complimented on your kindness than your clothes. It is more gratifying to be admired for your talents than your status. Accepting yourself as you are, and finding friends who love you because you *are* that person, will provide more happiness and comfort than any amount of popularity ever could.

Kelly Garnett

Uniform

It was a scene straight from the annals of teen nightmare scenarios: Over Saturday morning pancakes, my
parents announced they had enrolled me in a private
school. Not just any private school—an all-girls Catholic
school *with uniforms.* If I had been cutting class, smoking
cigarettes in my middle school's mint-tiled bathrooms, or
loitering about with small, sinister boys who glared at my
parents, I might have understood. But I hadn't even done
anything interesting enough to deserve this cruel decision. I petitioned my parents all summer with plea bar-
gains and threats, but when fall crept around, there I was
sighing resentfully as I slipped on my polyester skirt, but-
toned up my thin white blouse, tied a ridiculous tie
around my neck and stomped dramatically to my dad's
sedan in stiff, shiny penny loafers. He smirked at my
expense and handed me two new dimes. "Put them in
your shoes. That'll show those nuns."

Nuns? Dear God. I hadn't even considered nuns.

I had, however, considered my new classmates. My
public school friends and I had fretted all summer about
these unseen, private school–bred creatures—wealthy

snots, we imagined, with expensive purses and a million tortures planned for inferior classes like myself. When they turned sixteen, their daddies would buy them BMWs, which they would make a point of parking on the opposite end of the school lot from my hand-me-down clunker as though poverty were contagious. Unanimously, my friends agreed that they were lucky they weren't me. Now I had to suffer nuns, too?

The halls of Incarnate Word whirled with plaid. Matching girls skipped in all directions, hugging and squealing, "Omigod!" and, "How was your summer?!" Nuns and civilian teachers cruised amid the flurry. I went to my first class, sat down and didn't open my mouth for an entire semester.

By the beginning of spring, I'd mumbled enough words to make a few good friends—Sara, Cathy, Jamie and Anne—and learned that the country club crew, whom we called "The Buffies," kept their whispers about debutante balls and banquets to themselves. They couldn't be bothered to engage in the snobby insults and hair-pulling stunts I'd come to fear from a lifetime of bad teen movies. More importantly, such a small school couldn't even uphold a social hierarchy. All cliques were weighted equally—except for the Star Trek nerds, but no society is perfect. In this society, however, you were forced to get a personality. This wasn't like public school friendships when preppies drifted towards preppy-looking people. We were forced to look the same; what distinguished us was the person beneath the plaid, and it was time to figure out just who she was.

My parents had promised I could leave after one year if I truly, deeply hated private school, but after just an hour's deliberation, I decided to stay on, making up my absence to my public-school friends with true tales of nunsense. There was Sister Agnes who called everyone "my good American," Sister Clarita with one big leg and one normal one (she never spoke, only hissed), and her sister, Sister Ailbee, whose shifting hairline just had to be a wig. Sister Ailbee was also legendary for her perfect attendance at every basketball game, her passionate defense of the Trail of Tears and the time she broke off midsentence during her own lecture on the Great Depression to stare over our heads at the wall and chant, "I'm Abraham Lincoln."

Eventually, my routine polyester plaid getup made the same transition from creepy to, well, lovably creepy. Kneesocks were cute, almost disarmingly precious, and since I didn't need much practical everyday wear, I was free to spend my allowance on highly impractical party clothes for the liberating weekend. My old wardrobe of jeans and T-shirts couldn't compete with silver-sequined miniskirts and dresses lined in hot pink fur. Smart girls even got their driver's license pictures taken in uniform, their ties knotted high enough inside the frame to catch a sympathetic cop's eye. Most of them finagled their way out of speeding tickets with a warning. When I got cited for breaking my city's teen curfew, I wore my uniform to court and was sentenced to ten hours of community service pouring lemonade at the public library's weekly poetry readings. The guy ahead of me had to scrub barnacles off the police officers' boats. We knew what the uniform did to civilians; it was a superhero's disguise bestowing the powers of innocence and charm.

Private school had never been punishment, and it never became prison. Like high schools of all shapes and flavors, Incarnate Word was a rite of passage with bragging rights of its own. While I never wore pants to class, never cheered on my school at a football game or stared dreamily at the cute boy a few desks over, I did graduate with a well-carved sense of self and a solid group of girlfriends I'll know until we're all in grandmother shoes. And for the rest of my life I'll be able to juice up conversations with the simple boast: I survived an all-girls Catholic high school.

Amy Nicholson

A Perfect Score

Failure is success if we learn from it.

Malcolm S. Forbes

"Hey Lara," Susan called. "How about lunch? We haven't talked in so long."

"Can't. I've got a bio test next period," I yelled, rushing off to the library. I opened up my book and frantically crammed any extra information. *I need an A,* my mind kept repeating. *That would make another perfect quarter and a definite place on the honor roll.* I studied till the last minute of lunch and rushed to class.

Good, I thought, glancing over the first page. I quickly filled in the answers, smiling with confidence. When I reached the last page, my mind went blank. I read the question over, but the words started to jumble, and although I could picture the pages of the book, I could not read the text. I stared at a diagram of the plant cell. My mind wouldn't function. I started chewing the pen. *Concentrate, Lara, you studied this last night.* I tried to re-member what was written in the book. After studying until midnight the night before, I felt I had a good enough grasp on the material. I had fallen asleep with a mental picture of a plant cell. *So why can't you remember it now?* I asked myself. I glanced up at the clock. I had fifteen more minutes. *Okay, the round circle has to be the nucleus and the lines . . .* my mind wavered. The pen cap fell to the ground. I reached over and grabbed it clumsily. The fifteen minutes evaporated into three. Soon everyone left, and I was still staring at the paper.

"Lara, class ended seven minutes ago. I need you to pass in your test," Mrs. Phloem said, stretching out her hand. I quickly placed random names in the blank spaces and reluctantly handed her the test. Slowly gathering my belongings, I left the room.

After school, I went to the locker room and changed at the very back for basketball practice. I heard giggling up front but couldn't be bothered. There were more important subjects to deal with, like the biology test.

After practice, I quickly changed and walked home. The air felt nippy, my nose was frozen, and even with gloves on, I felt the cold air freeze my fingers. I shivered, wishing the sun were out. I disliked the short days and long nights of winter. It made my time feel compressed. Especially now, with basketball, my life seemed like a nonstop race. I awoke at six the next morning for school. Practices started at three thirty and I wasn't back home until eight.

That night after dinner I sat down to finish *The Great Gatsby*, which was due the next Friday. I thought "Great American Novels" would be the appropriately challenging English class for the semester. Unfortunately, with overly idealistic characters like Gatsby, the book truly felt like a waste of my time. Yet the fact remained I was afraid to open my biology text and check the answers, although I refused to believe I might have done poorly on the test. The worst grade I could receive is a B. That would just about keep in balance with my brother's perfect high-school record. How I wished my brother wasn't so perfect. It made me work twice as hard to prove myself to others. On the other hand it was a challenge, and I liked challenges.

Soon it was eleven-thirty. Finishing the book I pressed back into the chair. *Do I have anything else?* I asked myself, glancing at the table. Outside, thunder rumbled and interrupted my thoughts. Staring at the window, I watched drops of water slide down the glass pane. "It's the middle of January, and it's raining," I said aloud. "How profound."

The next day in biology I got my test back. I stared dumbfounded at the red marked: 76. *Not even a B minus,* my mind screamed. *Just average. It's over. No perfect record.*

When I reached home that night, I couldn't concentrate on my homework. I felt like a failure. Now I wouldn't reach my brother's standards. My brother was so smart that he got a scholarship to Harvard. How could I prove myself with a 76?

I sat at my desk, stuck on the same math problem for an hour. Sighing, I laid down the pencil. Outside the thunder clamored. I jumped at the unexpected sound and stared at the window. It was raining again. This was the third night. I reached over abruptly, unfastened the storm window and pulled it open. Sticking my head out, I yelled, "Stop it! I'm trying to concentrate!" I got sprayed with the sudden force of water. I retreated and closed the window. Laying my head on the cold glass I glanced down at the empty street. There was only one dim streetlight, which highlighted each drop of water. It reminded me of the way Gatsby had stood outside Daisy's house after the accident, waiting for the perfect life. It had never happened. "Hmm," I solemnly grinned. "Now, here I am, trying to make my life perfect," I said to my reflection. Sighing, I realized it would probably rain tomorrow and that I would probably be starting the new chapter on photosynthesis. Yet unlike a great

American classic, my story would continue, because I did have a second chance. "Wow," I smiled, "school can teach me a few lessons in life." It wasn't the most profound moment in my life, but turning the lights off I got under my bedcovers and thought, *Maybe tomorrow I'll have lunch with Susan*. The fact is, one test is not my life. Taking the time to build a friendship that will last all the exams of life and believing in myself and in doing my best will always be the ultimate best score.

Lalanthica V. Yogendran

Two Ways We Can Remember It

When I was in high school, the town I grew up in was pretty rough. None of my friends liked using violence, and I thought it was pretty much the worst turn any situation could take, but I think all of us had been in fistfights, been beaten up a few times, and generally accepted the fact that even though violence was terrible, it was a part of life. It wasn't that you used it as a tool, but when people made it necessary, you couldn't be afraid to step up and defend yourself, so they didn't hurt you.

The night Mikey was jumped, I remember that we were all playing pool at this place called the Hilltop. They didn't serve liquor, so teens could play pool there until eleven or twelve, even on weeknights. There were five of us there, and I was at the table, losing to Jens, as usual, since he was the best pool shark among us, when Dan got a page from Mikey. When he came back from the telephone by the bathroom, we could all tell something was wrong by the gray color of his face framing a small scowl of worry.

"We gotta go pick up Mikey," he said, the words coming out slowly. "I think something happened to him."

That was all he would say until Mikey jumped into Dan's van at the corner of Twenty-third and Potrero. Mikey's face looked like a very hardworking prizefighter's; it was speckled with livid bruises, his lip was split and one eye was already swelling shut. I had certainly never been worked over so badly, and I think each one of us winced a little when we first saw his busted mug.

"These guys came outta nowhere," said Mikey. "They saw me on the bus, and when I was getting off, I guess they musta followed me around the corner. Then I just heard this deep voice asking me for a light, and when I turned to look, I just saw a fist come up all fast and then Wham! and I was on the ground. Everything else was just a blur, man." He sounded like the most tired guy there ever was, like he had been dreading talking about it, but also felt like he was unloading a huge weight just by telling us. He was vague in his recollection of exactly who the guys were, and he could only give us a few very rough descriptions, which could have fit just about anybody with the same basic skin tone or body shape.

We took Mikey home, but he didn't want us to come in. I guess he was scared of telling his mom about it. We asked him if he wanted to go to the hospital, but he said he hated the hospital and just wanted to go home.

The next day in school, he had stitches in his lip, so I guess he had to go to the hospital anyhow, but he didn't say anything about it until the next week, when he saw the guy who had asked him for a light.

We had spent the intervening time recycling Mikey's story between us, talking about what we'd do if we could just find the guys who had beat up our friend. We never said anything when he was around, because we all knew Mikey would just rather forget all about it. But we were angry, and we wanted to feel like we could do something about it, so we talked and threw around fantasies of revenge and retribution.

Mikey saw the guy during lunch, at the supermarket near our school, where the guy apparently worked. Mikey said he had been behind the deli counter, chatting up some girl who worked there, too. Mikey said he had recognized him right away, and saw that his name tag read "Victor."

After school, Mikey went home as he had every day since he got jumped, but the rest of us all gathered at our usual spot above the old train tracks.

Now that we had a name and a regular location on the object of our anger, the plans could begin. Some wanted to jump him outside of his work, but Dan eventually convinced most of us that we should get some bats, follow him home, and get him there.

All of this scared the daylights out of me. As I said before, none of us were strangers to using our fists, but this was different. This was not the childish rough-housing of greedy or mean juvenile thugs, this was planned, organized violence that could get very real, very fast, resulting in serious injuries for this guy. I had this sick feeling of both terror and resolve—like the floor was dropping out of my stomach—but that wasn't going to stop me from doing what I had to. If we were going to use violence, I would be there. I felt it would be my duty, but I didn't want to, so I didn't know what to say.

I looked over at Jens, who had this look in his eyes that I have only seen a few times before or since. It was the look of supreme sadness, the sorrow that comes from a direct understanding of all the pain and hatred in the world. He looked at the ground, and then, in a very careful, clear voice, said something I will always remember.

"Guys, I'm as pissed as anyone about what happened to Mikey, and I don't think this guy deserves to get away with it, but we have to think about what this can cause. The way I see it, years from now, we can remember all this stuff in one of two ways: the first way is that we'll say,

'Remember when Mikey got jumped? Man, that sucked, but we looked out for him.' The other way is that we'll say, 'Remember when we beat up that dude, and he got killed, and one of us went to jail?' or 'Remember when one of us got killed because his boys decided to find us and put a bullet in us?' I think it'd be better if we choose the first way and think of some other plan to get this guy."

The words seemed to tumble out of him from some other place, like a hole in time had opened up and the guy he was going to become years from then had fed those words straight to his younger self. Silence overtook us, the way it does when someone is saying something exactly right even though no one else could see it before. Like ice water on red-hot iron, it cooled our anger, and we all accepted the wisdom of his words.

We came up with something better: we talked to the girl who was Victor's coworker. It turns out, she thought Victor was a total jerk and was only too pleased to help us pay him back. We concocted this plan to incriminate him for stealing liquor, which she assured us that Victor had bragged about to her in any case, and our plan went off without a hitch. He lost his job, and we heard he got slapped with a hefty fine, drug counseling and probation, so we figured that was good enough for our revenge.

Mikey wasn't happy about it anyway, but he was glad we wanted to help him and thanked us for deciding not to get violent with Victor.

I think we were all a little bit less than satisfied, but the retribution wasn't important. We had done our best to stand by a friend without being stupid or impulsive.

The crucial thing was that we had turned a corner in our lives. As I remember the events of those days, I look at them as one of those times that helped decide who I am, and that, at all times, I had a choice about shaping what kind of future I could have.

Evan Wynns

Losing Sight of the Shore

Each friend represents a world in us, a world possibly not born until they arrive, and it is only by this meeting that a new world is born.

Anaïs Nin

The night before I left home for college I don't recall getting much sleep. I had that nervous feeling in the pit of my stomach, and even though it was the middle of August, my hands were cold and clammy. As we pulled out of the driveway the following morning in my parents' minivan, I watched my house, my yard and my town getting farther and farther away. I gripped my pillow and sobbed all 340 miles to Whitewater, Wisconsin.

I thought about a lot of things on the way down and asked myself repeatedly why I hadn't chosen to attend a university a little closer to home. Was I insane? Why was I choosing to put almost five hours between myself and my family, friends and boyfriend? But I knew this was not the time to reevaluate my decision. I kept telling myself that I was going to Whitewater for the education

program, to play soccer, and to "expand my horizons."
The first few weeks were tough. When I wasn't at soccer
practice I was going through photos and other various
mementos with tears rolling down my face. I ran up quite
a phone bill that first month.

The whole soccer thing just wasn't for me, so about a
week and a half later, when the rest of the student body
moved in, I was anxious to get to know the girls on my
floor. I actually felt like I had the upper hand because I had
already been away from home for several days. It didn't
take long, and new friendships began to form.

We were all strangers who by chance were put together
in the same room, dorm, class and campus. Eventually
names became faces, and faces became friends. It's amazing how much you learn about someone in such a short
period of time. I felt closer to some of these people in just
three months than people I had known for years.

My first trip home was one I anticipated greatly. I even
had a countdown on my door. When the day finally
arrived, and I made the long haul back up to Spooner, I
remember feeling like I had been splashed in the face with
cold water. I guess I don't really know what I had
expected. My family didn't seem much different, and my
bedroom remained untouched. But the whole atmosphere
was changed; suddenly I felt like a visitor, and the place
where I had spent many years now seemed slightly foreign. I met up with a lot of old friends and attended a high-
school football game, but it's funny how out of place I felt.
I stared at the people who I used to talk with on the phone
for seemingly never-ending amounts of time, and somehow I did not have a lot to say.

I returned back to school and felt lost. I wasn't
extremely close to my new friends yet, but a lot had
changed with my old ones. I was going through the transition. It is a time to let go of the past—being careful not to

forget it, but instead focusing on the present and aiming for the future. If I hadn't gone through the transition I would have missed out on a lot of things. I would have missed out on late-night talks in the middle of the hall, water fights, the hair-dying-gone-bad experience and the infamous pumpkin launch from the fourth-floor window. (No one was hurt, but unfortunately for us, the act was committed just as the RA entered the building.)

As time wore on, I found my trips home were less frequent and made only to catch up with my family or see my boyfriend. I actually missed being at school, that place I had once found so dreadful.

The night my boyfriend and I broke up, the first people I told were the girls that lived on my floor, and when I had finally controlled my tears enough to make a phone call, it was to a girl who lived across campus.

College life is great. Yes, there are a lot of changes as you enter a world of procrastination, cramming and lack of sleep. There are many things to get used to, like living on a floor with sixty girls and twelve shower stalls. But it is a time to grow and become stronger. When the end of my first year came, I found it ironic that I was crying all the way back to Spooner for the summer, for the same reasons I had cried all the way to Whitewater. I didn't want to leave. But the friends I made will still be there when I return in the fall. They have come into my life for a reason, and I can't wait to see them again.

Marianne Melcher

Live Your Dream

The future belongs to those who believe in the beauty of their dreams.

Eleanor Roosevelt

After birth, we all are hurled,
into an ever-changing world.
We live our lives, we learn to love,
and are granted dreams from up above.

But as we grow, we learn to see,
we're living in reality.
With talent squandered, forgotten dreams,
the world's a scary place, it seems.

For people don't always learn to fly.
They lose their dreams, and let them die.
Their favorite things, what they do best
are lost, forgotten, laid to rest.

From this, we can all learn to keep
our treasures near, not buried deep.
Our fiercest loves, and great desires
are in our souls, our inner fires.

If you love music, learn to play.
Or if it's art, then draw each day.
Whatever you have the dream to do,
once it's found, keep it with you.

You'll meet with failure and stop to cry,
but you can do it if you try.
For the world will look so much more bright,
if you just keep your dreams in sight.

Katie Hays

Right Kick, Wrong Direction

*You don't get to choose how you're going to die,
or when. You can only decide how you're going
to live. Now.*

Joan Baez

I was eleven years old. This was my first soccer game.
As the tall, skinny kid stuck in the middle of the muddy
field, with little knowledge of the rules and regulations of
the game, I was nervous and apprehensive, but still
excited. With kids running at me from all directions, I
observed the skills that many of my teammates possessed.
Their motions appeared to be so smooth and effortless,
while their faces revealed their attachment to the game. I,
on the other hand, lacked the dedication that many of the
other kids had.

Little to my knowledge, this game turned out to be an
intense one. My team was trailing behind the entire game,
but toward the end, we tied it up. I watched as parents
yelled and screamed, filled with excitement and emotion.
Many of the parents, with their waving arms and beaming

eyes, seemed more involved in the game than their children.

Suddenly, it was my turn to kick the ball. This was my chance to reveal that I was as good as everyone else. I brought my leg back and was ready to kick with all my strength. I gave a good, hard kick—one of my better—but unfortunately, I had kicked the ball in the wrong direction. Seeing the disappointed faces of the members of my team, I felt my face go from pale white to bright red; I wanted to run home, faster than I ever ran in a soccer practice.

Over the next few years, I continued to participate in a variety of sports, trying to find the one where I would be the center of attention for the right reasons. That never happened. As the firstborn son, my father could not wait to toss the baseball around the backyard with me. Each time he would throw the ball, I somehow managed to trip on a shoelace or stumble over a rock. My father continued to push me, and during my elementary-school years it seemed that I might become quite the athlete. I was able to fake an interest and avoid the action when playing. At the same time, my little brother was suddenly not so little and began to dominate the family athletic domain. His ability and genuine passion for sports made me wonder why I was so different.

I began to feel like an outsider, not only with my family, but also with the whole male race. All my friends could play sports, and they all knew of my less-than-perfect abilities. I did have many friends to help ease the path of growing up without indulging in sports, but there were still the many instances when I was not invited for a foot-ball game. It was frustrating to have this inability when agility appeared to be such a significant aspect of a young child's life. Whenever I would be introduced to people, whether it be a kid in school or a friend of a parent, I was always asked if I played basketball—a natural question to a fourteen-year-old six-footer. When I responded "No," everyone would tell me that I should. But I did not want to, and I was never able to figure out why it mattered so much.

As I became a teenager, I put an end to all my phoniness about sports. When my parents finally allowed me to stop participating in Little League and other sports teams, I was filled with mixed emotions. I was happy that I did not have to go through another baseball practice, standing in the outfield, hoping a ball would never be hit in my direction. But on the other hand, I was a "reject." I did not go to basketball practice after school like everyone else. I felt alone.

Eventually, I realized that I was not a recluse, but that I enjoyed the company of other people, as well as taking part in activities. I recognized that I was not a social misfit, but a social butterfly. New friends helped me to discover my inherent sense of humor, along with my natural ardor to explore and appreciate the world around me. I began to focus on the other aspects of my life, the ones I enjoyed. In high school I identified my desire to become a leader, and I involved myself in different student organizations. I also pursued my interests in writing and film. I spent my time being productive, but more importantly, I felt good about myself and what I was doing.

My lack of ability for sports was something that separated me from many people, but also made me realize what in life I do enjoy. Now when faced with a challenge, I feel exactly like that little boy who stood, scared and uneasy, in that intimidating soccer field. The only difference is now that uneasiness is accompanied by a surge of confidence in my talent and capabilities.

Joseph Losardo

Label This!

You don't have to listen
To the rumors and hype
Or let others brand you
With a stereotype
You don't need the clothes,
Or the shoes, or the car
Just believe in yourself, and be who you are

You can try hard in school
Without being a geek,
'Cause there's way more to life
Than the popular clique
Joining the band doesn't make you uncool
It's those who say otherwise who are the fools.
Join a team, or a club, or try out for the play
Don't wait any longer, go for it today

You don't have to be great, just get out there and start
And whatever you do, let it come from the heart
Be it music, or writing, or drama, or sports,
Don't let anyone else make you think you fall short

Oh, the things you can do,
If you be who you are,
Just be true to yourself, and you will go far

Oh, the people you'll meet
Of all different kinds
Just forget about labels
And open your mind

Oh, the things you will learn
And the worlds you will see
If you say to yourself:
"I'm glad to be me!!"

Emily Adams

Star of My Own Movie

There is only one corner of the universe you can be certain of improving . . . and that's your own self.

Aldous Huxley

I always loved the movies. It didn't even matter if I went to see them alone. Once the lights faded and the previews began, I kept my eyes on the screen until the credits rolled and the lights came up again. In the movies, nothing seemed impossible; in fact, I liked to pretend that what was happening on-screen was happening in my own life, as well. In other words, I lived vicariously through the actresses on-screen, no longer an ordinary sixteen-year-old girl from a typical suburban neighborhood. I became the star of the cheerleading squad who leads her team to victory, or the orphaned teenager who bridges the gap between the races at her high school, or even the young woman who falls in love with a handsome nobleman from the nineteenth century. And I would always live happily ever after.

It wasn't the charming characters that I loved most of all, or even the exciting adventures they had. I liked the happy endings, the perfect happy endings. I wanted my life to be like that, happy and wonderful. I wanted to escape the stress of family and friends and school. It was all so overwhelming that oftentimes I felt paralyzed. My only escape from the reality that haunted me was ducking into a movie theatre.

I hadn't always been this way. As a young girl I was outgoing and friendly, and even involved in extracurricular activities. High school was different, though. I became quiet and withdrawn.

My parents were worried about me. They didn't understand why I was suddenly so sad. They pleaded with me to call old friends or get more involved with school. They didn't understand what the high-school pressures were like: the pressures to have the perfect body, the perfect grades and the perfect friends. Perfect just wasn't me. My ideal world was unattainable. I was average. No more, no less. Average. I spent my free time on the couch watching one rental movie after another until the lull of the screen would put me to sleep.

After promising my parents a thousand times that I would call one of my old friends, I finally agreed. The only number I knew by heart was Sarah's, so I called her. Sarah herself was pretty close to perfect: straight-A student, class president, off to Yale in the fall, beautiful, sweet, brilliant. We decided to meet for a pizza lunch.

We ate and talked and caught up on old times. She filled in the blanks of her life, and I smiled and told her everything in my life was good.

"Couldn't be better," I lied.

"You're lucky," she said honestly. "I can't tell you how stressed out I've been lately. . . . " She explained the pressures she was under, and even told me about some of her insecurities related to her future.

I couldn't lie to her.

"I could be better actually," I admitted.

I told Sarah everything. I told her how difficult it has been for me the past few years and how unbearable the pressure had been.

"I wish my life was the way it is in the movies," I sighed. "It would be so much easier." I looked down through my fingers, face in my hands.

"I understand," she said.

I looked up at her, questioning her with my eyes.

She told me that she would often escape her realities by filling her spare moments with TV and movies, fantasizing that her life could follow the simple plot lines. She was just like me.

"Then one day," Sarah explained, "I started to think about why I wanted to be like the people in the movies I was watching. What did those characters have that I didn't have? And then it occurred to me. They had their scripts already written out for them. They weren't real; they were somebody's idea, somebody's plan. I had ideas. I had plans. I had the ability to write my own script. If I alone had the power to determine the plot of my life movie, then why wouldn't I make it an inspiring one, a movie with a happy ending?"

She took my hand in hers.

"Cecile," she said, "you are the star of your own movie. Now all you need is your story."

I looked into her eyes and nodded, and then suddenly I began to cry. She was right. No other actress could fill my role. Not one. It was up to me to produce, direct and edit my life. I decided right then and there that I would write my own script. I would set my own goals from now on, goals that I knew I was capable of achieving. There can be no success without the possibility of failure. The only sure way of failing is by refusing to try.

I looked over at Sarah, my new costar.

"Thank you," I said squeezing her hand. The velvet curtain rose, and my film began to take on a glorious life of its own.

Cecile Wood

Oh, the Things That We Feel

Oh, the things that we feel as we walk through our years
As we look back and swim in the lakes of our tears

Oh, the things that we learn as we walk through our
    youth
As we lose our first love, as we lose our first tooth

Oh, we walk through our days with our heads in the sand
How we look up and find we are holding a hand

Oh, the things that we see as we look to the past
How we always assumed that forever would last

We question decisions and analyze words
Of a time that is gone, that flew south with the birds

We remember advice from a time so far back
And we see it's a gift, it is not an attack

We envision the faces of people we knew
Wondering what with their lives did they do

We look at old pictures, hear songs we once sung
We discover the beauty we missed being young

How we never were happy and never at ease
As we plunged into waters as deep as we pleased

To discover that beauty is not what we'd thought
It was there all along, it was not what we sought.

And we view our parents in a whole different light
Though we always knew deep down inside they were
    right

Oh, how they prepared us for oceans and streams
How they taught us to swim and to follow our dreams

We look up from the water to see that we're there
And we open our doors to the people who care

As we look back and swim in the lakes of our tears
Oh, the things that we feel as we walk through the years

Danielle Rosenblatt

Teenage Clichés

When you're a teenager, people unload clichés on you like it's their job. A perennial favorite is, "One day, you'll look back on this and laugh." Nothing used to infuriate me more than hearing that one from my parents when I was going through a crisis. *How,* I wondered, *could they minimize the heartbreak I experienced when my best friend switched schools? How could they find it funny that my hair, which I had dyed a vivid, electric ocean-blue a week before, was now snot green?*

It was outrageously offensive of them. And when I look back on it now, well, I just have to laugh.

Ever hear that Mark Twain quote about how when he was fourteen his father was so ignorant he couldn't stand to be around the man, and upon turning twenty-one was amazed at how much his dad had learned in seven years?

Another cliché, right? But sometimes clichés get that way for a reason. My parents were utterly clueless about the deep complexities of me. They were strict, irrational and understood nothing about being a teen. They came out of the womb forty years old. I would never be like them.

And today, when I hear myself say things like "Now,

let's not get hysterical," or "You're being very passive-aggressive," or even "It's important to understand the value of money," I can barely stop myself from whirling around to see where my mom and dad are hiding, throwing out their countless gems of wisdom.

But I'm not so far from my adolescence to forget certain things. In fact, I just barely escaped unscathed. Like when adults tell you, "These are the best years of your lives." I remember hearing that and feeling utterly dismayed, but not to worry—no matter who tells you that, you don't have to believe them. In fact, even my state senator said those words. I was at my high-school graduation and Chuck Schumer was up there at the podium, claiming that the next night, prom, was to be the best night of our lives. I turned and stared at my friend Jeanette in horror. The average life expectancy of an American woman is eighty. Did Chuck really mean to say that the pinnacle of my existence would arrive the next evening, less than one-fifth of my way through it?

Prom was great, actually—definitely not the best, but plenty of fun. A lot of moments in your teenage years will be. But more often than not, things won't turn out like a teen movie. The mean, popular girls may not see the errors of their ways in the end. The dorky kid everyone picks on most likely won't experience a miraculous physical and social transformation and go on to date the star athlete.

The scary part is, sometimes real life isn't much different from your teenage years. I still feel awkward pretty often. (The other day, I tripped getting on the train on the way to work and fell flat on my face in front of rush-hour crowds.) I still get zits. I still feel intimidated by the women who are taller, thinner and better dressed than I am.

At the same time, so much has changed. I sometimes wonder how thirteen-year-old Alanna would react if nineteen-year-old Alanna could go back in time and stop in for a visit. I envision the thirteen-year-old dropping her headphones, which are blaring Marilyn Manson, and backing away in terror, snot green hair flying. The nineteen-year-old looks so . . . normal! She highlights her hair! She gets manicures! She has Calvin Klein capris, lipstick, hip-hop CDs and, God help her, a self-help book! She has become one of the conformists she so despises.

Or have I? Maybe instead I've realized trying so desperately to be different is its own kind of conformity, and I should just like what I like without constantly second-guessing myself. After all, baggy black clothes don't make me a nonconformist. As one of my classmates told me in my first semester of college, just the fact that I wear clothes at all means I'm sticking to a societal norm. (I'm not advocating running around naked, here.) Maybe I've learned to channel my awkwardness into more productive outlets than green hair—like writing, for example.

Not everything becomes so clear. I'm still not completely sure if I'd be better off running a sheep farm in New Zealand or writing sitcoms in Los Angeles. But for the first time, that kind of confusion is exciting. Instead of feeling like I have no idea who I am, and the entire world is out to antagonize me, I see all these possibilities before me. I see a journey ahead, instead of a group of popular girls ready to pelt tennis balls at my head in gym class. It's hard to know how incredibly okay you'll feel once you exit your teen years. I remember when the Columbine massacres took place my sophomore year, I thought, *Yeah, I can see how something like this, as horrible as it is, could happen.* Not that I could ever envision doing such a thing or condone such behavior, but that sense of being cornered and needing to fight your way out—I got that. Now I think about how Dylan Klebold and Eric Harris were seniors, only weeks away from being through with high school forever, and I wish they could have had the perspective I have now. Because the worst of it really does end eventually.

Alanna Schubach

Who Is Jack Canfield?

Jack Canfield is one of America's leading experts in the development of human potential and personal effectiveness. He is both a dynamic, entertaining speaker and a highly sought-after trainer. Jack has a wonderful ability to inform and inspire audiences toward increased levels of self-esteem and peak performance.

He is the author and narrator of several bestselling audio- and videocassette programs, including *Self-Esteem and Peak Performance, How to Build High Self-Esteem, Self-Esteem in the Classroom* and *Chicken Soup for the Soul—Live.* He is regularly seen on television shows such as *Good Morning America, 20/20* and *NBC Nightly News.* Jack has coauthored numerous books, including the *Chicken Soup for the Soul* series, *Dare to Win* and *The Aladdin Factor* (all with Mark Victor Hansen), *100 Ways to Build Self-Concept in the Classroom* (with Harold C. Wells), *Heart at Work* (with Jacqueline Miller), *The Power of Focus* (with Les Hewitt and Mark Victor Hansen) and *Chicken Soup for the Soul Life Lessons.*

Jack is a regularly featured speaker for professional associations, school districts, government agencies, churches, hospitals, sales organizations and corporations. His clients have included the American Dental Association, the American Management Association, AT&T, Campbell's Soup, Clairol, Domino's Pizza, GE, ITT, Hartford Insurance, Johnson & Johnson, the Million Dollar Roundtable, NCR, New England Telephone, Re/Max, Scott Paper, TRW and Virgin Records. Jack has taught on the faculty of Income Builders International, a school for entrepreneurs.

Jack conducts an annual seven-day Living Your Highest Vision training program. It attracts entrepreneurs, sales professionals, corporate trainers, professional speakers, and others interested in creating and living their ideal life.

Look for Jack's latest book, *The Success Principles,* on the shelf in January 2005.

Self-Esteem Seminars
P.O. Box 30880
Santa Barbara, CA 93130
phone: 805-563-2935 • fax: 805-563-2945
Web site: *www.jackcanfield.com*

Who Is Mark Victor Hansen?

In the area of human potential, no one is more respected than Mark Victor Hansen. For more than thirty years, Mark has focused solely on helping people from all walks of life reshape their personal vision of what's possible. His powerful messages of possibility, opportunity and action have created powerful change in thousands of organizations and millions of individuals worldwide.

He is a sought-after keynote speaker, bestselling author and marketing maven. Mark's credentials include a lifetime of entrepreneurial success and an extensive academic background. He is a prolific writer with many bestselling books, such as *The One Minute Millionaire, The Power of Focus, The Aladdin Factor* and *Dare to Win* in addition to the *Chicken Soup for the Soul* series. Mark has had a profound influence through his library of audios, videos and articles in the areas of big thinking, sales achievement, wealth building, publishing success, and personal and professional development.

Mark is the founder of the MEGA Seminar Series. MEGA Book Marketing University and Building Your MEGA Speaking Empire are annual conferences where Mark coaches and teaches new and aspiring authors, speakers and experts on building lucrative publishing and speaking careers. Other MEGA events include MEGA Marketing Magic and My MEGA Life.

He has appeared on television (*Oprah,* CNN and *The Today Show*), in print (*Time, U.S. News & World Report, USA Today, New York Times* and *Entrepreneur*) and on countless radio interviews, assuring our planet's people that "You can easily create the life you deserve."

As a philanthropist and humanitarian, Mark works tirelessly for organizations such as Habitat for Humanity, American Red Cross, March of Dimes, Childhelp USA and many others. He is the recipient of numerous awards that honor his entrepreneurial spirit, philanthropic heart and business acumen. He is a lifetime member of the Horatio Alger Association of Distinguished Americans, an organization that honored Mark with the prestigious Horatio Alger Award for his extraordinary life achievements.

Mark Victor Hansen is an enthusiastic crusader of what's possible and is driven to make the world a better place.

Mark Victor Hansen & Associates, Inc.
P.O. Box 7665
Newport Beach, CA 92658
phone: 949-764-2640
fax: 949-722-6912
Visit Mark online at: *www.markvictorhansen.com*

Who Is Kimberly Kirberger?

Kimberly Kirberger is one of the most renowned and effective champions for teens today. Deeply committed to improving the often-torturous transition from adolescence to adulthood, Kimberly's books, public speaking, advice columns and teen-help organizations make it safer for teens to love and accept who they are. In the compassionate and loving voice that teens all over the world turn to and trust, Kimberly reassures the frightened, guides the confused and incites hope where often too little exists.

Kimberly's astonishing ability to capture the teen voice propelled her onto the #1 *New York Times* bestseller slot on more than one occasion, first as coauthor of *Chicken Soup for the Teenage Soul,* which catapulted her to international recognition. Kimberly's success inspired an outpouring of thousands of candid letters and intimate submissions from teens around the globe, which set the stage for *Chicken Soup for the Teenage Soul II* and *III,* both debuting at the #1 spot on the *New York Times* bestseller list. Her other releases in the *Chicken Soup* family include *Chicken Soup for the Teenage Soul Journal, Chicken Soup for the Parent's Soul, Chicken Soup for the College Soul, Chicken Soup for the Teenage Soul on Tough Stuff* and *Chicken Soup for the Teenage Soul on Love & Friendship.* Kimberly went on to create the *Teen Love* series, the first of which, a *New York Times* bestseller, has sold more than 700,000 books since its publication in 1999. *No Body's Perfect: Stories by Teens About Body Image, Self-Acceptance and the Search for Identity* and the accompanying Kimberly's latest projects, *No Body's Perfect Journal,* were released by Scholastic in January 2003.

Kimberly's lecture schedule includes nonprofit organizations, corporate groups and high schools. Kimberly's television appearances include *Geraldo,* MSNBC, Fox Family's *Parenting 101,* CNN, CBS's *Woman to Woman* and *The Terry Bradshaw Show.* She has written a cover story on "Teenagers Today" for *Life* magazine, as well as consulted and written for *Teen, Seventeen, Cosmo Girl, Teen People, Twist, J-14* and *Jump.*

Kimberly's words are compassionate, honest and practical. She's a benevolent force, inspiring our kids to love and accept themselves and lead lives of excellence. Kimberly lives in Southern California with her teenage son, Jesse.

Who is Mitch Claspy?

Mitch Claspy is the Vice President of Inspiration & Motivation for Teens, Inc. (IAM4Teens). Mitch has been involved with *Chicken Soup for the Teenage Soul* and IAM4Teens since 1997, and has guided the *Teenage Soul* books in both leadership and creative capacities since their inception. Mitch has contributed to all aspects of the organization including helping to found the Teen Letter Project, managing each book's editorial and permission processes.

Mitch has worked with a number of teens throughout the years in his various roles within the *Teenage Soul* organization. Mitch has enjoyed supervising volunteer teen Web site monitors, conducting teen reader groups, coaching young writers and outreaching to teens through the Teen Letter Project. He also helped to found the nonprofit organization Soup and Support for Teachers and Teens, which will provide free *Teenage Soul* books and curriculum support to the nation's teachers in their work with young people.

Mitch's interest in teen issues began as an undergrad at U.C. Santa Cruz, where he had the opportunity to work with teens on a weekly basis. Mitch has also managed and coordinated events for such organizations as Whole Life Expo, the Academy of Motion Picture Arts & Sciences and the American Film Market.

Mitch enjoys traveling every chance he can get, hiking, playing tennis, kayaking, dining with family and friends, working on his house in Venice, California, and spending time with his dog, Harley.

Mitch can be reached at:

1223 Wilshire Blvd. #514
Santa Monica, CA 90403
e-mail: *chickensoupforteens@yahoo.com*

Contributors

Emily Adams is twenty years old and is currently working on a B.A. with a major in music at Bishop's University. When she's not playing her clarinet, she can be found singing in the choir, hanging out with her Little Buddy, serving on the Students' Representative Council, volunteering, or just listening to Sarah McLachlan or Ani DiFranco. On a more personal note, she would like to formally dedicate "Label This!" to her good friend Shara, who taught her that it's okay to be different.

Donata Allison is a sixteen-year-old student. Her upcoming plans are to attend Central Bible College to become a youth pastor. She plans on bringing her brother along with her wherever God leads her after college. Without her little brother and God she would be a completely different person. She can be reached at *DnataA@yahoo.com.*

Scott T. Barsotti is from Pittsburgh, Pennsylvania. He graduated from North Allegheny High School in 1999 and Denison University (English) in 2003; he is currently pursuing a master of fine arts degree at The School of the Art Institute of Chicago. Scott is also a working playwright and a member of the Roundelay Theatre Company.

Al Batt is a husband, father and grandfather who lives on a farm near Hartland, Minnesota. He is a writer, speaker, humorist, storyteller and news-paper columnist. He does a regular television and radio show, contributes to numerous magazines and is an avid birder. He can be reached at *SnoEowl@aol.com.*

Mary Berglund currently teaches A.P. English in Grand Forks, North Dakota. While she was the sports editor and feature writer of her local newspaper for twelve years, she wrote hundreds of weekly columns and has compiled these for publication. She has three sons, all of whom work in athletics and public relations. She can be reached at *mary_berglund@yahoo.com.*

Donya Brown grew up in the small town of Tunkhannock, Pennsylvania. She's nineteen years old and currently lives with her boyfriend of seven years in Wilkes-Barre, Pennsylvania. She enjoys reading and writing, and she intends on beginning a novel in the fall. "Tear-Stained Eyes" is her first published piece and she's looking forward to building off this and using it as a starting point for her future writings. She believes that this was exactly the start she needed. She can be reached at *o0donya0o@yahoo.com.*

Irene Budzynski, R.N., is a medical-surgical nurse in a Connecticut city hos-pital. Married thirty-five years, she has three sons, and her spare time is spent surrounded by books, volunteering in the public library's used-bookstore. Her stories have appeared in *Heartwarmers of Spirit: Triumphs Over Life's Challenges* and *Chicken Soup for the Caregiver's Soul,* and have been heard on *Nightsounds Radio* (FM), an inspirational radio program. She can be reached at *irene_budd@yahoo.com.*

Cazzey Louis Cereghino, a singer-songwriter-actor-screenwriter-model-novelist, is a native of Milwaukie, Oregon. He resides in Los Angeles, California, with his quadruple bunkbed and couch on stilts. A Polar Bear Club member, Cazzey enjoys skydiving, bridge jumping, running marathons, bodybuilding, wiffle ball, traveling, spontaneity and embellishing. Check his on-screen and writing credits at *www.cazzey.com.*

Cheryl Costello-Forshey is a poet whose work has been published in the books, *Stories for a Faithful Heart, Stories for a Teen's Heart, Stories for a Teen's Heart 2, A Pleasure Place, Serenity for a Woman's Heart, Open My Eyes, Open My Soul* and numerous *Chicken Soup for the Soul* books. She can be reached at *costello-forshey@1st.net.*

Jennifer Danley grew up in Nebraska and plans on attending the University of Nebraska at Lincoln where she is going to major in journalism. "Let Me Live" was written when she was thirteen, though she continues to write. When it was written it was dedicated to her best friend, Morgan Farrell, and her mom, Lisa Chastain. She can be reached at *danley118@hotmail.com.*

Beth Dieselberg is a poet, writer, world traveler and lover of all languages. She graduated from Indiana University with a degree in Spanish and Portuguese, and is currently using her bilingual skills within the social service sector. She can be reached at *bdieselb@hotmail.com.*

Christina Dotson is an education major at Ashland University in Ohio. Her stories have been published in numerous magazines including *Guideposts for Teens,* as well as *Chicken Soup for the Christian Teenage Soul.* She would like to thank her family for their love and encouragement. She can be reached at *chrissyd@accnorwalk.com.*

Harold Eppley and **Rochelle Melander** are popular speakers and personal coaches. They have published six books, including *Timeouts with God: Meditations for Parents* and *The Spiritual Leader's Guide to Self-Care.* They can be contacted through their Web sites at *www.MelanderEppley.com* or *www. LifeRhymeCoaching.com,* by telephone at 414-963-1222, or by e-mail at *rochelle@liferhymecoaching.com.*

Sarah Erdmann is seventeen years old. She lives in Oconomowoc, Wisconsin. She enjoys writing stories, playing flute, participating in school plays and musicals, drawing, and painting. Sarah learned many important lessons early in life when her mom died of brain cancer. Sarah is planning on pursuing writing or art as a career and is looking forward to college. She can be reached at *Erddie1@cs.com.*

Brian Eule is a graduate of Stanford University and a current M.F.A. candidate in Columbia University's creative writing program. He is the author of the children's book *Basketball for Fun* (Compass Point Books, 2003). He can be reached at *brianeule@yahoo.com.*

Greg Faherty is a published author with more than six years of professional resume writing experience and over fifteen years of experience in technical, scientific, clinical, business, educational and creative writing. He's also a skilled proofreader and editor, as well as an author of four published educational study guides. Lastly, he has multiple publications in the fields of poetry and photography.

Lauren Fritsky is a recent graduate of La Salle University in Philadelphia, where she received a B.A. in English. She is originally from Brick, New Jersey. Lauren hopes to start a career as a journalist and eventually write a few books of her own. She can be reached at *K1702F@aol.com.*

Linnea Gits-Dunham has been an artist living and working in Chicago since 1993. She is also co-owner of a design consulting company in Chicago, Binthhaus and recently completed a design project with the furniture company Herman Miller for their Chicago showroom, as well as a lighting line at Manifesto showroom in Chicago. She currently released a print series for a children's alphabet that is available through Binthhaus at 312-243-7326, or the Chicago stationary company Alphabetique. She can be reached at *binthhaus@hotmail.com.*

Phyllis Anne Guilmette worked as a reporter and editor in New York, covering issues relating to the welfare of children, social issues, entertainment, crime and politics. She works as a freelance writer for several magazines. While writing, she is pursuing an advanced degree in education. She lives with her husband, an army pilot, and her daughter, Phylicia. She can be reached at *phillyanne@hotmail.com.*

Deiah Haddock is a student at Western Carolina University. Currently studying Spanish and psychology, she continues to write in her free time as a form of healing. Deiah is also a musician, playing and writing songs on the piano. She turned nineteen in 2004, and has been cancer free since May 2000! She can be reached at *spazzy21dmh@hotmail.com,* or visit her at *www.geocities.com/chemochick85.*

Cynthia M. Hamond has been published numerous times in both the *Chicken Soup for the Soul* series and Multnomah's *Stories for the Heart.* Her stories have been printed in major publications and magazines. She has received two writing recognitions, and her short story "Goodwill" has become a television favorite.

Katie Hays wrote "Live Your Dream" when she was fifteen.

Olivia Heaney is a student and a national laureate of the Canada Millennium Scholarship. She has won many national awards for leadership, speaking, community innovation and as a singer/songwriter. Olivia plans to pursue law. She enjoys volunteering and her future aspirations include traveling the world to become "the difference that makes a difference." She can be reached at *oliviaheaney@hotmail.com*.

Jeff Heisler is a freelance writer from Marshall, Michigan. You can learn more about him at *www.heislerink.com*.

Lauren Henderson is a nineteen-year-old young woman living in Kansas City, Missouri. She is finishing up her senior year in high school and will soon begin college courses. She writes on a daily basis and has plans to move to Los Angeles, California, in the future to pursue her writing career. She is currently in the process of completing her first screenplay. Lauren's Web site can be found at *www.weallhavestories.com*. She can be reached at *benzo@weallhavestories.com*.

Julie Hoover is currently a senior at Baylor University in Waco, Texas, and wrote her story when her sister first went off to college. She is studying health science and hopes to continue to physical therapy school after graduation. She is the president of the Baylor Water Ski Team, member of Phi Theta Physical Therapy Organization, and member of Pi Beta Phi Sorority. She gives honor to the Lord and would like to thank her family for always supporting her.

Arielle Jacobs will graduate from Tufts University in May of 2005 with a bachelor of arts degree in philosophy. She would like to say thanks to her wonderful friends, without whom this particular story (and a myriad of others) could not have taken place. She can be reached at *ariellejacobs88@yahoo.com*.

Neil Katcher is a working writer-producer in Los Angeles. He is currently producing "Mortified," a television pilot for Comedy Central. Previously, Neil served as Authentic Entertainment's director of development for two years, where he created and developed projects for cable networks including Discovery, VH1, Bravo, Comedy Central and Travel Channel.

Jim Lauer wrote his poem as a guide for children and their parents while he was chief medical officer at a comprehensive child and adolescent treatment center. Having been fortunate enough to receive most of these gifts as he was growing up, he reflected on what often was missing in the lives of children and teens he had been treating since 1966 as a family psychiatrist.

Dan Levine writes for magazines, newspapers, the Internet, film and television.

Peter Lim spent his childhood in Shaker Heights, Ohio, absorbing the '80s and trying to shake his fear of clowns. He received a B.A. in English from Ohio State University, before moving to San Francisco, California, where he now resides. He writes, and wins staring contests in his spare time. He can be reached at *tonydanzaisking@hotmail.com*.

Joseph Losardo received a bachelor of fine arts from New York University's Tisch School of the Arts in 2002. He also studied in Florence, Italy, and Buenos Aires, Argentina. After graduation, Joe began work in the film industry, but now focuses on writing. He can be reached at *jalosar@hotmail.com*.

Julie Lucas is a marketing communications expert with experience in education, broadcasting and First Amendment initiatives. She directs Illumination, a strategic marketing communications company and is education chair of the National Television Academy (NTA), which governs the Emmy Awards. For NTA, she coauthored a book of broadcast journalism lessons for high school with Av Westin (former executive producer of ABC's *World News Tonight* and *20/20*).

Melody Mallory is a seventeen-year-old high-school senior from Paris, Texas. She is an honor roll student and is involved in many clubs and activities including Extemporaneous Speaking, CX Debate, and One Act Play. She's a varsity cheerleader and loves playing softball and being with the people who mean the most to her. She would like to thank her parents for everything they've done for her and says she loves them very much!

Melissa Malloy is a "born and raised" Calgarian and comes from a loving family of six. She has been writing since the age of eight and aspires to be a published poet one day. During her teen years she battled through drug addiction, alcoholism, teen pregnancy and depression. She is very aware of the difficulties and the emotional roller coaster that can come with being a teenager. She also knows that people have the capacity to overcome any obstacle; all it takes is a little faith and a little hope. She is twenty-two years old and has a beautiful three-year-old daughter. She is now completely sober and is in post-secondary school, doing very well. She can be reached at *Karmalissa@hotmail.com*.

Cortney Martin is a newspaper reporter, fiction writer and magazine freelancer. She is a 2004 graduate of the University of Houston and plans to continue writing professionally and as a hobby. She is pleased to be a *Chicken Soup* contributor for the second time. She can be reached at *cortneymartin82@yahoo.com*.

Lizzy Mason is a graduate of Manhattan College with a degree in communications. She works in publishing as a publicist and is a resident of New York City. Her previous publications include an article in *Positive Teens Magazine* and poems in both *The Anthology of 11th Grade Poetry* and *An Anthology of Amateur Poets*.

Marianne Melcher graduated college and currently teaches math at Shell Lake High School. She enjoys spending time with her family, fiancé, friends and pets. In her free time she likes to read, write and work out. She wants to remind people that, "With God, all things are possible," and to always follow your dreams. She can be reached at *suzyq_54801@hotmail.com*.

Dinaw Mengestu is a freelance writer living in Brooklyn, New York, currently completing his first novel.

Eric J. Moore started writing and rambling at a young age. Various poems, essays and stories may be found in the spattering of high school, college, and local anthologies, as well as his photography and collages. Having relocated to the sunny traffic-laden city of Los Angeles, California, Mr. Moore still churns out endless journals of heartfelt swill.

Rachel Moore holds a B.A. in creative writing from Hampshire College. She can often be found browsing through her favorite bookshop or knitting in a café. She has also traveled extensively through Central America. Rachel lives and writes in San Francisco, California.

Rachel Louise Moore, age thirteen at the time of submission, is a college student and digital media designer. She enjoys creating1337 graphic art, the Mac OS and blogging. You can visit her blog at *www.yurmama.com*. She can also be reached at *Rachel@yurmama.com*.

Lauren Nevins is a magna cum laude graduate from Stony Brook University where she studied psychology, women's studies, and child and family studies. She has been working in early childhood education since graduating and is currently in her first year of a master's in social welfare program. She looks forward to becoming a professional counselor and will continue to pursue nonfiction writing based on her life. She can be reached at *laurennevins1980@yahoo.com*.

Amy Nicholson outlasted parochial high school and a football-centric college town before moving to Los Angeles, California, where she is a theater critic for the *LA Weekly*. Between plays, she invents quasi-Mediterranean recipes, teaches English and reviews documentaries for a mess of film festivals. She can be reached at *marthastewartrules@gmail.com*.

Carrie O'Maley is twenty-four years old and lives and works in New York City. She wrote "My Amazing Brother" in 1998, and her brother, Mark, still remains one of her closest friends. She can be reached at *venuschic4@aol.com*.

Rianna Ouellette received her bachelor of arts in classical studies from Bryn Mawr College in 2004. She enjoys reading and sewing.

Lindsay Ann Parker is a student at Appalachian State University majoring in radio and television. She is a member of Chi Omega Sorority. Her story was written in memory of Gray Griffin and is dedicated to his wonderful parents. She can be reached at *LP51894@appstate.edu.*

Laura Pavlasek is a twenty-one-year-old psychology major at Stephen F. Austin State University in Nacogdoches, Texas, and plans on attending graduate school in the future. She enjoys spending time with her boyfriend, Jacob, playing with her pug puppy, Louis, reading and going out on the weekends. She can be reached at *LMPavlasek@yahoo.com.*

Emily Peck is a sophomore at Northwestern University in Evanston, Illinois, where she is a poetry major. In addition to studying poetry, Emily enjoys singing, reading and watching old movies. She plans on being a professional writer. She can be reached at *Ptuniafish@aol.com.*

Sarah Provencal wrote her story when she was twelve and had forgotten all about it until *Chicken Soup* called and asked to publish it. She's happy to share it with all of you and hopes that it makes you smile.

Michael Punsalan graduated from the University of Dayton in 1998 with his bachelor of arts degree, and is currently studying for his master's degree. He has been published in both alternative press magazines and collections of work. Currently, he is working on his first novel, based on an emotionally charged, true story.

Sara Ronis is a university student who lives in Montreal, Canada. She wrote her story when she was fourteen and has also published a poem in *Teen Love: On Friendship.* She loves to hear from readers and can be reached at *dreamer17_@hotmail.com.*

Danielle Rosenblatt is a twenty-year-old college student who studies English and creative writing at the University of Pennsylvania. She is a writing coach to West Philadelphia elementary-school students who, she says, keep her excited about writing. To learn more about Danielle and read samples of her work you can visit her Web site at *www.xanga.com/home.aspx?user=dmrosenb.*

Alanna Schubach is a senior at American University majoring in journalism and Spanish and minoring in literature. She loves traveling, photography and not being a teenager anymore. Currently she is working with a friend on a comedic adaptation of *Crime and Punishment* set in a Long Island, New York, high school. She can be reached at *effbeye@aol.com.*

Patrick Seitz is a freelance writer, voiceover artist, actor and former high school English teacher. He is pursuing an M.F.A. degree in creative writing and writing for the performing arts at University of California, Riverside, where he focuses on screenwriting and playwriting. He can be reached at *patrick_seitz@msn.com,* or visit him online at *www.patrickseitz.com.*

Mary Shannon is a college writing teacher and the mother of two teenage boys. She is also the president of the board of directors of Alliance of Abilities, a day program for people with head injuries and other cognitive disabilities. You can find out more about this program at *www.integrity-house.org.*

Brittney Shepherd is a novice of many crafts.

Brittany Steward is sixteen years old and lives in Eau Claire, Wisconsin. Besides writing poetry, she enjoys dancing, spending time with her friends and, like most girls, shopping. Brittany has been reading the *Chicken Soup* books since the sixth grade and hopes someone will find comfort in her writing as she has in others.

Sarah Strickler began writing when she took creative writing classes her senior year of high school. She would like to thank her writing teacher, Mrs. Shanahan, for teaching her the art of writing. Sarah enjoys writing, dancing and volunteering. She hopes to continue her writing when she attends the University of Nebraska at Omaha.

Chris Sullivan is a writer and graduate student living in New York City. In addition to his research in emerging democracies and new methods to battle governmental and economic corruption, Chris maintains a Web site of his essays and humor writing at *www.chrissullivan.us.*

Bethany Trombley is a twenty-year-old student and is currently partnered in business with her fiancé, Jim. She is excited about expanding their business, helping others along the way and soaking up the sunshine on the beaches of the world writing all the while, of course. She can be reached at *bethykay2002@aol.com.*

Sarah Van Tine wrote her story as a reflection on how wonderful the Lord is in giving us what we need. For her, it was Brian. Brian is a great part of her life and never stops pushing her to be a stronger person spiritually and mentally. She believes you shouldn't just push yourself into the dating world but to trust that God will hand over that perfect guy for you and to not be discouraged if you haven't had a boyfriend by the time you think you should have had one. Three and a half years after their first date, Brian and Sarah are now engaged and will be getting married in two years. He was her first and only boyfriend. She can be reached at *sarah_lynn@verizon.net.*

Mark Whistler currently lives in Denver, Colorado and is the author of *Trading Pairs: Capturing Profits and Hedging Risk with Statistical Arbitrage Strategies—* published by John Wiley & Sons, Inc. He is also the key developer of PairsTrader.com, and has written for several publications including *The Motley Fool, Working Money* and *BullMarket.com.* Mr. Whistler comments that—though he often writes for rigid financial publications—contributing to *Chicken Soup for the Teenage Soul IV* is truly an honor and a blessing.

Rebecca Wicks is a British legal alien, living in New York City. She works in advertising, sings in the shower and writes freelance for various publications. Check out more on *www.beckywix.blogspot.com*. To contact her for writing assignments, or just to have a cup of tea, she can be reached at *beckywix@ hotmail.com*.

Jessica Wilson has a bachelor of arts degree in English and over seven years of writing and editing experience. She works out of her home for a tax law publishing company, CCH. She's currently enrolled in the Institute of Children's Literature writing program. She can be reached by phone at 770-222-6936 or by e-mail at *coxjessica@yahoo.com*.

Kristina Wong is a solo performer, writer, actor, educator, activist and filmmaker. She performs and teaches at universities throughout the country. She was born and raised in San Francisco, California, and now lives in Los Angeles. Her Web site is *www.kristinawong.com*.

Dallas Nicole Woodburn is a sixteen-year-old high-school junior from Ventura, California. She has self-published a book of short stories and poems, won national writing contests and appeared as a featured author in the book *So, You Wanna Be A Writer?* Dallas has also created a nonprofit foundation called Write On! that encourages kids to read and write through projects such as book drives and essay contests. Please visit her Web site at *www.zest.net/writeon*.

Heather Woodruff's story happened nearly ten years ago, and in case you were wondering, she and her brother did travel the world together. In one year, they saw twenty-three countries, and to this day he remains one of the best friends she has ever had. She can be reached at *hlw2977-work@yahoo.com*.

Rebecca Woolf is a freelance writer/photographer living in West Hollywood, California.

Evan Wynns was born in 1979, and with luck, is still alive. He has been an apprentice curry chef to an A-bomb survivor, plasterer, poet and wage slave, and is currently trying to get someone other than his friends interested in his first novel. He can be reached at *dutchmasta88@yahoo.com*.

Yaa Yamoah was born and raised in Ghana, West Africa. She has two stepsisters. She is the middle child. She moved to the United States to finish her last year of high school and to go to college. She recently graduated from college with a B.A. in communications. She is now living in New York City, and working at a public relations agency. One of her sisters attends school in New York City so it's not so bad. Life is treating her nicely. Her mom still lives in Ghana and Yaa visits her every Christmas.

Lalanthica V. Yogendran was born in Sri Lanka but calls Boston, Massachusetts, her home. With a degree in microbiology and research in infectious disease, she is looking to enter medical school in the coming year. She is involved in various community service activities and enjoys writing in her spare time. She can be reached at *vilashiniy@hotmail.com.*

Esther Young was born in Caracas, Venezuela, in 1984. She moved to California in 2000 for her last two years of high school. She currently attends Yale University, where she nurses a passion for film and travel. She still rides her bike all over campus. She can be reached at *chewiecookie@hotmail.com.*

Permissions

We would like to acknowledge the many publishers and individuals who granted us permission to reprint the cited material. (Note: The stories that are in the public domain or that were written by Jack Canfield, Mark Victor Hansen, Kimberly Kirberger or Mitch Claspy are not included in this listing.)

The Friend That You've Outgrown. Reprinted by permission of C. S. Dweck and Sheppard Dweck. ©2000 C. S. Dweck.

My Friend, Forever. Reprinted by permission of Melissa Malloy. ©2000 Melissa Malloy.

There Is No End in Friend. Reprinted by permission of Rebecca Woolf. ©2004 Rebecca Woolf.

Sketches. Reprinted by permission of Kristina Wong. ©2004 Kristina Wong.

Love Poem. Reprinted by permission of Cortney Martin. ©2000 Cortney Martin.

Unfaithful. Reprinted by permission of Chiara Tomaselli. ©2004 Chiara Tomaselli.

Bacon and Eggs. Reprinted by permission of Beth Dieselberg. ©1999 Beth Dieselberg.

Andy. Reprinted by permission of Scott T. Barsotti. ©2004 Scott T. Barsotti.

For Claire. Reprinted by permission of Rebecca Wicks. ©2004 Rebecca Wicks.

Jonathon. Reprinted by permission of Dan Levine. ©2004 Dan Levine.

Going Away. Reprinted by permission of Bethany Trombley. ©2001 Bethany Trombley.

SPF 1,000. Reprinted by permission of Lauren Henderson. ©2004 Lauren Henderson.

More than Just Sisters. Reprinted by permission of Julie Hoover. ©1996 Julie Hoover.

Just Being There. Reprinted by permission of Patrick Seitz. ©2004 Patrick Seitz.

I Hope You Dance. Reprinted by permission of Dallas Nicole Woodburn and Woody Woodburn. ©2004 Dallas Nicole Woodburn.

The Greatest Audience. Reprinted by permission of Greg Faherty. ©2004 Greg Faherty.

Understanding Jenny. Reprinted by permission of Cynthia Hamond. ©2004 Cynthia Hamond.

Chicken Soup for the Soul

Share with Us

We all have had Chicken Soup for the Soul moments in our lives. If you would like to share your story or poem with millions of people around the world, go to chickensoup.com and click on "Submit Your Story." You may be able to help another reader, and become a published author at the same time. Some of our past contributors have launched writing and speaking careers from the publication of their stories in our books!

Our submission volume has been increasing steadily — the quality and quantity of your submissions has been fabulous. We only accept story submissions via our website. They are no longer accepted via mail or fax.

To contact us regarding other matters, please send us an e-mail through webmaster@chickensoupforthesoul.com, or fax or write us at:

Chicken Soup for the Soul
P.O. Box 700
Cos Cob, CT 06807-0700
Fax: 203-861-7194

One more note from your friends at Chicken Soup for the Soul: Occasionally, we receive an unsolicited book manuscript from one of our readers, and we would like to respectfully inform you that we do not accept unsolicited manuscripts and we must discard the ones that appear.

Chicken Soup for the Soul

Improving Your Life Every Day

Real people sharing real stories — for nineteen years. Now, Chicken Soup for the Soul has gone beyond the bookstore to become a world leader in life improvement. Through books, movies, DVDs, online resources and other partnerships, we bring hope, courage, inspiration and love to hundreds of millions of people around the world. Chicken Soup for the Soul's writers and readers belong to a one-of-a-kind global community, sharing advice, support, guidance, comfort, and knowledge.

Chicken Soup for the Soul stories have been translated into more than 40 languages and can be found in more than one hundred countries. Every day, millions of people experience a Chicken Soup for the Soul story in a book, magazine, newspaper or online. As we share our life experiences through these stories, we offer hope, comfort and inspiration to one another. The stories travel from person to person, and from country to country, helping to improve lives everywhere.

Teenage years are tough, but this book will help teens as they journey through the ups and downs of adolescence. Teens will find support and inspiration in the 101 new stories from teens just like them. Stories in this book serve as a guide on topics about daily pressures of life, school, love, friendships, parents, and much more. This collection will show readers that as tough as things can get, they are not alone!

978-1-935096-72-6

Chicken Soup for the Soul

Teens Talk

HIGH SCHOOL

101 Stories of Life, Love, and Learning for Older Teens

Jack Canfield,
Mark Victor Hansen,
Amy Newmark & Madeline Clapps

Teens in high school have mainly moved past worrying about puberty and cliques, so this book covers topics of interest to older teens—sports and clubs, driving, curfews, self-image and self-acceptance, dating and sex, family, friends, divorce, illness, death, pregnancy, drinking, failure, and preparing for life after graduation. High school students will find comfort and inspiration in this book, referring to it through all four years of high school, like a portable support group.

978-1-935096-25-2

Chicken Soup for the Soul

Teens Talk Growing Up

Our 101 BEST STORIES

Stories about Growing Up, Meeting Challenges, and Learning from Life

Jack Canfield
& Mark Victor Hansen
edited by Amy Newmark

Being a teenager is hard—school is challenging, college and career are looming on the horizon, family issues arise, friends and love come and go, bodies and emotions go through major changes, and many teens experience the loss of a loved one for the first time. This book reminds teenagers that they are not alone, as they read stories written by other teens about the problems and issues they all face every day.

978-1-935096-01-6

The teenage years are difficult. Old friends drift away, new friends come with new issues, teens fall in and out of love, and relationships with family members change. This book reminds teenagers that they are not alone, as they read the 101 best stories from Chicken Soup for the Soul's library written by other teens just like themselves, about the problems and issues they face every day—stories about friends, family, love, loss, and many lessons learned.

978-1-935096-06-1